Jossey-Bass Teacher

Jossey-Bass Teacher provides educators with practical knowledge and tools to create a positive and lifelong impact on student learning. We offer classroom-tested and research-based teaching resources for a variety of grade levels and subject areas. Whether you are an aspiring, new, or veteran teacher, we want to help you make every teaching day your best.

From ready-to-use classroom activities to the latest teaching framework, our value-packed books provide insightful, practical, and comprehensive materials on the topics that matter most to K–12 teachers. We hope to become your trusted source for the best ideas from the most experienced and respected experts in the field.

Reading Comprehension Boosters

100 Lessons for Building Higher-Level Literacy
Grades 3–5

Thomas G. Gunning

JOSSEY-BASS
A Wiley Imprint
www.josseybass.com

Published by Jossey-Bass
A Wiley Imprint
989 Market Street, San Francisco, CA 94103-1741—www.josseybass.com

ISBN 978-0-470-39992-7

Printed in the United States of America

FIRST EDITION

PB PRINTING   10 9 8 7 6 5 4 3 2 1

About This Book

Reading Comprehension Boosters: 100 Lessons for Building Higher-Level Literacy, Grades 3–5 is a program designed to help your students acquire the higher-level reading, reasoning, and responding skills they need to cope with complex literacy demands, including high-stakes tests. The program consists of the following key components:

- *An overview of the program.* The Introduction provides a rationale for the program and describes its scope and sequence.

- *Motivational introduction to the program.* Mystery Passages are used to motivate students by having them engage in riddle-type tasks that also provide diagnostic information and lay the groundwork for upcoming units.

- *100 lessons.* The core of the book is the series of 100 lessons designed to introduce and reinforce key skills and strategies for literacy. Each lesson begins with a teaching guide that provides suggestions for introducing the skill or strategy and supplying guided and independent practice. Many lessons also contain suggested extension and assessment activities. Following the teaching guide are the Student Pages, which contain practice materials so that students can apply the strategies and skills that they have been taught. The Student Pages feature high-interest theme-related reading selections accompanied by questions and other activities designed to reinforce the skills and strategies that have been introduced.

- *An end-of-theme reflection for the teacher* that offers concrete suggestions for applying the strategies taught in the unit to whole books. This section also includes a bibliography of books relevant to the theme of the unit.

- *A culminating reflection for students* in which they think back on what they learned and how they can apply these new strategies and skills to school texts and outside reading. Also included is a list of books where they can find more information about the theme of the unit.

About the Author

Tom Gunning is professor emeritus at Southern Connecticut State University, where he was department chairperson and director of the Reading Clinic. He is currently an adjunct professor in the Reading/Language Arts Department at Central Connecticut State University, where he teaches courses in assessment and intervention. He has been a secondary school English teacher, a secondary school reading specialist, and an elementary school reading consultant. He was also the editor of *Know Your World Extra*, a periodical for struggling readers.

Gunning has been a consultant for elementary schools in areas that include improving the core curriculum, implementing response to intervention, and planning programs for severely disabled readers. Trained as a Junior Great Books discussion leader, he has used this approach with students in an urban elementary school. Recently he served as a hands-on consultant for a Reading First school.

Gunning is the author of *Creating Literacy Instruction for All Children* (7th edition); *Assessing and Correcting Reading and Writing Difficulties* (4th edition); *Developing Higher-Level Literacy in All Students*; *Closing the Literacy Gap*; and *Word Building, a Response to Intervention Program,* designed for students with decoding problems. He is also the author of a number of children's books, including *Strange Mysteries, Amazing Escapes,* and *Dream Cars.* He is the coeditor with Jim Collins of *Building Struggling Readers' Higher-Level Literacy: Practical Ideas, Powerful Solutions.*

Gunning was a contributing editor for *My Friend,* a nonprofit magazine for students in grades 1 to 8, and was a member of *Sports Illustrated for Kids* panel of experts to advise the editorial staff on the readability and suitability of this magazine's articles. He is a past president of the Readability Special Interest Group and is currently the group's membership chairperson.

Gunning has conducted research on group reading inventories, severe reading disabilities, intervention programs, readability, response to intervention, decoding processes and strategies, and literacy skills needed to cope with high-stakes tests.

Gunning has a bachelor's and a master's degree from Loyola University Maryland and earned a doctorate in the psychology of reading from Temple University in Philadelphia. As a Mellon Visiting Fellow at Yale University, he studied brain development and its implications for literacy instruction.

The impetus for *Reading Comprehension Boosters: 100 Lessons for Building Higher-Level Literacy for Grades 3–5* grew out of his lifelong work with struggling readers, recent work with struggling comprehenders in a Reading First school, and current work with students who are proficient decoders but poor comprehenders.

Contents

Introduction

Reading Comprehension Boosters: 100 Lessons for Building Higher-Level Literacy, Grades 3–5 takes a step-by-step approach. Key prerequisite skills are taught in each of the six units. Instruction is heavily scaffolded at first, but students are gradually led to independence. For deriving main ideas, for instance, students are taught to categorize, a key prerequisite skill. Students also select from possible main ideas in a multiple-choice format before constructing their own.

Because comprehension is a constructive process in which students create meaning based on their background knowledge, *Reading Comprehension Boosters* has been designed to build background knowledge. Topics are developed in depth so that students' background knowledge and ability to make generalizations are enriched. A theme approach has been taken because this allows for determining relative importance of information, comparing and contrasting, noticing similarities and differences, and drawing conclusions, all of them key thinking skills. Because vocabulary is a key component of comprehension, vocabulary is systematically developed. Once students have become familiar with the program, they are introduced to two vocabulary words in each lesson.

Because higher-level comprehension demands engagement, high-interest topics are featured. Students will read about such intriguing topics as guide horses, two-headed snakes, parachutes for planes, flying cars, children who help make the world a better place, and sleep patterns in people and animals.

Although *Reading Comprehension Boosters* features intriguing topics, its main function is to introduce students to key higher-level literacy strategies. It is essential that students then apply these skills to their content-area texts and trade books. *Reading Comprehension Boosters* provides brief, easy-to-read selections so that students can devote their full mental energies to learning the strategies. Once learned, the strategies can be applied to more challenging materials. Each unit is accompanied by a listing of books that extends the unit's topic. Suggestions for applying strategies to these materials are provided.

Strategies Presented

Reading Comprehension Boosters focuses on developing comprehension skills and strategies. *Strategies* are deliberate, planned procedures designed to help readers reach a goal (Afflerbach, Pearson, & Paris, 2008). Previewing, predicting, summarizing, visualizing, connecting, and questioning are strategies. In contrast to strategies, *skills* are automatic processes that are usually performed without conscious control. When strategies are applied automatically, they become skills. In this book, the emphasis is on teaching students to use strategies so that they will become skilled readers. Often, however, strategies and skills will be taught at the same time, so in some instances, both terms are used together.

Reading Comprehension Boosters focuses on the skills and strategies delineated in the National Assessment of Educational Progress (NAEP) Reading Framework. NAEP, also known as the Nation's Report Card, is the gold standard of assessment. Its framework represents a consensus on the key higher-level literacy skills and strategies. The latest framework, set out in Table I.1, which will be the basis of future assessments, has a cognitive emphasis and encompasses the following key areas: Locate and Recall, Integrate and Interpret, and Critique and Evaluate. This book develops the Locate and Recall and Ingrate and Interpret categories. Critique and Evaluate mainly consists of evaluating the quality of literary selections and is better presented in the context of reading full-length literature selections. However, detecting the difference between facts and opinions, a widely taught and assessed evaluative skill, is presented.

Scope and Sequence of the Program

Mystery Passages introduce the program. These passages motivate students by having them engage in riddle-type tasks that also provide diagnostic information and lay the groundwork for upcoming units. The remainder of this book is divided into six units. Each of the first five units reinforces a key strategy and develops one or more themes. The sixth unit provides added practice with all the strategies that have been introduced. Unit themes and skills/strategy focus are listed below:

Unit 1: Finding Main Ideas, Identifying Supporting Details, and Visualizing

  Theme A: The Wonderful World of Animals (Lessons 1–19)

  Theme B: Robots (Lessons 20–24)

Unit 2: Summarizing

  Theme: Animal Helpers (Lessons 25–37)

Unit 3: Inferring, Predicting, Concluding

  Theme: People Helping People (Lessons 38–63)

Unit 4: Facts and Opinions

  Theme: Inventions (Lessons 64–72)

Unit 5: Comparing and Contrasting

  Theme A: Confusing Animals (Lessons 73–78)

  Theme B: Famous People (Lessons 79–81)

  Theme C: Sleep (Lessons 82–87)

Unit 6: Review and Application

  Theme A: Transportation (Lessons 88–96)

  Theme B: One-Room Schoolhouses (Lessons 97–100)

Overriding Strategies

Within each unit, three overriding strategies are presented: using graphic organizers, making connections, and generating questions. These are in addition to the key strategy or strategies being introduced in that unit.

Table I.1 NAEP Framework on Key Higher-Level Literacy Skills and Strategy

Skills/Strategies	Supporting Skills/Strategies
Locate and Recall	
Locating details Determining main idea/supporting details	Locate supporting or other information. Categorize words and sentences. Use details to generate main idea. Support the main idea by citing details. Identify topic sentences. Use titles and headings to predict the main idea. Select the main idea when directly stated. Select the main idea when implied. Use graphic organizers to display the main idea and supporting details. Use a frame to state the main idea and supporting details. State the main idea and supporting details
Summarizing	Identify the best summary. Use frames to summarize. Use graphic organizers to summarize.
Integrate and Interpret	
Inferring/concluding	Generalize and draw conclusions based on facts, details, and examples. Support inferences and conclusions.
Predicting	Base predictions on text and background. Support predictions.
Explaining why	Infer causes or effects.
Imaging	Use visualizing.
Questioning	Learn to formulate questions. Turn titles and headings into questions.
Comparing/contrasting	Select essential elements for comparisons. Recognize words used to express comparisons and contrasts.
Connecting	Select pertinent connections. Justify and explain connections.
Critique and Evaluate	
Differentiating between facts and opinions	Supply a method of verification for factual statements.

Using Graphic Organizers

Graphic organizers are excellent devices for helping students engage in higher-level thinking and are used throughout the program. To get the most benefit from their use, focus on a few core organizers that display key thinking patterns. The following organizers are used in this program:

- Web—main ideas and details
- Frame matrix—comparison and contrast
- Sequence map—events arranged in chronological order
- Process map—steps arranged in order

Making Connections

Making connections deepens students' comprehension and, if the connection is to something in their lives, personalizes it. Students make three basic connections: text to text, text to self, and text to world. *Text-to-text connections* might consist of a connection made between two events or characters in a story or in the same article or connections made between a text being read now and one read in the past. The connection could also be to a TV show, movie, or Web site. The text could be visual or auditory or a combination. *Text-to-self connections* are those in which the reader makes a connection to an event, situation, or person in his or her life. *Text-to-world connections* are connections made between a text that is being read and something that is happening in the world.

Making a connection requires going beyond simply noting a similarity. The students should also give an example of the similarity and then establish a connection between the text element and the personal element, if they are making a personal connection. They would explain how the connection contributed to their understanding of the selection—for example: "When I was in third grade, our class collected books and school supplies for the children whose schools had been hit by hurricanes. That's like what the kids in Brandon's class did when they collected books for kids in hospitals and group homes." Because students' experiences vary greatly, some children will have difficulty making connections to some of the articles in the lessons. Therefore, connection questions are included in the students' practice exercises only for articles that lend themselves to construction of connections by all students. However, the teaching guide poses additional connection questions. These are to be used at your discretion if you judge that they are appropriate for your students.

Generating Questions

In addition to making connections, proficient readers generate questions. Encourage students to ask themselves questions as they read. One source of questions is to turn titles and headings into questions. The student then reads to answer the questions. This needs to be a flexible strategy. If the question doesn't work out because the title or heading didn't really suggest the main idea of the article or section, readers need to reword the question. Another excellent strategy is to ask why or how questions. Asking these questions causes students to think more deeply about their reading and fosters both better comprehension and increased retention.

Getting Started

To implement the program, determine students' reading levels. Make sure that they can read on at least a beginning third-grade level. The selections in the early units of the book are easy so that students can devote all their mental energies to constructing meaning without being sidetracked by figuring out difficult vocabulary and complex sentence structures. The selections gradually grow in difficulty, and they are heavily scaffolded at the start. Students are then gradually given more responsibility for their learning.

Start the program with the Mystery Passages, since these will motivate students, provide diagnostic information, and get students off to a promising start by placing emphasis on reading for meaning, integrating details, and thinking about what you are reading. Then proceed to Unit One. Units build on each other, so they should be presented in order. However, core programs take precedence, so if yours follows a different sequence, adjust the order of presentation.

Monitoring Progress

To monitor students' progress, note the nature and quality of their responses in discussions and also note how well they do on each lesson's exercises. Students should be able to obtain a score of 70 to 80 percent on the lessons. If they consistently score below 50 percent, the material is probably too hard, and if they consistently score 90 percent or above, the material is probably too easy. You might also use mazes, running records, or other external assessments to monitor progress.

Lessons

At least one lesson is provided for the introduction of each strategy/skill and subskill. All strategy/skill and subskill lessons have two parts: introduction and guided practice. A number of lessons also have an extension in which students delve more deeply into a topic or apply the target strategy/skill. Some lessons also have suggestions for assessment so that you can check students' progress.

In the introduction, you explain the strategy/skill, tell why it is important to learn, and then demonstrate or model how it is processed. In most introductions, you will think aloud as you use the strategy/skill so students can see what processes are involved. They can see that constructing meaning is an active endeavor.

Guided practice is just that: students practice the skill, but you provide help as needed and discuss their responses. As part of the lesson, assess students' progress. You can note how well students grasp a concept and how well they are able to apply a skill and make adjustments as necessary. Assessment is a two-way street. You might find that students need more instruction. And if you find that they have mastered a skill, move on to the next one. There are a number of suggested extensions. However, feel free to add your own. Most important of all, provide many opportunities to apply the skill being learned. If at all possible, enlist the efforts of content-area teachers so that they are using the same pedagogical language and fostering the same strategy or skill that you have introduced.

Assisting English Language Learners

In order to benefit from *Reading Comprehension Boosters*, English learners should be in at least the intermediate stage of English acquisition. At this stage, they have acquired between three thousand and six thousand words. Students at this level should be able to read third-grade-level passages with adequate comprehension. If you are in doubt about the level of students' language, consult with the English as a Second Language or bilingual teacher. Students might also have taken a language proficiency test. Even though English learners in the intermediate stage have acquired a sizable vocabulary, unfamiliar words will be a primary problem for them, so provide extra vocabulary instruction. Before these children read a selection, you might ask them to note any unfamiliar words in the selection so that these can be discussed. Figures of speech will be especially difficult for English learners because the words taken together don't mean what the individual words usually mean. Common expressions, such as "run up a bill" or "time is up," will be puzzling to them. Preview figurative expressions in articles that students are about to read.

English learners also need to develop their academic language: the words, grammar, and thinking skills necessary to understand written text and compose responses. It includes the technical language of subject matter or content-area topics, such as *habitats, shelter,* and *migration,* as well as the words used to express complex concepts or directions: *provide, analyze, organize, support, require.* Preteach the words and expressions used in directions and the words and expressions that students might need to respond to the questions. Frames, which are partially written responses, are used throughout this book in order to provide a model that students can use for constructing responses. In fact, providing instruction in academic language benefits all students.

Because English learners might have difficulty articulating a response even when they may know the answer, provide them added time and prompts: "Can you tell me more?" "Can you tell me why the stonefish is said to be the most dangerous fish in the world?" "How strong is its poison?" You might post sentence starters for discussions: "I think _____ was the most important invention. And here is why I think that: _____."

During discussions, focus on meaning rather than on correcting errors, which can be embarrassing and discouraging to English learners. Instead, you might rephrase what the student said as long as you judge that this will not be demeaning to the student or discourage him or her from responding in the future. In a rephrase, you correctly restate the student's linguistically incorrect statement. If the student says, "Albert lost hims backpack," you might say, "Yes, Albert did lose his backpack."

Introducing the Program

Introduce the program to students by explaining its purpose and discussing how it will help them become better readers and writers, Highlight some of the interesting topics that they will be reading about: two-headed snakes, flying cars, parachutes for planes, and inventors who were not much older than they are. Read with them and discuss the Message to Students, which can be reproduced from page 7.

Using Mystery Passages to Introduce Reading Comprehension Boosters

Use Mystery Passages to introduce *Reading Comprehension Boosters.* These are brief informational selections that have been inverted so that the main idea or topic is not revealed until the last segment has been read. Students read the Mystery Passages in segments, and after each segment, they make a prediction as to what the paragraph is about.

Reading Comprehension Boosters will help you become a better reader. In the stories you are given, you will read, reason, respond, and reflect.

Read: You will be reading about a number of interesting topics in the articles in the lessons, such as strange animals, robots, animals that help people, and inventors. You will be building your background knowledge. Background knowledge helps you to understand what you read. Reading is hard when you are meeting a lot of new ideas. The more background knowledge you bring to an article or story, the better you will understand it. The articles also build vocabulary. The more words you know in an article or story, the better you can understand it.

Reason: Reasoning means to think. Having background knowledge and a good reading vocabulary are important, but they aren't enough. You also have to be able to think about what you read. The lessons will show you how to get main ideas, understand important details, make inferences and draw conclusions, make connections, picture what you are reading, tell the difference between facts and opinions, and compare ideas.

Respond: Responding means to answer. Do you sometimes have a hard time writing the answer to a question even though you know the answer? The lessons will show you how to write your answer and how to explain or prove your answer.

Reflect: Reflecting means to think carefully. In these lessons, you will be asked to reflect on your work. By thinking carefully about what you have read and written, you can become a better reader and writer.

Mystery Passages are an almost magical technique that motivates students, provides invaluable information about students' reading processes, and builds students' comprehension abilities. Students enjoy solving mysteries. When working with struggling readers, I have found Mystery Passages to be the technique they like best and provided me with best information about their thinking processes. Mystery Passages yield information about a student's ability to make predictions, integrate details, and make and support inferences.

A Mystery Passage should be on the student's instructional level and should be about a familiar topic. Otherwise the student will not have the background needed to make predictions. For example, a passage about polar bears would not be appropriate for students who have no knowledge of these bears.

Administering a Mystery Passage as a Diagnostic Instrument

In preparation for reading a Mystery Passage, the student is told that she or he will be reading an article in parts and that after reading each part, he or she is to try to guess what the mystery animal is. After reading each part, the student is asked, "What do you think the mystery animal is?" and then, "What makes you think that?" to explain the reasoning for his or her response. After the student has completed reading all the separate segments, he or she is asked to reread the passage and then retell the entire selection. Students' responses are analyzed in light of the following questions (Wade, 1990; Gunning, 2010):

- How well was the reader able to hypothesize the identity of the animal?

- How well did the reader support her or his hypotheses with reasons, inferences, or predictions?

- At what point did the reader guess the identity of the animal?

- What information from the text did the reader use?

- Did the reader integrate information from the passage with information from previously read passages? Did he or she use clues in additive fashion?

- Were the reader's inferences and predictions logical?

- How did the reader make use of background knowledge?

- How well was the reader able to identify key information in the passage?

- What strategies did the reader use?

- How did the reader handle unfamiliar words or puzzling portions of the text?

Note in particular how much background knowledge students have and how well they make use of it. Note also how well students integrate information from succeeding segments and how logical their reasoning processes are.

When Mystery Passages are administered individually, record and then analyze each student's responses. When these passages are administered to a group, ask the students to record their own responses. After students have completed recording their responses, discuss them. This gives students the opportunity to expand on their responses. Give students one clue segment at a time. Otherwise they may read down the page and locate the identity of the mystery animal.

A sample Student Page follows for a Mystery Passage.

Mystery Animal

- It is a very large animal. When fully grown, it might weigh up to 1,500 pounds or even more.

  My prediction:

  _____

  Reason(s) for my prediction:

  _____

  _____

- It is a powerful swimmer. It can swim for ten hours or more.

  My prediction:

  _____

  Reason(s) for my prediction:

  _____

  _____

- It is a fast swimmer. It can swim six miles in an hour's time.

  My prediction:

  _____

  Reason(s) for my prediction:

  _____

  _____

- It doesn't mind the cold. It swims in icy water and sometimes floats on large sheets of ice.

  My prediction:

  _____

  Reason(s) for my prediction:

  _____

  _____

- It has a built-in life jacket. It has two coats of hair. The inner coat is made of fine white hair and keeps it warm. The outer coat is made up of longer hairs. These hairs are hollow. The hollow hairs are like tiny life jackets or tubes.

  My prediction:

  _____

Reason(s) for my prediction:

_____

_____

The two coats of hair help keep the polar bear on top of the water.

What were the main things that you learned about the mystery animal?

_____

_____

_____

_____

Source: Gunning (2010).

Analyzing Students' Performance on Mystery Passages

Students to whom the think-aloud Mystery Passage is administered fall into five main categories (Wade, 1990; Gunning, 2010):

- *Good comprehenders,* who use information from the text and background knowledge to generate and support their hypotheses. They are flexible and change their hypotheses when new information in the text calls for this.

- *Non–risk takers,* who stick closely to the text and are reluctant to offer a hypothesis. They fail to make adequate use of background knowledge. Nearly one in five students in Wade's testing was a non–risk taker. Most were younger readers or struggling readers.

- *Nonintegrators,* who fail to put together information from various segments of the text. They might pose a new hypothesis based on the current segment of text without regard to the segments they have already read.

- *Schema imposers,* who hold on to their first hypothesis and interpret information in succeeding passages to fit their schema. About one in ten students in Wade's testing was a schema imposer. Schema imposers might overrely on background knowledge because they have difficulty processing the text.

- *Storytellers,* who rely heavily on background knowledge to create a plausible scenario that might have little to do with the text. As with schema imposers, they may have difficulty processing text and find it easier to create their own meaning rather than construct meaning from the text. About one in twelve students in Wade's testing was a storyteller.

Using the Assessment Results

Use the assessment results to plan an instructional program. If students' prediction strategies and skills are weak, emphasize making and justifying predictions. If students fail to integrate ideas, include questions and activities that require putting details together.

Using Mystery Passages as an Instructional Tool

Mystery Passages can also be used as an instructional tool (Smith, 2006). Use the polar bear Mystery Animal passage for diagnostic purposes and the remaining passages for instructional purposes. Of course, you will be gathering additional diagnostic information as you observe students. Besides being intrinsically interesting to students, Mystery Passages put a focus on reading for meaning, predicting, integrating information, using background knowledge, and thinking about what one reads. These are foundational skills and so provide a good starting point for a program designed to boost comprehension. The core lessons in this book more fully develop these and other strategies and skills

Introduction

Discuss the Mystery Passage about the polar bear. Ask students to tell what clues indicated that the creature was a polar bear. Explain that we use clues from the passage plus background knowledge and our thinking skills to help predict what the mystery animal might be.

Guided and Independent Practice

Have students complete the Mystery Animal exercises that follow. Directions are the same for an instructional focus as they are for a diagnostic focus. Students read a segment, write down what they think the mystery animal is, and then tell what makes them think that. After completing all the segments, they reread the whole passage and tell what they learned about the mystery animal.

Do the first exercise that follows, "The Most Dangerous Animal," cooperatively with students. Then have them try doing the other exercises on their own, providing help as needed. Discuss their responses. Pay particular attention to the kinds of reasoning processes that they use and whether they read for meaning and integrate information from the article. These skills will be especially important as students work their way through *Reading Comprehension Boosters*. The purpose of Mystery Passages is to get students interested in this program and also to start to remind them to read for meaning, integrate ideas, and think about what they read.

Extension

Compose similar passages for student practice, or adapt passages so that the main idea comes last. As students read, encourage them to use their background knowledge and thinking skills. Also use prompts that lead them to integrate details in a passage. Have students apply these skills to the upcoming exercises. In Unit One, for instance, the focus is on recognizing and deriving main ideas. This requires integrating the details in passages.

Mystery Animals

Use the clues to solve the mystery. After each clue, write down what you think the mystery animal is.

The Most Dangerous Animal

- What is the most dangerous animal in all of Africa?

  My prediction:

  _____

  Reason(s) for my prediction:

  _____

  _____

- The most dangerous animal in all of Africa is a huge beast. It can weigh more than 8,000 pounds. Even though it is huge and has short legs, it can run very fast. It can run faster than any human and most other animals.

  My prediction:

  _____

Reason(s) for my prediction:

_____

_____

- Its mouth is gigantic and its teeth huge. It can chomp alligators and small boats in half. Atop its head are sharp horns.

My prediction:

_____

Reason(s) for my prediction:

_____

_____

Many animal scientists believe that the hippo is the most dangerous creature in Africa. Hippos have killed more people than any other wild animal.

What were the main things that you learned about the mystery animal?

_____

_____

_____

_____

Longest-Living Land Animal

- Besides humans, what is the longest-living land animal?

  My prediction:

  _____

  Reason(s) for my prediction:

  _____

  _____

- The longest-living animal is slow moving. And it eats mostly grass and other plants.

  My prediction:

  _____

  Reason(s) for my prediction:

  _____

  _____

- Although it's slow moving, the longest-living animal has a good way to protect itself: it can crawl into its hard shell.

  My prediction:

  _____

Reason(s) for my prediction:

_____

_____

The longest-living land animal is a tortoise. A tortoise is a turtle that lives on land. A tortoise by the name of Harriet lived to be 175 years old. And a tortoise by the name of Tui Mali holds the record for living the longest. She lived for 188 years.

What were the main things that you learned about the mystery animal?

_____

_____

_____

_____

The Lion Killer

- Lions have the title "King of the Beasts," but there is an animal the size of a medium-sized dog that can kill a lion. Can you guess what the animal is?

  My prediction:

  _____

  Reason(s) for my prediction:

  _____

  _____

- The animal weighs just 50 pounds. It's a good digger. It often digs an underground burrow. Its burrow can be 50 feet long.

  My prediction:

  _____

  Reason(s) for my prediction:

  _____

  _____

- The mystery animal lives in Asia and North Africa, but it has relatives that live in North America. Its relatives spend much of their time in trees.

  My prediction:

  _____

Reason(s) for my prediction:

_____

_____

• The lion-killing animal has a covering that helps to keep it safe. But the covering is not a shell.

My prediction:

_____

Reason(s) for my prediction:

_____

_____

• The lion-killing animal is covered with quills that are more than 1 foot long. If an enemy approaches, it rattles its quills as a warning. If the enemy doesn't heed the warning, the lion-killing animal runs backward and sticks the unlucky enemy with dozens of long, sharp quills.

My prediction:

_____

Reason(s) for my prediction:

_____

_____

Using their deadly quills, crested porcupines have killed lions that are ten times their size.

What were the main things that you learned about the mystery animal?

_____

_____

_____

_____

The Largest Animal Without a Backbone

- Scientists have been hunting for this giant animal for hundreds of years. It is the largest invertebrate (in-VER-tuh-brit). An invertebrate is an animal that doesn't have a backbone.

- My prediction:

_____

Reason(s) for my prediction:

_____

_____

- Until a few years ago, no one had ever seen one alive. The only thing scientists had seen were dead giants that had washed up on shore or were floating in the sea.

My prediction:

_____

Reason(s) for my prediction:

_____

_____

- Search after search turned up nothing. Some searchers hooked up cameras to submarines. And some searchers tied cameras onto the backs of whales. But the searchers had no luck.

  My prediction:

  _____

  Reason(s) for my prediction:

  _____

  _____

- Then some Japanese scientists came up with a good idea for finding one of the giants. The beaks of the giant animals had been found in the bellies of whales, so they decided to follow a pod of whales.

  My prediction:

  _____

  Reason(s) for my prediction:

  _____

  _____

- The scientists hoped the whales would lead them to the giant creature.

  My prediction:

  _____

Reason(s) for my prediction:

_____

_____

- As they followed the whales, the scientists dropped a long line with food on it into the water. Underwater cameras were focused on the bait. The plan worked. One day with the bait just about 3,000 feet under the sea, one of the giants went after the bait.

My prediction:

_____

Reason(s) for my prediction:

_____

_____

The underwater cameras took pictures of the giant squid as it tried to eat the bait.

What were the main things that you learned about the mystery animal?

_____

_____

_____

_____

Unit One has two themes. The first theme explores the world of animals. It looks at unusual animals and ways in which animals take care of their young and help each other. The second theme explores the world of robots. It describes some of the main ways in which robots are used—some of which will undoubtedly be surprising to students—and concludes with a story about a pet robot. Place books and articles on the topic in your classroom library. The skills/strategy focus for the first unit is deriving the main idea and supporting details. Visualizing is also introduced.

Teaching the Main Idea and Supporting Details

Grasping the main idea of a selection is a foundational skill. In this book, the main idea is a summary statement that includes the details or ideas in a selection. It is what all the other sentences are about. The main idea is more specific than the topic. Whereas the topic is the subject, the main idea is the general idea that is expressed about the topic. A topic might be "guide dogs." A general idea about guide dogs might be, "Guide dogs are carefully trained." Unless students grasp the main idea, they have no basis for organizing information and run the risk of getting lost in details.

Grasping the main idea is also a prerequisite for summarizing, outlining, and taking notes. Grasping the main ideas requires the ability to see similarities among details, note differences, and classify or categorize details. Without the prerequisite skills of noting likenesses and differences and being able to classify details, students will have difficulty deriving or recognizing main ideas. The major problem that students have with selecting or constructing main ideas is not including all the details. Students tend to select or construct a main idea that is too narrow. Deriving the main idea requires the following subskills:

- Categorizing words and sentences
- Identifying topic sentences
- Using titles and headings to predict the main idea
- Selecting the main idea when directly stated
- Selecting the main idea when implied
- Using graphic organizers to display the main idea and supporting details
- Using a frame to state the main idea and supporting details
- Stating the main idea and supporting details

Theme A ▷ The Wonderful World of Animals

Lesson 1 ▸ Identifying Topic Sentences

Objectives: To prepare for identifying main ideas, students apply their concept of main idea by choosing from the sentences in a paragraph the one that includes all the others. In preparation for choosing a topic sentence, students categorize groups of words.

Introduction: Explain to the students that an important reasoning skill is being able to see similarities and differences and then tell how things are the same or different. Explain that being able to see similarities and differences will help them better understand the materials they read. Using a series of items that are similar, such as those listed next, ask students to tell how they are the same. Then have them provide a category label:

collies, poodles, German shepherds (dogs)

crows, robins, blue jays, eagles (birds)

tigers, lions, leopards, panthers (wild cats)

bass, tuna, flounder, cod (fish)

Explain that just as words can be classified, so too sentences can be classified and given a label. Write the following sentences, or similar ones, on the board, and explain to students that one sentence acts as a label and includes all the other sentences. Ask them to read the sentences and identify which one tells about the others:

Buffalo can smell a pool of water that is three miles away.

Buffalo have sharp senses.

Buffalo can see moving animals or people as far away as a mile.

Buffalo also have good hearing.

Most zebras have large black stripes that cover their bodies.

Some zebras have gray, brown, yellow, or red stripes.

Not all zebras look alike.

Some zebras have spots, instead of stripes, on most parts of their bodies.

Some zebras have stripes, but the stripes are so faded that the zebras appear to be all white.

Discuss why "Buffalo have sharp senses" and "Not all zebras look alike" are the main idea sentences. Emphasize that these sentences include the ideas in the other sentences in their group.

Guided and independent practice: Once students have grasped the idea of classifying sentences, have them complete the exercises on the Student Pages. Discuss students' responses. Help them to see that the sentence that includes all the others is the topic sentence. Explain, too, that they can check their responses by seeing if all the other sentences are included in the topic sentence. If one or more don't fit, then they need to choose another topic sentence. To assess students' progress, note whether students can categorize. In prepublication tryouts of these materials, a number of students demonstrated mastery of this skill, but a smaller number showed a definite need for it. Provide added instruction and practice for those who need it.

Extension: Provide added practice if needed. If students have grasped the concept of the inclusive topic sentence, go to Lesson 2. However, continue to have students classify and categorize as the occasion arises. In math they might classify numbers; in geography, places or landforms; in science, rocks or metals or animals.

The articles in this section will take you into the world of animals. They will tell you about an animal that kills snakes, a two-headed snake, how animals help each other, and how animals keep themselves safe. At the same time, you will be learning how to understand main ideas and their supporting details.

Lesson 1: Identifying Topic Sentences

The *main idea* is what a paragraph or longer piece of writing is all about. Some paragraphs have main idea sentences. The main idea sentence is also known as the *topic sentence.* The topic sentence can be thought of as a box in which all the other sentences in the paragraph can be placed.

To show you how topic sentences work, a paragraph has been broken up. Its sentences are listed below. See if you can find the topic sentence. Keep in mind that it will be the sentence that includes all the other sentences. Underline the topic sentence. Then look at the other sentences to make sure that the main idea sentence tells about them:

Birds sing to tell other birds where they are.

Birds sing for a number of reasons.

Birds sing to find mates.

Birds sing to warn other birds to stay away from their homes.

Credit: Norma Kable.

The topic sentence is, "Birds sing for a number of reasons." It includes all the other sentences. The other sentences explain that birds sing to tell us where they are, to find mates, and to warn other birds to stay away from their homes. All of these sentences help support the main idea: birds sing for a number of reasons.

Now underline the topic sentence in each of the following lists of sentences:

<u>The way a bird sings depends on where it is.</u>

Birds that are low to the ground sing in low sounds.

Birds in bushes sing in medium sounds.

Birds in the treetops sing in high sounds.

Many birds know just one song.

Chipping sparrows and black-capped chickadees sing two or three songs.

The brown thrasher can sing 2,000 or more songs.

<u>Some birds can sing more songs than others.</u>

The pygmy marmoset is so small that it could fit in your hand.

At birth, a pygmy marmoset weighs only about half an ounce (15 grams).

<u>The pygmy marmoset is the smallest monkey in the world.</u>

Grown-up pygmy marmosets are only about 5 inches (13 centimeters) long, but they have an 8-inch (20-centimeter) tail.

The pygmy marmoset weighs just 4 to 7 ounces (113 to 199 grams).

Pouch rats grow to be 13 to 17 inches (33 to 43 centimeters) from the tip of the nose to the base of the tail.

The pouch rat's tail is as long as its body.

African Gambian pouch rats are the largest rats in the world.

Pouch rats can weigh 6 or more pounds (2.7 kilograms).

The cheetah is built to go fast.

The cheetah has large nostrils and lungs so it can pull in more air.

With its large heart, the cheetah pumps blood faster.

The cheetah has a long, thin body so that it can cut through the wind.

The cheetah has long, powerful legs.

The cheetah has special paw pads and claws that keep it from slipping.

Objectives: Students apply their concept of main idea by choosing from the sentences in a paragraph the one that includes all the others. Students verify their choice by underlining supporting details.

Introduction: One strategy for deriving the main idea of a paragraph is to seek out the topic sentence, which is generally, but not always, the first sentence. Of course, the reader can't tell if a particular sentence is the topic sentence until she or he has read all or most of the paragraph. Explain to students that now they will be choosing the topic sentence in a paragraph rather than from a list as they did in Lesson 1.

Model how you determine whether the first sentence seems to be stating a main idea and how, if it does seem to be, you note as you read the paragraph whether the details are supporting the hypothesized main idea. If some sentences are not supporting the main idea, then you seek another main idea sentence. Show how the main idea might be presented in a middle or even the final sentence. Also explain that not all paragraphs have topic sentences. Use the following paragraph or one of your choosing to model the process. As you read the paragraph, tell students what is going on in your mind so that they gain insight into the thinking processes for this lesson.

> Indians gave birds names that fit what they did or how they looked. Indians called the woodpecker the "tree digger." The waxwing was given a name that means "top of head sticking up." That is just what the head feathers of the waxwing do. The small but loud house wren was given a name that means "making big noise for its size." The snipe, a bird with a long beak, was known as "bill dragging on the ground."

Your think-aloud might go something like this:

Reading the first sentence: "It looks like this might be the main idea. Let's see if the rest of the sentences tell how Indians gave birds names that fit."

Reading the second sentence: "Okay. It tells how the woodpecker got its name. This fits in with the idea of how the Indians gave birds names that fit."

Reading the third and fourth sentences: "Yes, these sentences also tell how Indians gave birds names that fit."

Reading the last sentence: "All of these sentences are telling about how the Indians gave birds names that fit, so that's the main idea of the paragraph."

Help students determine the main idea of the following paragraphs. Discuss students' responses. Ask them to explain their responses by showing how the topic sentence they chose includes all the others.

> For Indians, buffalo were very important. Buffalo meat was a main food for many tribes. Tents, ropes, and leather bags were made from buffalo hides. Even the horns were useful to the Native Americans. Horns were used to make spoons.

> Owls make their homes in a number of different places. Most owls make their homes in trees. As you probably can guess from their name, barn owls often make their homes in barns. But they also make their homes in caves and old mines. Some owls live in giant cactus plants. Some owls even live underground. Burrowing owls make their nests in burrows once used by prairie dogs or foxes.

Guided and independent practice: Have students complete the first item in the Student Pages for Lesson 2 and compare their responses with that provided. Then have students complete the remaining items. When they have finished, discuss their responses. Ask them to explain their responses by showing how the topic sentence they chose includes all the others. To assess students' progress, note whether students can select the correct topic sentence and explain their choice.

Extension: Provide additional practice materials. Cut up brief paragraphs that contain a topic sentence. Have students place the topic sentence at the top of a column and the supporting details under the topic sentence. This manipulative activity helps students better see the relationship between the main idea and its supporting details. After students achieve proficiency classifying sentences in a list, have them select the main idea in brief, well-constructed paragraphs. As students are reading in their content-area texts or are reading informational trade books, have them identify topic sentences. Explain and show them how they can use the topic sentence to help them comprehend what they are reading. The topic sentence will enable them to organize the information that they are reading. Also have them compose or develop topic sentences in their writing.

Lesson 2: Nile Crocodiles

Now see if you can find the topic sentence when it is in a paragraph. Not all paragraphs have a topic sentence, but this one does. Often the topic sentence is found first, but it can come anywhere in the paragraph. As you read, notice the details that support the main idea.

Nile Crocodiles

Nile crocodiles are good parents. The mother crocodile lays her eggs in a carefully made nest that she then covers with sand. The mother stands guard over the nest for three months. The father crocodile helps out. He is there to chase away enemies. As the time for the babies to hatch comes near, the mother crocodile listens carefully. When the babies are ready to hatch, they call out. The mother crocodile quickly uncovers the nest. The mother crocodile then carries each newly hatched baby down to the water. If the streams dry up, the mother searches for water holes. Then she carries the babies there.

What is the topic sentence for this paragraph? Write the topic sentence on the line below. Remember that the topic sentence tells the main idea of a paragraph. It tells what the paragraph is all about. The other sentences in the paragraph support the topic sentence.

_____

_____

The topic sentence is, "Nile crocodiles are good parents." The paragraph mainly tells why Nile crocodiles are good parents. It tells how the mother and father guard the nest and how the mother crocodile uncovers the nest when it is time for the babies to hatch. It tells how the mother helps the babies get to the water. All of these details tell why Nile crocodiles are good parents.

Now find the topic sentence in the next paragraph. Write the topic sentence on the lines after it.

> Should an enemy appear, the mother crocodile has an unusual way of keeping her babies safe. She grabs them and tosses them into her mouth. They couldn't be in a safer place. Seeing the large jaws and the many teeth of the Nile crocodile, hungry animals leave in a hurry. They look for food elsewhere.

_____

_____

The topic sentence is, "Should an enemy appear, the mother crocodile has an unusual way of keeping her babies safe." The paragraph then explains how the mother crocodile puts the eggs in her mouth if an enemy appears, and this frightens the hungry animal.

Find the topic sentence in the following paragraph. Write the topic sentence on the lines.

> Nile crocodiles help each other. When a school of fish is headed their way, crocodiles work together. They gather in a half circle and force the fish to swim toward the middle where they are easily snapped up. Nile crocodiles also work together when it gets very

hot. They dig large dens where they can go to get away from the heat.

_____

_____

Underline two details from the paragraph that support your answer.

Find the topic sentence in the next paragraph. Write the topic sentence on the lines following it.

Being fierce, the Nile crocodile doesn't have many enemies. However, Nile crocodiles are in danger from people. Nile crocodiles are hunted for their hides, which can be used to makes shoes and boots and belts. Their meat can be eaten, and oil from their bodies can be used to make medicines. Farmers sometimes hunt Nile crocodiles because they attack their sheep, cows, and other animals.

_____

_____

Underline two details from the paragraph that support your answer.

Objectives: Students use titles to help predict main ideas and information from the title and article to identify the main idea.

Introduction: Titles, especially those of nonfiction articles, are one of the most useful sources for predicting or creating a hypothesis as to what the main idea might be, but students don't automatically use them. Discuss with students titles of nonfiction books and how those titles announce what the book is about. Explain that titles of articles are also helpful in predicting what the main idea of an article is. Explain to students that the way to see if their prediction about the main idea is right is to see what all or most of the sentences in the paragraph are talking about. Model the process using the following or a similar paragraph.

Insect Disguises

You can look right at a walking stick and not see it. The walking stick looks just like a twig on a tree branch. Another insect looks just like a leaf. It even rocks back and forth so that it looks like a leaf blowing in the wind. And there is an insect that looks just like a stone. Since birds don't eat sticks, leaves, or stones, birds leave the insects alone. The insects' disguises help keep the insects safe.

This paragraph is mainly about

    a. where insects live.

    b. why some insects make their homes in trees.

    c. how insects use disguises to hide from birds.

    d. the kinds of insects that birds eat.

    Discuss students' responses. Stress that the answer is what all or most of the sentences are talking about.

Guided and independent practice: After discussing titles and how they help the reader think about what the main idea for an article might be, have students read the title "Snake Killer" in the Student Pages for this lesson and predict what they think the article might be about and what they think the author might tell them about snake killers. For English learners, discuss the expression italicized in the following sentence: "Flying up above the mongoose, the hornbill *can spot the mongoose's enemies.*"

After students make their predictions, have them read the article to see how their predictions play out. Encourage students to change their predictions as they read if their predictions are not working out. Have students circle the correct answer after the article and then check their answers. Discuss the answers with the students. Also talk over how the title helped them to figure out what the paragraph was mainly about. To assess students' progress, note whether students can select the correct title and justify their choices.

Extension: Discuss titles of books and articles, and note whether the titles suggest the main idea of the book or article. This works best with nonfiction titles. As students compose titles for pieces they have written, guide them so that they create titles that contain or suggest the main idea. Have students use the titles from articles in children's periodicals to make predictions. Online articles are available at http://teacher.scholastic.com/scholasticnews/index.asp and http://www.timeforkids .com/TFK/, as well as other sources.

Lesson 3: Snake Killer

Topic sentences can help you discover what the main idea of an article is. A title can also help you discover the main idea. A good title tells what an article is going to be about.

Read the title of the following article. What do you think it will be about? To find out what a paragraph is mainly about, use the title and topic sentence as clues. Also ask yourself, "What are all or most of the sentences telling me?" Circle the letter of the correct answer.

Snake Killer

The mongoose is a champion fighter. It hunts and kills snakes, even poisonous ones. The mongoose is very fast. When a snake tries to strike the mongoose, the mongoose leaps out of its way and jumps on the back of the snake's neck. Then it bites into the snake's neck and kills it.

1. This paragraph is mostly about

   a. a snake's enemies.

   b. how mongooses kill snakes.

   c. where mongooses are found.

   d. how fast mongooses are.

Helping Each Other

Mongooses and hornbills help each other. A bird known as the hornbill follows the mongoose as it hunts for food. When the mongoose finds a nest of ants or other food, the hornbill invites itself to dinner. Why does the mongoose let the hornbill come along and even eat some of the food? Flying up above the mongoose, the hornbill can spot the mongoose's enemies. Even an animal brave enough to kill snakes has enemies. When it spots an enemy, the hornbill gives a warning cry.

2. This paragraph is mostly about

    a. what hornbills eat.

    b. why a mongoose has enemies.

    c. how the mongoose finds food.

    d. how the hornbill and mongoose help each other.

Lesson 4 ▶ The Hornbill Alarm Clock

Objectives: Students use (1) titles to help predict main ideas and (2) information from the title and article to identify the main idea.

Introduction: Encourage students to use the titles of articles to predict what the main idea of an article might be. After students make their predictions, have them read the article to see how their predictions play out. Encourage students to change their predictions as they read if their predictions are not working out.

Guided and independent practice: Have students circle the correct answers in the Student Pages and then check their answers. Discuss answers with students. Also talk over how the title helped them to figure out what the paragraph was mainly about. Encourage students to make a connection by telling who or what their alarm clock is.

Lesson 5 ▶ Chasing Crowned Eagles Away

Objectives: Students use titles to help predict main ideas and information from the title and article to identify the main idea.

Introduction: Encourage students to use the titles of the articles to predict what the main ideas of the articles might be. After students make their predictions, have them read the article to see how their predictions play out. Encourage students to change their predictions as they read if their predictions are not working out.

Guided and independent practice: Have students circle the answers they think are correct and then check their answers. Discuss the answers with the students. Also talk over how the title helped them to figure out what the paragraph was mainly about.

Lesson 4: The Hornbill Alarm Clock

Read the paragraphs, and answer the questions that follow them.

The Hornbill Alarm Clock

Like most other birds, the hornbill wakes up early. It flies over to where the mongoose is sleeping. It calls the mongoose. First, it calls softly. But then it calls louder. It keeps on calling until the mongoose wakes up. The hornbill is an alarm clock with wings.

1. This paragraph is mostly about

   a. why birds wake up early.

   b. what alarm clocks do.

   c. why the mongoose sleeps later than the hornbill.

   d. how the hornbill is like an alarm clock.

Monkeys Helping Hornbills

Without really meaning to, monkeys help keep hornbills safe from danger. Hornbills are large birds. Many of them live in large rain forests. Hornbills are also very loud. But even though they are large and loud, hornbills have enemies. One of their most feared enemies is the crowned eagle. When it spreads its wings, the crowned eagle is six feet across. It has very sharp claws. The crowned eagle is big enough and tough enough to eat monkeys and hornbills. When they spot a crowned eagle, monkeys give out a cry that sounds like the bark of a dog. This warns the other monkeys. They quickly go into hiding. Monkeys also call out a warning when leopards are around. Hornbills take action when they hear the warning call that crowned eagles are near, but they don't do anything when they hear the warning call that leopards are in the area. Leopards eat monkeys, but they don't eat hornbills.

2. This paragraph is mostly about

    a. how monkeys warn hornbills of danger.

    b. why hornbills are afraid of crowned eagles.

    c. why hornbills aren't afraid of leopards.

    d. what hornbills are like.

Lesson 5: Chasing Crowned Eagles Away

Read the paragraphs, and answer the questions that follow them.

Chasing Crowned Eagles Away

Hornbills don't run for cover when they hear that a crowned eagle is near. Instead they call each other. Then they head for the spot where the crowned eagle is. When a crowned eagle sees a flock of hornbills approach, it is surprised and puzzled. And it is probably frightened too. It doesn't know what the hornbills are going to do. And it doesn't wait around to find out. The crowned eagle flies away.

---

1. This paragraph is mostly about

   a. why hornbills don't run for cover.

   b. why hornbills are afraid of crowned eagles.

   c. why hornbills call each other.

   d. how hornbills get rid of crowned eagles.

Hiding Babies

Hornbills have a special way of keeping their young safe. Hornbills build their nests in holes in trees or rocks. After she lays her eggs, the female hornbill closes up the opening to her nest and stays inside. Only a thin opening to the nest is left. The male hornbill stays outside the nest. The male hornbill passes food through the tiny slit in the nest for the female hornbill and the baby birds.

2. This paragraph is mostly about

    a. how hornbills keep their young safe.

    b. how hornbills find food.

    c. where hornbills live.

    d. how much hornbill babies eat.

Objectives: Students use titles or information, or both, in an article to construct the main idea of an article.

Introduction: Most paragraphs do not have a topic sentence, so it is necessary to construct a main idea. This is done by reading the paragraph and determining what all or most of the sentences in the paragraph are about. Explain this to students and go over the following steps with them.

To build an implied main idea:

1. Use the title or heading, if there is one, to guess what the main idea might be.

2. Read the sentences in the paragraph.

3. Ask yourself, "What are all or most of these sentences telling me?" The answer to that question is the main idea.

Show students how you would determine the implied main idea of the following paragraph. Then invite the class to help construct a topic sentence for the paragraph.

Kangaroos

The red kangaroo can grow to be 7 feet tall and weighs up to 200 pounds or more. The gray kangaroo is also a large kangaroo. It isn't quite as tall as the red kangaroo, but it weighs more. A kangaroo known as the swamp wallaby is smaller than the red and the gray kangaroos. The swamp wallaby is about 3 feet high and weighs about 50 pounds. The rat kangaroo is the smallest kangaroo. Rat kangaroos are barely 9 inches high. The rat kangaroo is about the size of a rabbit.

Guided and independent practice: After discussing and posting steps for building a main idea, have students read the title of the article in the Student Pages, "The Tree Hyrax," and use that to guess what the main idea might be. After students make their guesses, have them read the article to see how their guesses work out and to change the guesses if necessary. Have students circle the correct answer after the paragraph and then check their answers. Discuss the answers with the students. Also talk over how the title helped them to figure out what the paragraph was mainly about. Follow the same procedure with "The Noisy Tree Hyrax," the next paragraph in the Student Pages for the lesson.

Extension: Discuss titles of books and articles, and note whether the titles suggest the main idea of the book or article. This works best with nonfiction titles. As students compose titles for pieces they have written, guide them so that they create titles that contain or suggest the main idea. Have students use the titles from articles in children's periodicals to make predictions.

Lesson 6: The Tree Hyrax

Sometimes a paragraph or article doesn't have a topic sentence. You have to figure out what the main idea is. To get the main idea when there is no topic sentence, follow these steps:

1. Use the title or heading, if there is one, to guess what the main idea might be.

2. Read the sentences in the paragraph.

3. Ask yourself, "What are all or most of these sentences telling me?" The answer to that question is the main idea.

Read the following paragraphs. Then circle the letter of the correct answer.

The Tree Hyrax

The tree hyrax is small and furry. Its fur is dark brown or black, with some gray or yellow mixed in. It looks like a rabbit, except that it has small, rounded ears. And it has only a stump for a tail. The tree hyrax has four toes on its front feet but only three on its hind feet.

1. This paragraph tells mostly

   a. where a tree hyrax lives.

   b. what a tree hyrax looks like.

   c. how big a tree hyrax is.

   d. how the tree hyrax got its name.

The Noisy Tree Hyrax

The tree hyrax begins making noises when the sun sets. First it squeaks and whistles. Then it squeals. It ends up by screaming. One scientist said that it sounds like an angry child.

2. This paragraph tells mostly

    a. why the tree hyrax makes noise.

    b. what kinds of noises the tree hyrax makes.

    c. where the tree hyrax lives.

    d. when the tree hyrax makes noise.

Lesson 7 ▶ Strange Catfish

Objectives: Students use a title and supporting details to identify a main idea and construct a web to display the main idea and supporting details.

Introduction: Have students read the title of the first paragraph in the Student Pages, "Strange Catfish," and use that to guess what the main idea might be. Encourage them to change their guesses as necessary. Also explain to students that they will be using a web to show the main idea and details. Chances are that students have used webs in the past. Explain that the main idea goes in the center and the supporting details go in the circles attached to the middle circle. Have students fill in the web for the article and then check their webs with the sample web. Discuss their responses and what they learned about catfish.

Guided and independent practice: Have students read the second paragraph in the Student Pages: "Fish That Use Disguises." Discuss students' responses. Have them justify their selection of the main idea by explaining how the details support the main idea. They might also talk about the different kinds of disguises that fish use.

Extension: Provide opportunities for students to complete webs. Ultimately have students create webs of their own. Graphic organizers are of most value when students create their own.

Lesson 8 ▶ Insect Sounds

Objectives: Students use (1) a title and supporting details to identify a main idea and (2) a web to display the main idea and supporting details.

Introduction: Have students read the title of the article in the Student Page, "Insect Sounds," and use that to guess what the main idea might be. Encourage them to change their guesses as necessary as they read.

Guided and independent practice: Discuss students' responses. Have them justify their selection of the main idea by explaining how the details support the main idea. Encourage students to add the names and sounds of other insects to the web.

Assessment: Note whether students are able to select the main idea and justify their choice. If not, model the process and provide more practice.

Lesson 7: Strange Catfish

Read the articles, and answer the questions that follow:

> ### Strange Catfish
>
> One kind of catfish is called the glass catfish. Its body is like a thin piece of glass. You can look through its skin and see its insides. Another kind of catfish is called the upside-down catfish. This strange fish often swims on its back. But the strangest catfish of all is the walking catfish. The walking catfish can "walk" on land by using its tail and fins to push itself along the ground.

Credit: Norma Kable.

1. Which of the following sentences best states the main idea of this paragraph?

    a. One kind of catfish swims upside down.

    b. There are some mighty strange creatures in the catfish family.

    c. The walking catfish is the strangest catfish of all.

    d. One catfish has a body that is like a thin piece of glass.

2. One way of showing main ideas and details is to use a web. The main idea or main word goes in the center. The supporting details are placed around the center circle. Part of the web here has already been filled in. Fill in the web's empty circles.

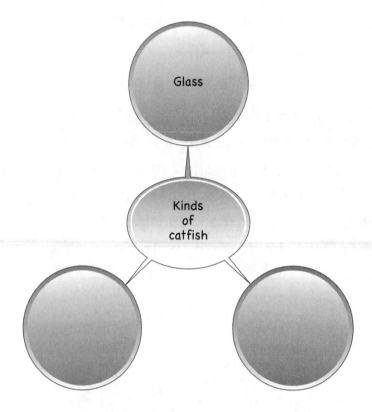

Compare your answers with those in the sample web below. The words that you use might be different, but the ideas should be similar.

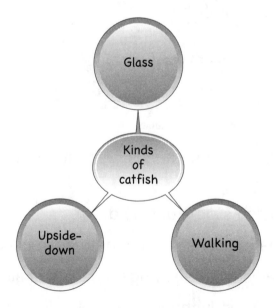

Fish That Use Disguises

Some fish use their shapes and colors to hide themselves. They disguise themselves. The leaf fish is very flat and is brown with white spots. It looks just like a leaf floating on the water. But if a small fish swims nearby, it soon shows that it is not a dead leaf but a live predator. It quickly opens its very large mouth and eats the smaller fish. The flatfish can make its body very flat. As it lies on the bottom of the sea, it can make its body match the sea bottom. The stonefish also hides on the bottom of the sea. It looks like a rock. When a fish swims by, the stonefish quickly gobbles it up. To protect itself from sharks and other dangerous creatures, the stonefish has thirteen poisonous spines. Pipefish have long, thin bodies. With their tubelike bodies, they can easily hide in seaweed. They can also change color so they can match the color of the seaweed where they are hiding.

3. Which sentence best states the main idea of this paragraph?

   a. The pipefish has the best disguise.

   b. The stonefish is the most dangerous fish.

   c. Some fish use disguises.

   d. Fish often eat other fish.

4. Fill in the web's empty circles.

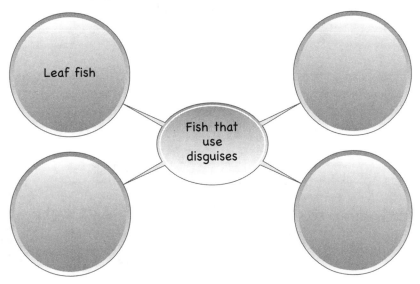

Lesson 8: Insect Sounds

Read the article, and answer the questions that follow it.

> ### Insect Sounds
>
> Insects can't speak, but they can be heard. Crickets make noises by beating their wings together. Some grasshoppers rub their back legs against their wings. They look like violin players. Termites beat on their wooden homes. They sound like tiny drummers.

1. Which sentence best states the main idea of this paragraph?

    a. Insects make sounds in many different ways.

    b. Most insects use their wings to make noise.

    c. Termites have a strange way of making noise.

    d. Some animals use their wings to make noise.

2. Fill in the web's empty circles:

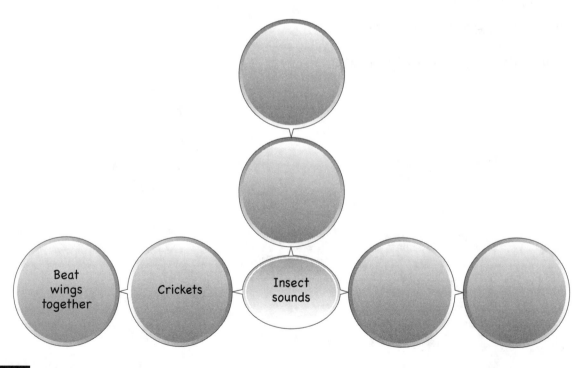

Objectives: Students use a web and frame to help construct a main idea and supply supporting details.

Introduction: Review the steps for inferring a main idea, and help the class determine and construct the main idea of the following paragraph. Explain that the wording of the topic sentence can vary but should contain the main idea of the paragraph, which is what all the sentences in the paragraph are about.

> When the honey guide makes noise, the honey badger lifts its ears. The honey guide is a bird that lives mainly in Africa. It eats beeswax, but it can't open the beehive to get the wax. The honey badger is a small, furry animal that likes honey, but it has trouble finding it. Finding honey is easy for the honey guide. Once it has found the honey, the honey guide starts chattering. When the honey badger hears the chattering, it comes running. It soon digs its way into the beehive. The honey badger eats the honey, and the honey guide eats the beeswax.

Introduce answer organizers and frames, which are designed to help students construct responses. Answer organizers tell students what kinds of responses are needed. In this lesson, students are asked to supply a main idea and three supporting details. Frames help students frame their responses. They supply key words and phrases and provide blanks for students to fill in a portion of the responses. These aids provide structure and the kind of language needed for constructed responses. Ultimately, answer organizers and frames are faded so that students are responding on their own. To introduce answer organizers and frames, have students read the title of the article in the Student Pages, "Watch the Ears," and use that to guess what the main idea might be. Encourage them to change their guesses as necessary as they read. Also point out the answer organizer and frame, and explain that these will help them write their answers.

Guided and independent practice: Discuss students' responses. Have them justify their construction of the main idea, and compare their completed frames with the sample provided. Explain that their wording might differ from the samples, but the ideas should be approximately the same.

Lesson 9: Watch the Ears

Read the article, and answer the questions that follow.

Watch the Ears

A zebra's ears are worth watching. If a zebra's ears are standing straight up, it's a sign that the zebra is feeling calm. If the zebra's ears are pointed forward, then danger may be near. Ears pointed forward mean that a zebra is afraid. If a zebra's ears are pointed backward, you better hope that there is a fence between you and the striped creature. Ears flattened backward are a sign of anger. The zebra may be getting ready to attack.

Credit: Norma Kable.

1. Fill in the empty circles in the web.

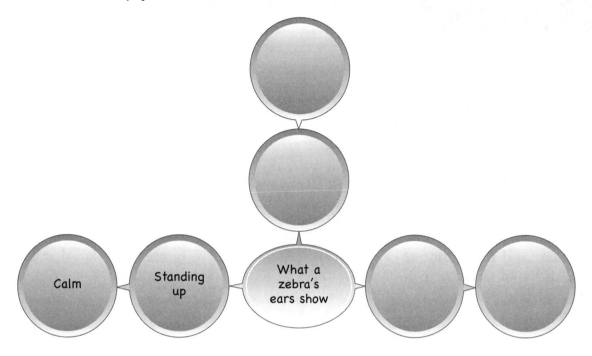

2. Tell what the main idea of the article is. Also tell why it is the main idea. Fill in the frame paragraph. Use the information in the web to help you fill in the frame paragraph.

The main idea of this article is that a zebra's ears show

_____.

The main idea is supported by information from the article. The article explains that if the zebra's ears are straight up, the zebra is feeling

_____.

If the zebra's ears are pointed forward,

_____.

If the zebra's ears are pointed backward,

_____.

Lesson 10 ▶ The Whale Shark

Objectives: Students use an answer organizer and frame to help construct a main idea and supply supporting details.

Introduction: Have students read the title of the article in the Student Pages, "The Whale Shark," and use that to guess what the main idea might be. Encourage them to change their guesses as necessary as they read. Also have them complete the answer organizer and frame.

Guided and independent practice: Discuss students' responses. Explain that there are different ways of wording responses, but the ideas should be approximately the same.

Lesson 11 ▶ Keeping Safe

Objective: Students use an answer organizer to help identify a main idea and supply supporting details.

Introduction: Have students read the title in the article in the Student Pages, "Keeping Safe," and use that to guess what the main idea might be. Encourage them to change their guesses as necessary as they read. Also have them complete the answer organizer and frame.

Guided and independent practice: Discuss students' responses. Explain that there are different ways of wording responses, but the ideas should be approximately the same.

Lesson 10: The Whale Shark

Read the article, and answer the questions that follow it.

The Whale Shark

The whale shark was named for its size. It is a shark, but it is as big as a whale. A whale shark is about 30 feet (9 meters) long. Some whale sharks have grown to be 60 feet long (18 meters). That is as long as four large cars parked in a row. A whale shark can weigh as much as 72,000 pounds (32,658 kilograms). That is about how much 20 large cars would weigh. The only sea creatures bigger than the whale shark are the large whales.

1. What is the main idea presented in this article? Use information from the article to support your answer. Write your answer in the boxes.

What is the main idea? (What are all the sentences talking about?) Write the main idea below.	What details support the main idea? (Which details are giving examples of the main idea? See if you can find two.) Write the details below.

2. Fill in the frame answer. Use the boxes above to help you.

The main idea of this article is that the whale shark

_____.

The main idea is supported by information from the article. The article explains that the whale shark is

_____

and

_____.

Lesson 11: Keeping Safe

Read the article, and answer the questions that follow it.

> ### Keeping Safe
>
> Some fish have unusual ways of keeping themselves safe. When puffer fish are in danger, they fill themselves with water or air. They puff themselves up to twice their normal size. This makes the puffer fish look frightening. It makes them harder to eat, too. Porcupine fish also double their size by gulping water or air when attacked. But a porcupine fish is covered with needles. These needles lie flat until the porcupine fish swells up. Then they stick out. Any enemy who tries to bite a porcupine fish gets a mouthful of cuts.

1. Write your answers in the boxes.

What is the main idea? (What are all the sentences talking about?) Write the main idea below.	What details support the main idea? (Which details are giving examples of the main idea? See if you can find two. Be sure to explain how each way of keeping safe works.) Write the details below.

<table>
<tr><td></td><td></td></tr>
<tr><td></td><td></td></tr>
</table>

2. Fill in the frame answer. Use the boxes above to help you.

The main idea of this article is that some fish

_____.

The main idea is supported by information from the article. The article explains that the puffer fish can

_____.

This helps the puffer fish because

_____.

The porcupine fish can

_____.

This helps the porcupine fish because

_____.

Copyright © 2010 by John Wiley & Sons, Inc.

Lesson 12 ▶ Alligators

Objectives: Students identify and use the main idea to create a title.

Introduction: Review the concept of a good title. Remind students that a good title tells what an article or story will be about and also tries to get the reader interested. Explain that the title of the article in the Student Pages, "Alligators," is too general to be a good title. Explain to students that they will be reading the article to get the main idea and also to think of and write a better title.

Guided and independent practice: Have students compare their completed responses with the sample response. Explain that there are different ways of wording responses, but the ideas should be approximately the same. Then have students create a better title for "Rhinos and Tickbirds," the next article in the Student Pages. Discuss students' responses. Explain that titles can differ but should give or at least hint at the main idea of the article.

Lesson 13 ▶ Parrotfish

Objectives: Students identify and use the main idea to create a title.

Introduction: Have students read the title of the article in the Student Pages. Discuss the fact that "Parrotfish" is too general to be a good title. Explain to students that they will be reading the article to get the main idea and also to think of and write a better title.

Guided and independent practice: Discuss students' responses. Explain that titles can differ but should give or at least hint at the main idea of the article. Talk over how the parrotfish keeps itself safe while it sleeps.

Assessment: Note whether students are able to create a title that reflects the article's main idea. If they have difficulty, model the process and provide more practice.

Lesson 12: Alligators

Read both of the articles, and answer the questions that follow them.

Alligators

With its strong jaws and slashing tail, the alligator is a killer. But it can be a helpful animal too. Alligators dig large holes about five or six feet deep. When winter comes, the holes are warm homes. The holes also hold water. So when water is hard to find, the holes become the alligators' wells. Other animals can drink from the wells, too. Water from the alligators' wells also keeps many kinds of plants alive. Everyone knows that alligators can be killers. But during very dry times, alligators can be lifesavers.

This article is called "Alligators." What could be another title for it? Use information from the article to support your answer. To answer this question, first decide what the main idea is. Then think up a title that tells what the main idea is. Write your title. Explain that this is a good title because it tells what the main idea is. Then tell what the main idea of the article is. Give details from the article that support the main idea. Use the frame to help you.

1. A good title for this article is

_____ .

This is a good title because the main idea of the article is that

_____ .

The main idea is supported by information from the article. The article explains that

_____

_____ .

The article also tells that

_____

_____ .

Now compare your answer with this sample answer:

> A good title for this article is "Helpful Alligators." This is a good title because the main idea of the article is that alligators can be helpful. The main idea is supported by information from the article. The article explains that alligators dig holes and that these holes fill up with water and become wells that other animals can drink from. The article also tells that the water can help keep plants alive.

Your answer does not have to be exactly like the sample, but your title should give the main idea, and you should explain why your title tells what the main idea is.

Rhinos and Tickbirds

Animals can be a big help to one another. The tickbird spends much of its time on the back of a rhino. It eats bugs off the rhino's back. In return for a free ride and a free meal, the tickbird acts as a lookout. The rhino has poor eyesight, so the tickbird watches for danger. Should a dangerous animal appear, the tickbird gives out a warning cry.

2. This story is called "Rhinos and Tickbirds." What could be another title for it? Use information from the article to support your answer.

A good title for this article is

_____.

This is a good title because the main idea of the article is that

_____

_____.

The main idea is supported by information from the article. The article explains that

_____

_____.

Lesson 13: Parrotfish

Read the article, and answer the questions that follow it.

Parrotfish

Parrotfish have a clever way of keeping themselves safe while they sleep. Before it goes to sleep, a parrotfish makes itself a sleeping bubble. The liquid for the bubble comes out of small openings around the parrot's head. It's a little like the way sweat comes out of small openings in our skin, only the liquid that oozes out is thicker than sweat. The bubble hides the parrotfish's scent so its enemies have a difficult time locating it. The slimy bubble also has a very bad taste. The bad taste keeps other sea creatures from trying to eat the parrotfish as it sleeps. The sleep bubble also acts like a burglar alarm. Should a sea creature bite or push against the bubble, the parrotfish will awaken and escape.

This story is called "Parrotfish." What could be another title for this story? Use information from the article to support your answer.

A good title for this article is

_____

_____.

This is a good title because the main idea of the article is that

_____

_____.

The main idea is supported by information from the article. The article explains that

_____

_____.

Lesson 14 ▸ Meerkats

Objective: Students use headings to help identify main ideas.

Introduction: Explain to students how headings can be used to help them get the main ideas of a longer article—one that has several sections. Tell students that whereas a title gives the main idea of the whole article, headings give the main ideas of the sections in the article. Show students headings in textbooks and magazines. Explain that often headings can be turned into questions and that they can then read to answer the questions and that this will help them understand what they are reading. Then do a think-aloud as you explain how you use headings. Point out the title and headings in the article in the Student Pages, "Meerkats," and encourage students to use the title and headings as they read the selection. Help them turn the headings into questions.

Guided and independent practice: Discuss students' responses. Ask them if and how using subheads helped them to understand better what they were reading.

Extension: Review the use of headings as students read textbooks, informational books, and other materials that have headings. Also have students supply headings when they write expository pieces.

Lesson 15 ▸ Two-Headed Snakes

Objectives: Students identify supporting details that provide explanations, and use headings to identify main ideas.

Introduction: Encourage students to use the title and heading to find main ideas and supporting details as they read "Two-Headed Snakes" in the Student Pages.

Guided and independent practice: Discuss students' responses. Explain how using headings, besides announcing main ideas, can help readers locate information. For instance, using the heading, "Why Two-Headed Snakes Live Longer in Zoos," could help readers find the answer to the question: "Why are two-headed snakes better off in a zoo than they are in the wild?"

Lesson 14: Meerkats

This article has headings in addition to a title. The title tells you the main idea of a whole article. The headings tell you what the main idea of a section of the article is. The first heading tells you the main idea of the first part, the second heading tells you the main idea of the second part, and so on. As you read the article, use the headings. You can turn the headings into questions. For the first heading in the article, you can ask yourself, "How do meerkats keep safe?" For the second heading, you can ask yourself, "What do meerkats eat for dinner?"

Read the article, and answer the questions that follow.

Meerkats

1   Meerkats are built for life in the desert. The black rings around their eyes are like sunglasses. They help keep the bright desert sun from getting in the meerkats' eyes. Meerkats have very small ears. They can close up their ears so that sand doesn't blow in them during a sandstorm.

Keeping Safe

2   If you see a meerkat, chances are it is standing up on its hind legs and looking all around. Meerkats have lots of enemies. When they are outside their homes, at least one meerkat acts as a guard or sentry. If it sees an enemy, it calls out a warning. Meerkats let out a barking cry if they spot an eagle or other birds of prey flying overhead. Meerkats give a hooting sound if they spot a fox or other animal that is attacking from the ground.

Meerkats don't always run from their enemies. If they spot a hawk, snake, small fox, or other small predator, they march at it. They growl and bark at the predator as loud as they can. As they get closer, they jump up and down. Most predators take the hint and run, fly, or crawl away.

Eating Dinner

3   Meerkats eat beetles, spiders, worms, birds, eggs, small snakes, lizards, and roots of plants. They also eat small rats and mice. Meerkats even eat scorpions (SKOR-pea-unz). Scorpions are poisonous spider-like creatures. But meerkats aren't harmed by scorpion poison. Meerkats first bite off the scorpion's stingers and then eat the rest of the scorpion.

1. Section 1 is mainly about

   a. where meerkats live.

   b. how meerkats are built for desert life.

   c. what life in the desert is like.

   d. how big meerkats are.

2. What question does section 3 answer?

   a. Why do meerkats eat scorpions?

   b. What do scorpions look like?

   c. Where do meerkats find their food?

   d. What do meerkats eat?

3. What is the "Keeping Safe" section of the article mainly about?

   _____

   _____

Lesson 15: Two-Headed Snakes

Read the article, and answer the questions that follow it.

Two-Headed Snakes

1   They say that two heads are better than one. But that isn't true if the two heads belong to one snake. For one thing, each head has a mind of its own. Sometimes one snake head wants to go one way, and the other wants to go the other way. They end up going nowhere. Another problem is that they fight over food. While they're deciding whether to go after a mouse or other animal, the animal will escape. An even bigger problem is that one head might see the other head as being food and attack it and even try to swallow it.

Why Two-Headed Snakes Live Longer in Zoos

2   Two-headed snakes don't have a chance in the wild. While they're fighting or figuring out which way to go, another animal will grab them and eat them. In captivity, two-headed snakes can live for a long time. One pair named Thelma and Louise lived in a zoo for seventeen years.

3   Scientists are now studying two-headed snakes. They want to see if the snakes can learn to work together to catch food.

Credit: AP Photo/James A. Finley.

1. Why is having two heads a problem for snakes? Use information from the article to support your answer. Write two details that the author included to show that having two heads is a problem for snakes.

Main Idea	Support
For a snake, having two heads is a problem:	Detail 1: Detail 2:

2. Why are two-headed snakes better off in a zoo than they are in the wild? Write your answer on the lines. If you don't remember why, go back to paragraph 2 and find the sentence that explains.

_____

_____

_____

_____

_____

Lesson 16 ▶ The Mouse That Howls

Objectives: Students will identify main ideas and provide explanations.

Introduction: Encourage students to use the title and heading as they read "The Mouse That Howls" in the Student Pages.

Guided and independent practice: Discuss students' responses to the questions. Have students locate and read sentences from the article that provide support for questions 2 and 3.

Assessment: To assess students' progress, note whether they are using headings and how well they are using them. You might ask students to tell how they are using headings and how the headings help them.

Lesson 16: The Mouse That Howls

Read the article, and answer the questions that follow it.

The Mouse That Howls

1 Did you know that there is a mouse that howls? Grasshopper mice don't like other mice to come into their territory (TAIR-uh-tor-ee). If other mice do come into the place where the grasshopper mice live, the grasshopper mice bark and howl.

What Grasshopper Mice Eat

2 Most mice eat seeds or bread or cheese. But grasshopper mice eat grasshoppers, beetles, and even other mice and scorpions and small snakes. Grasshopper mice aren't harmed by the poison of scorpions and snakes.

Fierce Fighters

3 Grasshopper mice are small. They weigh only about half an ounce (14 grams). But they are fierce fighters. They have long claws, sharp teeth, and strong jaws. They are also very fast on their feet and can catch their prey in a flash. Grasshopper mice are said to be like tiny wolves.

1. The first paragraph tells mostly

    a. why the grasshopper mouse howls.

    b. how the grasshopper mouse howls.

    c. what other animals do when the grasshopper mouse howls.

    d. how loud the grasshopper mouse howls.

2. Why are grasshopper mice able to eat poisonous snakes and poisonous scorpions? Write your answer on the lines.

_____

_____

3. Why is the grasshopper mouse said to be like a tiny wolf? Write your answer on the lines.

_____

_____

Lesson 17 ▶ The Fish That Fishes

Objectives: Students visualize, supply supporting details, and provide explanations.

Introduction: Based on a review of thousands of studies over a period of three decades, Marzano and associates (2000) found nine instructional techniques that were highly effective in improving student achievement. One of these is "representing knowledge" by creating graphic organizers, creating pictures or models, dramatizing or portraying, and imaging. Knowledge can be stored verbally or nonverbally. Storing knowledge nonverbally in addition to verbally greatly increases both understanding and retention.

Have you ever had the experience of seeing a movie that was based on a book that you read and being disappointed because the characters or scenes didn't look the same as those you had created in your mind as you read the book? Imaging is a powerful strategy for enriching the experience of reading. To introduce visualizing, describe the strategy. You might ask students whether they have ever read a story or book and then watched a movie or TV version of the story or book. Discuss how the movie or TV version might have differed from the book version and how sometimes people prefer the version that they created in their minds to the one they saw on the screen or TV.

Explain the value of visualizing. Use a think-aloud with a high-imagery passage to show students how you use this strategy. Read aloud some high-imagery passages and have students draw the images that they create. Because each of us has a different background of experience and unique processing abilities and propensities, images are personal. In a class of twenty students, you can expect twenty different versions of a visualized main character or scene.

Explain to students that their images will be personal to them because each of us is a special person with different experiences and backgrounds. However, the image should adequately and accurately reflect the text that students are reading or hearing. Students must concentrate so that their images are rich in detail but accurate in portraying the information provided in the piece. To provide some carefully guided practice, have students create images for the following high-imagery descriptions.

> When Laura walked behind Ma on the path to the barn, the little bits of light from the lantern leaped all around on the snow. The night was not yet quite dark. The woods were dark, but there was a gray light on the snowy path and in the sky there were a few stars [Wilder, 1935].

Komodo dragons are the biggest lizards in the world.... Komodo dragons walk on curved legs. Their tails swish back and forth to help them balance. They hold their heads high so they can see and smell any nearby animal [Maynard, 2007].

Encourage students to use the title of the article in the Student Pages, "The Fish That Fishes," to guess what the main ideas will be. Encourage them to make pictures in their mind to visualize what the fish that fishes looks like and what it does. Encourage inclusion of detail. Because some students have more artistic ability than others, place the focus on the content rather than the quality of the drawings. Demonstrate how stick figures might be used. As an alternative, have students write a description rather than create a drawing.

Guided and independent practice: Discuss students' responses. Ask for volunteers to show their drawings. Explain that drawings will differ because each of us has a different background of experience and different ways of looking at the world, but also explain that the drawings should show what was in the article. Display a picture of an anglerfish from a book or the Internet, and have students compare their drawings with what the fish actually looks like.

Assessment: To assess students' progress, note their drawings and written and oral descriptions of their images. Note too whether they are creating images on their own. From time to time, ask them what they are doing to make meaning as they read. Ask them to tell what strategies they are using and how these strategies are helping them comprehend better.

Extension: Have students extend imaging to fiction reading and reading in the content areas. Encourage them to create images as you read selections aloud to them. Ask questions such as the following to prompt students to elaborate on their images: "What are you picturing? What does the main character look like? How tall is he? What is he wearing? What is he doing? What expression does he have on his face? Is he frowning or smiling?" You might show students illustrated versions of the same story and discuss how different authors created different illustrations. Continue to model visualizing and encourage students to visualize as they read.

Lesson 17: The Fish That Fishes

Making pictures in your mind can help you to become a better reader. As you read the article about the fish that fishes, try to make pictures in your mind that show what the fish looks like and what it does.

The Fish That Fishes

Anglerfish (ANG-glur-fish) get their food in a surprising way. They fish for it. Anglerfish have a spine that grows out of their back fin. The spine can be very long or very short, but it bends over the mouth of the anglerfish like a fishing rod. On the end of this living fishing rod is a part that looks like a bug or a worm. The end part also lights up with a blue-green light. Most anglerfish live deep in the ocean. It is very dark deep in the ocean, so if the bait didn't light up, other fish wouldn't be able to see it.

The anglerfish has a round body and a very large mouth that is full of sharp teeth. When other fish stop to look at the lighted bait or try to eat it, the anglerfish snaps them up. Anglerfish have large jaws, so they can eat fish that are as big as they are, or even bigger. The anglerfish's teeth point inward so its prey cannot escape. Anglerfish are usually dark. That way, other fish can't see them. All they see is the bait.

1. In the column on the left, draw a picture that you made in your mind as you read about the anglerfish. In the column on the right, tell what your picture shows.

What I Pictured in My Mind as I Read	What My Picture Shows

2. How does the anglerfish catch its prey? Write your answer on the lines.

_____

_____

3. Why does the fake bait have to be lighted?

_____

_____

4. Why is the anglerfish able to catch fish that is bigger than it is?

_____

_____

Lesson 18 ▶ The Goliath Birdeater Spider

Objectives: Students visualize, supply supporting details, and provide explanations.

Introduction: Encourage students to use the title to guess what the main ideas in the article in the Student Pages, "The Goliath Birdeater Spider," will be. Encourage them to make pictures in their mind to visualize what the Goliath birdeater spider looks like and what it does.

Guided and independent practice: Discuss students' responses. Have volunteers show their drawings. Explain that drawings will differ because each of us has a different background of experience and different ways of looking at the world, but explain, too, that all of the drawings should show what was in the article. Display a picture of a Goliath birdeater spider from a book or the Internet, and have students compare their drawings with what the spider actually looks like.

Lesson 19 ▶ Giant Squid

Objectives: Students visualize, supply supporting details, and provide explanations.

Introduction: Encourage students to use the title of the article in the Student Pages, "The Giant Squid," to guess what the main ideas will be. Encourage them to make pictures in their mind to visualize what the giant squid looks like and how it moves through the water.

Guided and independent practice: Discuss students' responses. Ask for volunteers to show their drawings. Explain that the drawings will differ because each of us has a different background of experience and different ways of looking at the world, but explain that all of the drawings should show what was in the article. Display a picture of a giant squid from a book or the Internet, and have students compare their drawings with what the giant squid actually looks like.

Assessment: Note students' ability to visualize. If they have difficulty, model the process, and provide more practice.

Lesson 18: The Goliath Birdeater Spider

Read the article, and answer the questions that follow it.

The Goliath Birdeater Spider

The Goliath (guh–LIE–eth) birdeater spider's name isn't quite right. *Goliath* means "large" and it is the biggest spider in the world, but it doesn't eat birds. However, it does eat mice. It also eats crickets and other bugs.

How the Goliath Birdeater Kills Its Prey

The Goliath birdeater can hurt its prey in two ways. Its hairs have sharp points on the end. It can stick its prey with those. It can also bite. It has sharp fangs. The fangs carry venom that poisons their prey. The venom can kill mice and a cricket but isn't strong enough to kill a person. But the bite can be painful.

A Frightening Sight

Goliath birdeaters can be a frightening sight. They are hairy and very large. From leg tip to leg tip, they are 12 inches (30 centimeters) across.

1. In the column on the left, draw a picture that you made in your mind as you read. In the column on the right, tell what your picture shows.

What I Pictured in My Mind as I Read	What My Picture Shows

2. How does the Goliath birdeater kill its prey?

_____

_____

3. The article is called "The Goliath Birdeater Spider." What might be another title for this article?

_____

Explain your answer with information from the article. Write your answer on the lines.

_____

_____

_____

Lesson 19: The Giant Squid

Read the article, and answer the questions that follow it.

The Giant Squid

Giant squids, it seems, sometimes fight with whales. Toothed whales prey on giant squids. But giant squids fight back. No one has ever seen a giant squid fight a whale. But they have found marks on whales that were made by the tentacles (TEN-tuh-kuhlz) of a giant squid.

What a Giant Squid Looks Like

A giant squid has a long body. At the upper tip of its body are its fins. It uses these to guide itself through the water. Next comes the mantle. The mantle is the main part of the squid's body. Squid have a hard shell, but the shell is inside the mantle. Connected to the mantle is the funnel. A giant squid jets through the water by forcing water through the funnel. Sitting on top of the mantle is the head. The head holds a very large brain. Growing out of the head are eight arms known as "tentacles" (TEN-tuh-kehlz). Two of the tentacles are longer than the other six. From the tip of the fins to the tip of the longest tentacles, a giant squid can measure 60 feet (18 meters) or more.

Giant Eyes

No other creature has eyes as big as the giant squid has. Its eyes are as big as basketballs. It is very dark deep beneath the sea. The giant squid uses its giant eyes to find food.

How a Giant Squid Catches Its Prey

Giant squids eat fish, smaller squid, and other sea creatures. When it spots prey, the giant squid grabs it with its long tentacles. Their tentacles have suckers that hold onto the victim. Inside the suckers are hooks that are known as teeth. The teeth are as sharp as knives. With its two long tentacles and six shorter ones, the squid pulls the prey into its mouth. It cuts up the victim with its sharp beak. Its beak is so strong that it can snap a steel underwater cable in two. (An underwater cable is thicker than your fist.)

How a Giant Squid Escapes from Its Enemies

Giant squids are tough fighters. With their tentacles and sharp beaks, they can put up a fierce fight. But they would rather flee than fight. The giant squid has a special trick to escape from a whale or other enemy. When attacked, it shoots out a blob of black ink. The ink forms the shape of a squid. While the enemy animal is looking at the blob of ink, the squid turns a whitish color so it is hard to see. Then it squirts water out of its funnel and jets away.

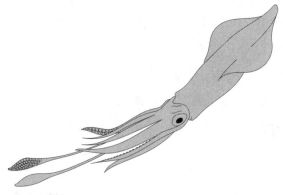

Credit: Clipart.com

1. In the column on the left, draw a picture that you made in your mind as you read about how the giant squid catches its prey or escapes from an enemy. In the column on the right, tell what your picture shows.

What I Pictured in My Mind as I Read About How the Giant Squid Catches Its Prey or Escapes from an Enemy	What My Picture Shows

2. In the empty boxes, write the missing steps that tell how a giant squid escapes from its enemies:

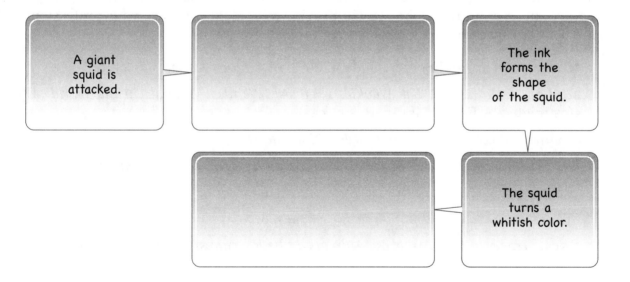

3. Why does the giant squid have such large eyes? Write your answer on the lines.

_____

_____

End-of-Theme Reflection

Discuss with students what they have learned about getting main ideas and supporting details and how they are using these skills. Ask what they have learned about animals and what they would still like to know. Have available copies of related books or other materials that extend the theme and encourage students to read them. Although the brief articles that students have read so far are building background knowledge and reading skill, students need to apply these skills to full-length selections. So that students might apply the skills and strategies that they have learned, select books that are well structured and have headings. Demonstrate to students how you use titles and headings to help you determine main ideas and grasp supporting details. Have them answer questions such as these:

- What were the main things that you learned from that book?

- What are the three to five most important ideas in the book?

- What strategies did you use to help you understand what you were reading?

The readability levels of the books listed below have been provided by Accelerated Reading (AR), except where noted otherwise. One book also has a three-digit Lexile designation. All are on a grade 3 to 5 reading level. However, readability formulas do not measure concept load, background needed to read a book, or interest level. You might want to examine the books you provide to students and use your professional judgment as to whether the books are appropriate for them.

Berger, Melvin, and Berger, Gilda. (2009). *Dangerous Animals.* **4.2**

Hanna, Jack. (2009). *The Wackiest, Wildest, Weirdest Animals in the World.* **4.9** (estimated by Follett Library Resources)

Kalman, Bobbie. (2005). *Endangered Komodo Dragons.* **5.6**

Landau, Elaine. (2008). *Alligators and Crocodiles: Hunters of the Night.* **4.1**

Redmond, S. (2003). *Tentacles: Tales of the Giant Squid.* **3.5**

Thomson, Sarah L. (2006). *Amazing Snakes.* **3.2**

West, Tracey. (2009). *Amazing Animals of the Rainforest.* **5.2** (estimated by Follett Library Resources)

Williams, Brenda. (2008). *Amazing Birds.* **4.3, 750**

Zoobooks magazines (zoobooks.com)

What did you learn about getting the main idea? How have you used what you have learned? Write your answer on the lines.

_____

_____

_____

_____

What did you learn about animals? Write your answer on the lines.

_____

_____

_____

Which animal was the most interesting to you? Why? Write your answer on the lines.

_____

_____

_____

Which animal was the most surprising to you? Why? Write your answer on the lines.

_____

_____

_____

Here is where you can go to find out more about some of the animals in this section:

Berger, Melvin, and Berger, Gilda. (2009). *Dangerous Animals*. New York: Scholastic. Gives facts about lions, tigers, grizzly bears, hippopotamuses, hyenas, rattlesnakes, and other dangerous animals. Asks true-false questions.

Hanna, Jack. (2009). *The Wackiest, Wildest, Weirdest Animals in the World*. Nashville, TN: Thomas Nelson. Describes the platypus, pufferfish, lion, anaconda, and other strange animals.

Kalman, Bobbie. (2005). *Endangered Komodo Dragons*. New York: Crabtree. Tells how Komodo dragons live and why they are endangered and gives fascinating facts about them.

Landau, Elaine. (2008). *Alligators and Crocodiles: Hunters of the Night*. Berkeley Heights, NJ: Enslow Elementary. Has colorful photos and lots of interesting facts about these creatures.

Redmond, S. (2003). *Tentacles: Tales of the Giant Squid*. New York: Random House. Describes the giant squid and tells how it lives.

Thomson, Sarah L. (2006). *Amazing Snakes*. New York: HarperCollins. Explains where snakes live and how they catch food and keep safe from enemies.

West, Tracey. (2009). *Amazing Animals of the Rainforest*. New York: Scholastic. Describes freshwater dolphins, gorillas, leopards, monkeys, and other animals.

Williams, Brenda. (2008). *Amazing Birds*. Milwaukee: Gareth Stevens. Has lots of interesting information about a number of birds.

Zoobooks. This magazine describes a different animal each month. zoobooks.com.

Theme B > Robots

Theme B, which explores the world of robots, provides additional practice with previously introduced main ideas and supporting details skills and strategies. In Lesson 22, students are introduced to the use of context clues to derive the meanings of words that may be new to them. Vocabulary knowledge is a key determiner of comprehension. One way to improve comprehension is to build students' vocabularies. To build vocabulary, Theme B introduces two potentially difficult words in each selection. In addition, students are provided with practice in using context. Instruction in context clues improves students' chances of deriving the meaning of a word from the context. This means that while reading for fun or to complete assignments, students will have a better chance of deriving the meanings of unfamiliar words and adding them to their vocabularies.

Review of Topic Sentences

Objectives: Students identify topic sentences and supporting details.

Introduction: Review the concept of topic sentences. Using the following paragraph or a similar one, model once again how you determine whether the first sentence seems to be stating a main idea and how, if it seems to be, you note as you read the paragraph whether the details are supporting the hypothesized main idea. If some sentences are not supporting the main idea, you seek another main idea sentence. Explain that the main idea might be presented in a middle or even an ending sentence and that not all paragraphs have topic sentences.

Factory robots can do a lot of jobs. Factory robots can paint products. Factory robots can weld pieces of metal together. They can put products into boxes and seal the boxes shut.

After reviewing topic sentences, have students complete the exercise in the Student Pages for this lesson.

Guided and independent practice: Discuss students' responses. Note that the topic sentences appeared in different places in the paragraphs.

The stories in this section are about robots. As you get more practice understanding main ideas and supporting details, you will be learning what robots are like and the various jobs that they do.

Lesson 20: Review of Topic Sentences

The topic sentence gives the main idea of a paragraph. Not all paragraphs have a topic sentence, but the one in the following article does. Often the topic sentence is the first one, but it can be anywhere in the paragraph. As you read this article, notice the details that support the main idea.

Robots

Robots make good workers. They never get tired. They can work 24 hours a day, 7 days a week, 52 weeks a year. And they never get bored. They can do the same job over and over again. They can put car parts together and paint cars faster and better than people can. And they won't get sick from paint fumes (fyuoomz) or burn themselves with a welding torch.

1. What is the topic sentence for this paragraph? Remember that the topic sentence tells the main idea of the paragraph. It is what the paragraph is all about. The other sentences in the paragraph support the topic sentence. Write the topic sentence on the lines. Underline sentences in the paragraph above that support the main idea.

_____

_____

_____

Read the next paragraph, and answer the questions after it.

Most robots that can move around have wheels. But some robots move on treads like those on a tank. With treads, they can go through mud and up hills easily. Some robots look and move like insects. They have three pairs of legs. With their six legs, these robots can climb into and out of holes and ditches. One kind of robot has just one leg. It uses that leg to hop by springing up into the air. Robots, it seems, have a number of ways of moving around.

2. Write the topic sentence on the lines. Underline sentences that support the main idea. *Hint:* The topic sentence is not always the first sentence in the paragraph,

_____

_____

_____

Lesson 21 ▶ Sawfish

Objectives: Students identify main ideas and supply supporting details.

Introduction: Explain to students that some titles just hint at the main idea. Tell them that they are going to read an article that is titled "Sawfish." Ask them what they think the article might be about. Remind them that all the articles in this unit are about robots. Encourage them to think about both parts of the word *sawfish*. After students make their predictions, have them read the article to see how their predictions play out. Encourage students to change their predictions as they read if their predictions are not working out.

Guided and independent practice: After students have circled their answers to the questions after the article, discuss their responses and especially reasons for their choices. Stress the need to support responses. Discuss the nature of the underground forest and the way that Sawfish cuts down the trees. Discuss any words that posed problems.

Extension: Have students visit the Sawfish Web site at http://www.tritonlogging.com/engineering.html to find out more about Sawfish.

Lesson 21: Sawfish

Some titles tell you exactly what an article is going to be about. But other titles just hint at the article's main idea. The title of this article is "Sawfish." What do you think it will be about? Keep in mind that all the articles in this theme are about robots. What kind of a robot might be called "Sawfish"? Read the article, and answer the questions that follow it.

Sawfish

1 A robot by the name of Sawfish saws down trees that are underwater. In some places, dams have been built and nearby forests have been flooded. There are about 100 million trees that are underwater. The trees are dead, but they are not rotten. For human lumberjacks, cutting the trees down is dangerous and difficult. Lumberjacks are people who cut down trees. Some of the trees are hundreds of feet underwater. But for Sawfish, cutting the trees down is no problem, no matter how big they are or how deep the water is.

2 Sawfish is a small submarine with a very large saw. It also has TV cameras. An operator on land uses these cameras to guide Sawfish. When it gets to a tree, Sawfish puts its arms around the bottom of the tree's trunk. Then it pulls out a heavy plastic bag and wraps it around the tree trunk. It quickly fills the bag with air from a tank that it carries. Then it saws across the bottom of the tree. It saws below the air-filled bag. After the tree has been cut through, Sawfish lets it go. The air-filled bag wrapped around the tree's trunk carries the tree to the surface.

Credit: Triton Logging.

1. Paragraph 1 is mainly about

    a. what lumberjacks do.

    b. where trees grow.

    c. how Sawfish got its name.

    d. what Sawfish does.

2. Paragraph 2 is mainly about

    a. what Sawfish looks like.

    b. how Sawfish cuts down trees.

    c. what trees are used for.

    d. where Sawfish works.

3. In the boxes, write the missing steps that tell how Sawfish cuts down a tree and sends it to the surface:

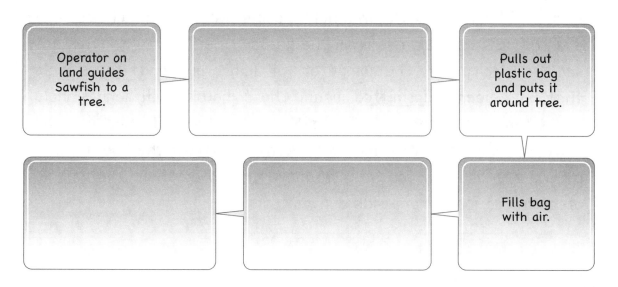

Rovers

Objectives: Students identify main ideas and supporting details and use context clues.

Introduction: This lesson introduces students to the use of context clues. In the article in the Student Pages and most of the ones that appear after it in this book, two words that students may not know are underlined. Students are to use context to derive a possible meaning for each of the two words. In the vocabulary questions in the exercise, students select from four definitions the one that best defines each underlined word.

To introduce the use of context clues, explain that each article will now have two words that are underlined. Tell students that if these words are new to them, they should use the context to help them make a good guess as to the meaning of each underlined word. When reading the selection, they can make a quick guess so they don't interrupt the flow of their reading. However, when they are answering questions about the words, they should look at the four possible definitions. Then they should go back to the article and take a close look at the way the words are used in the article. Next, they go back to the vocabulary question and select from the four definitions the one that best tells what each word means.

Explain to students that when using context, often it is helpful to think about what the article has said so far and also to read beyond the sentence in which the underlined word appears. Do a think-aloud as you model the process of using context. To make the think-aloud authentic, you might select a passage that has some words that are unfamiliar to you. Then guide students as the class cooperatively uses context with the following sample paragraph:

Someday robot suits might help people who are too weak to get around. The robot suits will help people walk, sit in chairs, and even go up stairs. Signals from the person's nerves and muscles are sent to a computer. The computer will figure out what the signals that have been <u>transmitted</u> mean. The computer will send signals to tiny motors in the suit. The <u>miniature</u> motors will help lift and move the person's arms and legs. With help from the robot suits, people who are now too weak to move around on their own will be able to lead more independent lives.

In the paragraph, the word *transmitted* means

a. fixed.

b. sent.

c. found.

d. passed.

In the paragraph, the word *miniature* means

a. costing a lot of money.

b. very quiet.

c. very easy to make.

d. very small.

After the class has used context to derive the meanings of the underlined words, introduce the article in the Student Pages for this lesson entitled "Rovers." Discuss what a rover is. Ask students to predict why robots might be called "rovers." Have students look at the illustration in the lesson. Have them tell what they notice about Rover and where they think it might be. Remind students that reading the title and headings and looking at illustrations can help them to read with more understanding. Have students predict what the article might tell them about the Rovers. Also remind students that they will be using context to get the meanings of the underlined words in the article.

Guided and independent practice: After students have completed the exercises, discuss their responses. Discuss in particular their responses to the vocabulary items. To provide added practice with the new vocabulary words, include them in the discussion of the article. Have students tell why the Rovers are said to be well equipped and also how they are able to analyze soil samples.

Assessment: Note whether students are going back to the selection to find the target vocabulary words and to see how the words are used in the article. If they have difficulty, model the process and provide more practice.

Extension: Have students visit the Rovers' Web site at http://marsrovers.nasa.gov/home/index.html to get the latest information on the robots.

Lesson 22: Rovers

Read the article, and answer the questions that follow it.

Rovers

1 Some robots are telerobotic. *Tele* means "distant" or "far away." Telerobotic robots are directed by people, but the people are someplace else. The most famous telerobotic robots are the Rovers.

Rovers Depend on People on Earth

2 Rovers have been sent to Mars. Right now there are two Rovers on Mars. Their names are *Spirit* and *Opportunity*. In 2011, a third Rover will be sent to Mars. Drivers on Earth start a Rover's engine. Then they guide it as it travels on flat land or goes over dunes and up hills. The operators guide it very carefully. If *Spirit* or *Opportunity* gets stuck in the sand, the operators can try moving the wheels in different ways. But if that doesn't work, the Rovers might be stuck there for all time. There are no tow trucks on Mars.

Rovers Have What They Need for Their Work

3 The Rovers are well <u>equipped</u> for exploring Mars. Both Rovers are packed with cameras and sensors. Sensors can pick up sounds and movement. With their cameras, they can take long shots of Mars and they can take close-ups. They have magnifying cameras that make a grain of sand look like a giant boulder. The Rovers have robot arms so they can pick up soil or rocks. Then they can use instruments on board to <u>analyze</u> the samples of the soil so that scientists on Earth can learn what the samples are made of. The Rovers even have a tool that they can use to dig inside rocks. That way the scientists on Earth can see what is inside

the rocks and also have the Rovers pick up bits on the inside of the rock and analyze them.

Rovers Are Slow Movers

4 The Rovers move slowly and carefully. A Rover might travel only a hundred yards in an hour. And most days it travels only a few hundred yards. *Spirit* took more than two months to climb up a tall hill and another two months to climb back down again.

Credit: NASA.

1. A good title usually tells what the main idea of an article or story is. The title of this article is "Rovers." What could be another good title for this article? Circle the letter of the title that you think is best. Then explain your answer with information from the article. Use the frame to help you answer the question.

   a. "Telerobotic Robots"

   b. "Robot Helpers"

   c. "The Red Planet"

   d. "Robots on Mars"

2. "_____"

is a good title because it tells the readers what this article is going to be about. The article tells why the robots

_____.

The article tells how the robots

_____

and how the robots

_____

_____.

The article also tells

_____

_____.

These details show that the title tells the main idea of the article.

3. Paragraph 2 is mainly about

    a. how many Rovers are on Mars.

    b. how people on Earth operate the Rovers.

    c. why the Rovers are on Mars.

    d. why the Rovers can go up and down hills.

4. Paragraph 3 is mainly about how Rovers

    a. move on Mars.   c. are guided.

    b. help explore Mars.   d. go up hills.

5. According to paragraph 2, why do the drivers on Earth guide the Rovers very carefully?

    a. Rovers are hard to guide.

    b. If the Rovers get stuck, there is not much they can do to help them.

    c. It took a long time to build the Rovers.

    d. Rovers can do many of the things that a person could do.

Sometimes there are new words used in the articles that you read. One way to learn new words is to use clues in the article to guess a new word's meaning. The following questions are asking you to choose the meanings of two words from the article. First look at the words below that are in *italics*, which means the letters are slanted. Next, read the possible meanings that are listed in answer choices **a** to **d**. Then go back to the paragraph and see how the words are used. In the article, the words are underlined. Then for each word, circle the letter of the best meaning.

6. In paragraph 3, the word *equipped* means

    a. is easy to run.

    b. works well.

    c. has parts that have been fixed.

    d. has things that are needed.

7. In paragraph 3, the word *analyze* means

    a. keep away from.

    b. lift up.

    c. break into small parts.

    d. find out what something is made of.

Lesson 23 ▶ T-52

Objectives: Identifying main ideas and supporting details and using context clues.

Introduction: Write the title of the selection on the board. Note that T-52 doesn't give much of a clue as to what the article might be about. Have students look at the illustration to see what T-52 looks like. Ask students to predict what the article might tell about T-52.

Guided and independent practice: After students have completed the exercises, discuss their responses. Talk over why T-52 is able to rescue people in places where humans might not be able to go. Also discuss why T-52 is described as a mammoth bulldozer. Ask how a mammoth bulldozer would be different from a regular bulldozer. Also discuss what some possible titles might be. Remind students that the titles that they create should tell what the main idea is and that they need to explain why the title they have made up gives the main idea.

Assessment: Note students' performance on this and previous exercises. Have they mastered key skills? If not, provide additional instruction and practice.

Lesson 24 ▶ The Pet Contest

Objectives: Students identify main ideas and themes, and use context clues.

Introduction: Ask how many students have pets. Have them tell what kind of pets they have. Ask if they have ever been in a pet contest. Have them read the story to find out about a boy by the name of Jason and his unusual pet.

Guided and independent practice: Discuss what Jason's pet was and why he had a robot dog for a pet. Discuss why the robot dog was not expensive. Discuss what the theme of the story is. Discuss why "Make the best of what you've got" is the theme of the story. Note that although the boy preferred having a real dog, he had fun with the robot dog. To foster making connections, give examples of times when you made the best of what you had and invite students to tell about a time when they made the best of what they had. Discuss responses to the other questions.

Lesson 23: T-52

Read the article, and answer the questions that follow it.

T-52

1   One telerobotic robot was built mainly to <u>rescue</u> people from danger. The T-52 Rescue Robot will go into burning buildings, pick up people or objects, and return.

2   T-52 is a giant of a robot. It stands 10 feet tall and weighs 10,000 pounds. It looks like a <u>mammoth</u> bulldozer with arms. With its powerful arms, T-52 can lift 1,000 pounds.

3   T-52 has seven cameras built into it. Standing outside the burning building, T-52's operator can watch on one of seven screens known as monitors and see what's going on inside the building. Using wireless controls, the operator directs T-52's movements.

Credit: TMSUK.

The article is called "T-52." What could be another title for it? This time make up a title on your own. Explain your answer with information from the article. Remember the title should tell what the main idea of the article is. Use the frame to help you answer the question.

1. Another title for this article is

"_____."

This is a good title because the article tells that

_____.

The article also tells how

_____.

These details show that the title tells the main idea of the article.

2. According to paragraph 3, an operator uses T-52 to see what's going on inside a building by

a. watching TV screens.

b. sitting inside the T-52.

c. using mirrors.

d. standing just behind the T-52.

3. Paragraph 2 is mainly about

a. how T-52 is operated.

b. who controls T-52.

c. what T-52 looks like.

d. why T-52 is needed.

4. In paragraph 1, the word *rescue* means

a. save from danger.

b. help with a problem.

c. explain what is happening.

d. take care of.

5. In paragraph 2, the word *mammoth* means

a. very unusual.

b. very large.

c. very frightening.

d. very friendly.

Lesson 24: The Pet Contest

So far, you have been reading nonfiction articles about robots, but there have been lots of stories written about robots. Here is a story about a boy and his robot pet. Read the story, and answer the questions that follow.

The Pet Contest

1   I had forgotten about wanting a dog until the principal came on the loudspeaker and said there was going to be a pet contest. The winners of the contest were getting a book of their choice at the bookstore around the corner. Two things I like: that's books of my own and dogs. Mom and Dad would like to get me a dog, but they can't. We live in an apartment that has a no-pets rule. You can't have a dog or a cat or even a bird. If the owner finds out you have a pet, out you go.

2   I wouldn't want to get kicked out. I like the apartment. It's right across the street from the park. That's where I spend most of my free time. And the rent is cheap. Mom and Dad work hard. But they don't make all that much money.

3   When I got home from school, Mom asked me how everything was. "Fine," I said. But the look on my face didn't match my words. Mom kept at me until I told her about the pet contest. I could see that she wished that she could let me get a pet. That night, she and Dad had a long talk.

4   The next night Dad came home carrying a big box. He had a wide smile on his face. "Got a surprise for you, Jason," he said, as he handed me the box. "Open it."

5   The box was kind of heavy. I like to guess what's inside boxes before I open them. But this one had me puzzled. I quickly opened the box. There, staring me in the face, was a dog. But the dog didn't bark or even move. I looked over at Dad.

6 "You've got to charge him up," Dad said. You see, Dad had gotten me a robot dog. I was surprised because the dog looked <u>expensive</u>. I knew money was tight. I didn't want Dad spending it on a fake dog. But Dad said he bought it from a guy at work. The dog was broken. So the guy sold it cheap. Dad is great at fixing things. He ordered some spare parts and got the dog working again.

7 I would <u>prefer</u> having a real dog, but it was kind of fun playing with the robot dog. I named it Robbie, and I taught it some tricks. I taught it to sit up and roll over. I also taught it to go get a ball when I throw it. That's a hard trick. I can't throw the ball too far. Robbie won't be able to see it. Its camera eyes can see for only about 20 yards.

8 When the day of the contest rolled around, I shined up Robbie and made sure he was charged up. Kids brought in all kinds of pets. There were pet dogs of all sizes and lots of pet cats. There were also pet fish and pet birds and pet hamsters. Prizes were being awarded for the best-behaved pet, the smartest pet, the biggest pet, and the most unusual pet. When the judges looked at Robbie, they got a puzzled look on their faces. They began talking among themselves. Some of the judges said that the contest was only for live pets. But then one of the judges said that the rules didn't say that the pets had to be live animals. The judges asked, "What can your pet do?" Robbie did all his dog tricks. He sat up. He rolled over. He ran after the ball that I threw and brought it back to me. And then I had him do some tricks that only robot dogs can do. He played a song with his built-in CD player. And he took my picture with his built-in camera. The judges were surprised.

9 Robbie didn't win first prize. The judges decided that should go to a real live pet. But Robbie got a prize for most unusual pet. To tell you the truth, I would still rather have a real live dog. But in the meantime, I'm going to hang on to Robbie.

1. What is the theme of the story that you just read? The main idea of a story is its theme. The theme is an idea that the author is trying to get across. Often it's a lesson about life. The theme of a story might be, "Share with others," "The best things in life are free," or "To have friends, you have to be a friend." Think about the story. What was the author saying in the story?

   a. Make the best of what you've got.

   b. Dogs make good pets.

   c. Contests are fun.

   d. We can learn things from our pets.

Did you pick "Make the best of what you've got"? That is the theme of the story. Jason wanted a dog to enter in the school's pet contest, but he understood that he couldn't have a real dog. The apartment where his family lived didn't allow pets. Jason trained his robot dog and entered it in the school's pet contest.

2. Paragraph 7 is mainly about

   a. what Jason thought of Robbie.

   b. the tricks that Jason taught the dog.

   c. how Jason took care of Robbie.

   d. why people like robot dogs.

3. In paragraph 6, the word *expensive* means

   a. hard to get.

   b. costing a lot of money.

   c. having many parts.

   d. hard to learn how to use.

4. In paragraph 7, the word *prefer* means

   a. stay close to.

   b. stay next to.

   c. do not care much about.

   d. would rather have.

End-of-Theme Reflection

Discuss the end-of-theme reflection that appears on the Student Pages that follow. Have available copies of the books suggested here or others that extend the theme and encourage students to read them. Although the brief articles that students have read so far are building background knowledge and reading skill, students need to apply these skills to full-length selections. So that students might apply the skills and strategies that they have learned, select books that are well structured and have headings. Demonstrate to students how you use titles and headings to help you determine main ideas and grasp supporting details. Have them answer questions such as:

- What were the main things that you learned from that book?

- What are the three to five most important ideas in the book?

- What strategies did you use to help you understand what you were reading?

The readability levels of the books listed below have been provided by Accelerated Reading (AR). All are on a grade 3 to 6 level. However, readability formulas do not measure concept load, background needed to read a book, or interest level. You might want to examine the books and use your professional judgment as to whether the books are appropriate for your students.

Davis, Barbara J. (2010). *The Kids' Guide to Robots*. **5.3**

Hyland, Tony. (2008). *How Robots Work*. **5.7**

Hyland, Tony. (2008). *Space Robots*. **6.0**

Kortenkamp, Steve. (2009). *Space Robots*. **3.5**

What did you learn about getting the theme of a story? How might you use what you have learned? Write your answers on the lines.

_____

_____

_____

_____

What did you learn about robots? Write your answer on the lines.

_____

_____

_____

Which of the robots that you read about do you think is most useful? Write your answer on the lines.

_____

_____

What else would you like to know about robots? Write your answer on the lines.

_____

_____

_____

Here are some books where you can find out more about robots:

Davis, Barbara J. (2010). *The Kids' Guide to Robots*. North Mankato, MN: Capstone Press. About a number of different kinds of robots and the jobs they do.

Hyland, Tony. (2008). *How Robots Work*. Mankato, MN: Smart Apple Media. Explains how robots move, use their senses, and do different kinds of jobs.

Hyland, Tony. (2008). *Space Robots*. Mankato, MN: Smart Apple Media. About the Rovers on Mars and other space robots.

Kortenkamp, Steve. (2009). *Space Robots*. North Mankato, MN: Capstone Press. About some of the discoveries that robots might make in space.

UNIT 2

> **Summarizing**

Unit Two explores various ways in which animals help people. The strategy focus is on summarizing. To open the unit, discuss with students some ways in which animals might help people. Place books and articles on the topic in your classroom library. You might also bookmark useful Internet sites.

Teaching Summarizing

When a group of researchers analyzed studies in the use of strategies to determine which strategies resulted in the greatest gains in comprehension, summarizing was number one. In addition to enabling students to organize and recite information, summarizing is also a check on their understanding. An inability to summarize is a sign that comprehension is lacking and calls for a rereading. Building on the previous unit, summarizing requires the ability to identify the main idea and supporting details. It also requires the abilities to select the most important information, combine details, and condense and paraphrase. The major problem that students have with summarizing is failure to discriminate between essential and unimportant details so that the summary becomes a retelling. Students might also have difficulty organizing information so that their summary is just a random listing of whatever they can remember.

The summary should begin with a main idea statement and then include essential supporting details. To develop the ability to summarize, the following activities are provided:

- Identifying the best summary
- Using frames to summarize
- Using graphic organizers to summarize

Theme

Animal Helpers

Objectives: Students learn the importance of and characteristics of a good summary and identify the best summary.

Introduction: Introduce the skill of summarizing by relating it to common oral summaries. Ask students to tell about their favorite book or the most interesting thing that they learned in school so far this week. After students have told about their favorite book or most important thing they have learned, tell them that they have just summarized. Explain that summarizing is telling the main idea and most important details. Tell students that if they have done any of the following activities, they have summarized:

- Told someone at home what they did at school

- Told about a trip that they took

- Told the main parts of a story that they read

- Told the main parts of a movie that they saw or a game that they watched

Tell students that in addition to summarizing orally, we summarize in writing. For example, they might be asked on a test to tell briefly what a story or article was about or to tell what happened to the main character. Or they might be asked to write a summary of a book that they have read. Explain, too, that they have read summaries. Locate and discuss the summaries provided at the end of textbook chapters and the blurbs on book jackets or recommended reading lists.

Students learn best when they make connections between what they are learning and their own experiences. They might not realize that they have been composing summaries much of their lives. To introduce the concept of summarizing, explain how you use summaries. For example, if you see the principal and the principal asks how your day went, you don't give every detail; you tell the principal only the most important information. Explain to students that summarizing is the most important reading and writing skill that they will learn.

Before students can summarize, they need to know what a good summary is like. Provide examples of well-crafted summaries and the selection in the Student Pages that was summarized. Help students discover what makes an effective summary. Ask: What do you notice about the summaries? What is in the first sentence of each summary? (Emphasize that it is the main idea.) What comes next? How does the summary end? To provide practice in recognizing the key elements of a summary, have students read "How Dogs Help Disabled People" in the Student Pages for this lesson. Have students read the title of the article and predict what the story might tell about ways in which dogs help disabled people. Have students read the selection to see how their predictions play out.

Guided and independent practice: Discuss students' choices for the best summary. Have them explain their selections. Discuss what they learned from reading the selection. Discuss types of assistance given with which they might be unfamiliar. As part of the discussion, use the vocabulary words from the selection. Have them tell how hearing ear dogs <u>alert</u> their owners when the dogs hear certain sounds and how <u>mobility</u>-assist dogs help owners who lack mobility. Also discuss students' responses to the vocabulary questions. Discuss the structure of the piece: How did the author organize the ideas? Help students see that the author used a structure of main idea and details.

The section is about ways in which animals help us. The articles are about how animals help people who can't see, can't hear, or can't walk. And it also tells how animals help boys and girls become better readers.

Lesson 25: How Dogs Help Disabled People

Now that you have finished Unit One and have had lots of practice with main ideas and supporting details, you are ready to learn how to summarize. Summarizing is the most important reading and writing skill of all. When you summarize, you tell only the important information or events. As they read, good readers create a summary in their minds. They might also stop after reading a section and check to see if they can summarize what they have read. If they can't summarize, this is a sign that they didn't understand what they read, so they read the section again.

Summaries can be spoken or written. In a spoken summary, we just tell the important things. You probably have made spoken summaries, but you might not have known it. You have made a spoken summary if you have done any of the following:

- Told about your favorite music group.

- Told what you learned in science class.

- Told the main parts of a story that you read.

- Told a friend about a book that you read.

A written summary is similar to a spoken summary. In a written summary, you tell the main idea first. Then you write the most important supporting details. You write the details as briefly as you can. The summary should be much shorter than the full article or story.

To help you understand what a good summary is like, read the following articles. After reading each article, select the best summary in the questions that follow.

How Dogs Help Disabled People

Dogs can help disabled people in many ways. A guide dog becomes the eyes for a blind person. It helps its owner get from place to place. A hearing ear dog <u>alerts</u> its owner when it hears certain sounds. A <u>mobility</u>-assist dog becomes its owner's helping hands. It helps its owner by picking up objects and bringing them to its owner. It picks up objects that the owner has dropped or can't reach. It can also pull its owner's wheelchair, carry things in a backpack, and open and close doors. It can even help its owner get dressed. Dogs that assist disabled people are known as service dogs.

1. Circle the letter of the best summary.

   a. Dogs can help disabled people in many ways. Dogs that assist disabled people are known as service dogs.

   b. Service dogs can help disabled people in many ways. Guide dogs help the blind. Hearing ear dogs help the deaf. Mobility-assist dogs help people who can't get around or do things for themselves.

   c. Service dogs can help disabled people in many ways. Guide dogs help the blind. Hearing ear dogs help the deaf. Mobility-assist dogs help people who can't get around or do things for themselves. A mobility-assist dog becomes its owner's helping hands. It helps its owner in many ways. It helps its owner by picking up objects and bringing them to its owner. It picks up objects that the owner has dropped or can't reach. It can also pull its owner's wheelchair, carry things in a backpack, and open and close doors. It can even help its owner get dressed.

d. Dogs can help disabled people in many ways. Dogs that assist disabled people are known as service dogs. One kind of service dog is the guide dog. A guide dog becomes the eyes for a blind person. It helps its owner get from place to place.

The best summary is choice **b**. It gives the main idea and the main supporting details. It uses just a few words. The summary in choice **a** does not give all the main details. It does not tell what guide, hearing, and mobility dogs do. The summary in choice **c** is much too long. The summary in choice **d** tells about only one kind of service dog.

2. In the article, the word *alerts* means

   a. keeps away from.

   b. warns of danger or difficulty.

   c. runs away.

   d. helps with.

3. In the article, the word *mobility* means

   a. the ability to move around and do things.

   b. helping people who are in need.

   c. keeping people from harm.

   d. knowing what to do.

Lesson 26 ▶ 4 Paws for Ability

Objectives: Students select the best summary, identify main ideas and supporting details, use context clues, and create a title.

Introduction: Have students read the title of the article in the Student Pages and predict what the selection might be about. Discuss what "paws" might suggest about the kind of animal being talked about and what "4 Paws for Ability" suggests about what the animals might be doing to help people. Have students read the selection to see how their predictions play out.

Guided and independent practice: Discuss students' choices for the best summary. Have them explain their selections in the Student Pages. Also discuss students' responses to the vocabulary and comprehension questions. Discuss how Karen's dog helped her when she became ill and what she did after she recovered. Discuss, too, the kinds of people whom dogs from 4 Paws for Ability might help. Discuss the structure of the piece: How did the author organize the ideas? Help students see that the author mainly used a sequence-of-events structure.

Extension: For more information, go to the 4 Paws for Ability's Web site at http://www.4pawsforability.org/.

Lesson 27 ▶ Where Service Dogs Can Go

Objectives: Students select the best summary, identify main ideas and supporting details, and use context clues.

Introduction: Have students read the title and predict what the selection might be about. Have students read the selection to see how their predictions play out.

Guided and independent practice: Discuss students' responses. Discuss with students why service dogs have certain privileges. Ask students if they have ever seen a service dog accompanying its owner in a store or restaurant or on a plane, bus, or subway.

Lesson 26: 4 Paws for Ability

Read the article, and answer the questions that follow it.

4 Paws for Ability

1 Service dogs can be lifesavers. Karen Shirk was at home alone, except for her service dog, Ben. Karen had been <u>ill</u>. She had just come home from the hospital a few days ago. Now she was having difficulty breathing. Karen was growing weaker and weaker. The phone rang. She was much too weak to get to the phone. Luckily Ben had been trained to get the phone and bring it to his owner. Ben picked up the ringing phone and dropped it next to Karen. Ben also began barking. The caller was Karen's father. He could hear that Karen's breathing was very weak. And he could hear Ben barking. It was Ben's way of asking for help. Karen's father called for an ambulance. Within minutes, Karen was being rushed back to the hospital. Karen was given good care at the hospital and was soon <u>recovering</u> from her illness. Ben had saved her life.

2 Not only had Ben saved Karen's life, he has also helped her in many other ways. He gets her food and water from the refrigerator. He picks up objects that she has dropped. And he carries packages for her. Mostly, though, he has been a good friend.

3 After she recovered, Karen decided to help others. Karen had waited six years to get a service dog. There were many other people who wanted dogs, but there were not enough dogs for all of them. Karen started 4 Paws for Ability and began raising service dogs. So far she has placed more than fifty dogs.

1. Circle the letter of the best summary:

a. After her service dog saved her life, Karen Shirk decided to help other disabled people get service dogs.

b. After her service dog saved her life, Karen Shirk decided to help other disabled people get service dogs. She started 4 Paws for Ability and has placed more than fifty service dogs.

c. After her service dog saved her life by getting the phone and barking into it, Karen Shirk decided to help other disabled people get service dogs. She didn't want them to have to wait a long time for a service dog the way she did. She started 4 Paws for Ability and has placed more than fifty service dogs.

d. After coming home from the hospital, Karen Shirk was at home alone, except for her service dog, Ben. Karen was having difficulty breathing. She was growing weaker and weaker. The phone rang. She was much too weak to crawl to the phone. Luckily Ben had been trained to get the phone and bring it to his owner. Ben picked up the ringing phone and dropped it next to Karen.

2. What question does paragraph 2 answer?

a. How did Ben help Karen?

b. How long did it take to train Ben?

c. What kind of a dog was Ben?

d. What made Ben a good helper?

3. In paragraph 1, the word *ill* means

a. hungry.

b. sick.

c. tired.

d. quiet.

4. In paragraph 1, the word *recovering* means

    a. feeling too sick to work.

    b. having trouble getting work done.

    c. being helped by others.

    d. getting better after being sick.

5. The title of the article is "4 Paws for Ability." What could be another title for it? Explain your answer with information from the article.

_____

_____

_____

_____

_____

Lesson 27: Where Service Dogs Can Go

Read the article, and answer the questions that follow it.

Where Service Dogs Can Go

Service dogs have certain <u>privileges</u>. They can go where no other dogs can go. As long as they are <u>accompanying</u> their owners, service dogs can go into food stores and restaurants. Other dogs cannot. Service dogs can travel on trains and planes. Other dogs can also travel on planes and trains. But usually they have to be placed where boxes and suitcases are kept. Service dogs can sit at their owner's feet. If a service dog owner is sick and in the hospital, the owner's dog can visit it. Service dogs can go just about anyplace a person can go.

1. Circle the letter of the best summary:

a. Service dogs can travel on trains and planes. Other dogs can also travel on planes and trains. But usually they have to be placed where boxes and suitcases are kept.

b. Service dogs can go just about anyplace a person can go. They can go into food stores, restaurants, and hospitals. They can travel on trains and planes and stay with their owners.

c. Service dogs can go into food stores and restaurants. Other dogs cannot. Service dogs can travel on trains and planes. Other dogs can also travel on planes and trains. But usually they have to be placed where boxes and suitcases are kept.

d. Service dogs have certain privileges. They can go where no other dogs can go. As long as they are with their owners, service dogs can go into food stores and restaurants. Service dogs can go just about anyplace a person can go.

2. In the article, the word *privileges* means

   a. duties that are important.

   b. rewards for working hard.

   c. rights that others might not have.

   d. things that are fun to do.

3. In the article, the word *accompanying* means

   a. resting on.

   b. having fun.

   c. running from.

   d. going with.

Lesson 28 ⟩ Service Dogs at Work

Objectives: Students select the best summary, identify supporting details, use context clues, and create a title.

Introduction: Have students read the title and predict what the selection might be about. Have students read the selection to see how their predictions play out and then complete the exercises.

Guided and independent practice: Discuss students' predictions and what they learned about service dogs. Also discuss students' completed summaries. Share with students some of the best summaries so they can see that summaries may be worded in a variety of ways, but all of them contain the essential information. Also discuss students' responses to the vocabulary questions. Ask them if they have ever seen a service dog at work. Discuss how dogs inform people that they are service dogs and what people should do if they notice a service dog. Discuss why service dogs should not be distracted.

Lesson 29 ⟩ Morris Frank and Buddy

Objectives: Students summarize, identify main ideas and supporting details, and use context clues.

Introduction: Have students read the article title and see what they notice about it. Point out that the title doesn't give much information. Ask what the names seem to suggest. Lead students to see that *Morris Frank* is most likely the name of a person and *Buddy* might be the name of an animal. Have students read the selection to see how Buddy helped Morris Frank.

Guided and independent practice: Discuss how Buddy helped Morris Frank and how Morris Frank happened to get Buddy. Also discuss students' completed summaries. Share with the class some of the best summaries so they can see that summaries may be worded in a variety of ways but all contain the essential information. Also discuss students' responses to the comprehension and vocabulary questions. Discuss, too, where Mrs. Eustis was residing when she wrote an article about using dogs to help the blind and what Morris did after he obtained Buddy.

Extension: You might want to read to students or encourage them to read the account of Buddy in Eva Moore's book *Buddy: The First Seeing Eye Dog* (New York: Scholastic Books, 1996).

Lesson 28: Service Dogs at Work

Read the article, and answer the questions that follow it.

Service Dogs at Work

1 Many service dogs wear special vests. Some vests have patches on them. The patch tells what kind of work the dog is doing. The patch might say "Hearing Dog" or "Search Dog." The vest and the patch <u>inform</u> people that the dog is working.

2 Most people don't know what to do when they see a service dog. If you notice a service dog at work, the best thing to do is to do nothing. Don't talk to the dog. Don't call it. Don't feed it. Don't pet it. The dog is working. It is helping its owner, so don't <u>distract</u> it. Taking the dog's attention away from its work makes its job harder.

1. Finish writing the summary by filling in the frame. Include only the most important information. Leave out any unnecessary words.

Many service dogs wear special vests to let people know

_____

_____ .

If you see a service dog at work,

_____

_____.

Now compare your answers with the sample answers:

Sample answers: Many service dogs wear special vests to let people know
they are working. If you see a service dog at work, don't distract it.
Your answers do not have to be exactly like this one, but your summary
should say that many service dogs wear special vests to let people know
they are working. It should also say you shouldn't distract a service dog.

2. In paragraph 1, the word *inform* means

  a. call to or yell.

  b. look like or be like.

  c. tell or let know.

  d. help with or carry.

3. In paragraph 2, the word *distract* means

  a. draw attention away from something.

  b. forget about for a long period of time.

  c. look at carefully and for a long time.

  d. understand fully and be able to explain to others.

Lesson 29: Morris Frank and Buddy

Read the article, and answer the questions that follow it.

Morris Frank and Buddy

1 The year was 1927. A friend was reading an article from a magazine to Morris Frank. Frank couldn't read the story himself. He was blind. The article was by Dorothy Eustis (YOU-stiss). She was an American woman <u>residing</u> (ree-ZIDE-ing) in Germany. In her magazine article, she explained how dogs there were being trained to help blind people get around. Morris Frank got a friend to send a letter to Mrs. Eustis. In his letter, Morris Frank asked if he could <u>obtain</u> one of those guide dogs. With Mrs. Eustis's help, Frank got a guide dog by the name of "Buddy." Soon he was taking Buddy around the United States. He showed people how trained dogs could help the blind. Mrs. Eustis heard about the good job Frank and his dog were doing. She came back to the United States. In 1929, she started The Seeing Eye.

2 At The Seeing Eye, dogs are trained to help the blind. And blind people are taught how to use their dogs. In that first year, seventeen blind people were given dogs and trained to use them. Since then, thousands of Seeing Eye dogs have been trained and given to blind people.

1. Finish writing the summary by filling in the frame. Include only the most important information. Leave out any unnecessary words.

Morris Frank and Buddy were the reason The Seeing Eye was started in the United States. After hearing about guide dogs helping the blind in Germany, Morris Frank

_____.

Morris was given

_____.

After hearing what a good job Morris's dog was doing, Mrs. Eustis

_____.

2. This article tells mainly

    a. when dogs were first raised to help the blind.

    b. why Morris Frank wanted a guide dog.

    c. how The Seeing Eye got started in the United States.

    d. how blind people are helped by The Seeing Eye.

3. According to paragraph 1, why couldn't Morris Frank read the article himself?

    a. He had never learned to read.

    b. He couldn't see.

    c. He had forgotten his glasses.

    d. The article was written in a language that Frank did not know.

4. Time charts can be used to help you summarize main happenings or events and put them in order. In the chart write the missing steps in the boxes.

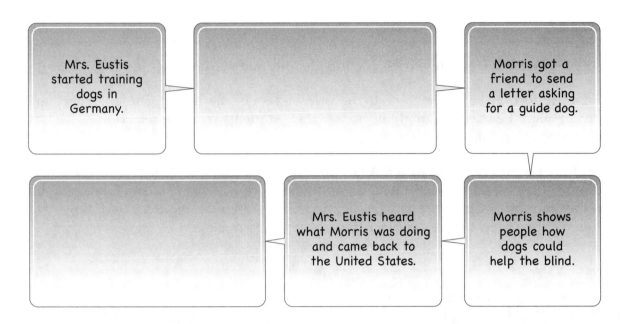

Mrs. Eustis started training dogs in Germany.		Morris got a friend to send a letter asking for a guide dog.
	Mrs. Eustis heard what Morris was doing and came back to the United States.	Morris shows people how dogs could help the blind.

5. In paragraph 1, the word *residing* means

    a. living in a place.

    b. taking a long trip.

    c. helping people who are sick.

    d. looking around for something that is lost.

6. In paragraph 1, the word *obtain* means

    a. want.

    b. get.

    c. use.

    d. call.

Lesson 30 ▶ Raising Puppies for The Seeing Eye

Objectives: Students summarize, identify details, and use context clues.

Introduction: Have students read the title of the article in the Student Pages and predict what the selection might be about. Have students read the selection to see how their predictions play out and complete the exercises.

Guided and independent practice: Discuss students' predictions and their completed summaries. Also discuss students' responses to the comprehension and vocabulary questions. Discuss, too, why puppy raisers attend meetings and how your students might feel about volunteering to be a puppy raiser.

Lesson 31 ▶ Getting to Know Their Dogs

Objectives: Students summarize, identify details, and use context clues.

Introduction: Have students read the title of the article in the Student Pages and predict what the article is about and what it will tell them. Have students read the selection to see how their predictions played out. Explain to students that they will be asked to write a brief summary about it.

Guided and independent practice: Discuss students' predictions and their completed summaries. Share with the class some of the best summaries so they can see that summaries may be worded in a variety of ways but all will contain the essential information. Stress the importance of including key information. Suggestions for polishing summaries can be introduced once students have a good idea of what kind of information should be included in a summary. Also discuss students' responses to the comprehension and vocabulary questions. Discuss how the people who are blind become acquainted with their dogs and why the final trip that they take is a good test of their ability to handle a Seeing Eye dog.

Assessment: Note students' ability to use a frame to summarize. If they have difficulty, model the process and provide more practice.

Extension: For more information, go to The Seeing Eye's site at http://www.seeingeye .org.

Lesson 30: Raising Puppies for The Seeing Eye

Read the article, and answer the questions that follow it.

Raising Puppies for The Seeing Eye

1   The Seeing Eye has a puppy-raising program. It is for young people between the ages of nine and nineteen and adults. People who sign up for the program join a puppy-raising club. The puppy-raising club meets once a week. At the club, the puppy raisers are given tips for caring for their puppies. The puppies <u>attend</u> along with their owners. Going to meetings with their owners helps the puppies get used to being around lots of people.

2   Puppy raisers take care of their puppies for fourteen to eighteen months. During that time, the puppy raisers learn to love their puppies. They feel sad when they have to give their puppies back to The Seeing Eye. But at the same time, the puppy raisers feel happy and proud. They are happy that they were able to help raise a puppy so a blind person would have a better life. As one puppy raiser explained, "Being involved in this program has taught me a lot about <u>volunteering</u> your time and giving of yourself." If the puppy raiser has done a good job, he or she can ask for another puppy to raise. Some young people have raised as many as seven puppies.

1. Finish writing the summary by filling in the frame. Include only the most important information. Leave out any unnecessary words.

The Seeing Eye has a puppy-raising program for young people. Puppy raisers take care of

_____.

The puppy raisers feel sad when

_____

_____.

But they feel happy and proud because

_____

_____.

2. According to paragraph 1, the puppies go to meetings with the puppy raisers so they

    a. will not feel lonely.

    b. get used to being with people.

    c. can learn new skills.

    d. can get to know better the person raising them.

3. According to paragraph 2, how long do puppy raisers keep their puppies?

    a. Fourteen months to a year and a half

    b. A year and a half to two years

    c. Two years to two and a half years

    d. Two to three years

4. In paragraph 1, the word *attend* means

    a. talk or speak to.

    b. find out or discover.

    c. go to a meeting or other happening.

    d. want to or hope to.

5. In paragraph 2, the word *volunteering* means

    a. helping out even though you don't have to.

    b. working hard for a long time.

    c. doing your very best at all times.

    d. trying to do a new job.

Lesson 31: Getting to Know Their Dogs

Read the article, and answer the questions that follow it.

Getting to Know Their Dogs

People who are blind meet their guide dogs at The Seeing Eye in Morristown, New Jersey. There they stay a month to become <u>acquainted</u> with their dogs, and they learn to handle their dogs. At first the blind people and the Seeing Eye dogs take short trips. They take two trips a day: one in the morning and one in the afternoon. Then they take longer trips. They learn to work with their dogs to cross streets, take buses, and go into all kinds of stores, shops, and restaurants. During their <u>final</u> week at The Seeing Eye, they take a trip to New York City with their dogs.

1. In the time chart write the missing steps in the boxes:

2. Finish writing the summary by filling in the frame. Include only the most important information. Leave out any unnecessary words.

People who are getting guide dogs stay at The Seeing Eye for a month so they can and learn to

_____ .

The people learn to work with their dogs to cross streets, take buses, and go to many different kinds of

_____ .

3. How do the blind people spend most of their time during the day at The Seeing Eye?

    a. Eating or resting

    b. Taking trips

    c. Learning how to take care of their dogs

    d. Talking with their teachers

4. In the paragraph, the word *acquainted* means

    a. spent some time with each other.

    b. watched or looked out for.

    c. knew or began to know someone or something.

    d. assisted with or gave some help to.

5. In the paragraph, the word *final* means

    a. close by.

    b. almost.

    c. next.

    d. last.

Lesson 32 ▶ Guide Horses

Objectives: Students use graphic organizers to summarize and use context clues.

Introduction: Have students read the title of the article in the Student Pages and predict what the selection might be about. Have students read the selection to see how their predictions play out and complete the exercises.

Guided and independent practice: Discuss students' predictions and their completed summaries. Also discuss students' responses to the comprehension and vocabulary questions. Discuss, too, why miniature horses might be used as guide horses and why they seem to have an instinct for guiding people who are blind.

Extension: For more information, go to the Guide Horse Foundation's Web site at http://www.guidehorse.org.

Lesson 33 ▶ Hearing Ear Dogs

Objectives: Students use headings to identify main ideas and supporting details, use graphic organizers to identify and summarize main ideas and details. and use context clues.

Introduction: Just as with titles, headings are useful for predicting or creating a hypothesis as to what the main idea might be, but students don't automatically use them. Using a think-aloud with an article that contains headings, show students how you use the headings to help you comprehend the article. Explain how you might even turn the headings into questions and read to answer these questions. For English learners, discuss the meaning of the italicized expression in this sentence: "Owners of hearing ear dogs say getting their dogs has *turned their lives around.*"

Guided and independent practice: After discussing headings and how they help readers better understand the main ideas in an article, have students use the headings in "Hearing Ear Dogs" in the Student Pages to get the main idea of each section of the article. Encourage students to turn each heading into a question and read to answer the question. Have students do this under your guidance, and discuss the article section by section. Then have students respond to the questions. Discuss some of the things that hearing ear dogs must become accustomed to and some of the sounds that they might need to respond to. While discussing students' responses, ask them to tell how headings helped them better understand the article.

Lesson 32: Guide Horses

Read the article, and answer the questions that follow it.

Guide Horses

Dogs have been guiding blind people for more than seventy years. Now horses are also being trained to guide the blind. Guide horses aren't regular horses. They are miniature horses. They are about the same size as guide dogs. Horses, it seems, have an <u>instinct</u> for helping the blind. When a horse in a herd goes blind, one of the other horses becomes its guide. Horses are smart. They can be trained to <u>perform</u> all the tasks and jobs that a guide dog is required to do. And they can do some things better. Horses are better at spotting danger than dogs are. Horses have eyes on the sides of their heads, so they can see what is on the side of them as well as what is in front of them. Horses are also stronger than dogs. They can carry packs for the blind person. And horses can walk long distances without getting tired. Horses live longer. Guide dogs live for only about ten to fifteen years. Horses live for thirty to forty years. And horses don't chase cats or get fleas.

Credit: Erik S. Lesser.

1. Summarize the article by filling in the web.

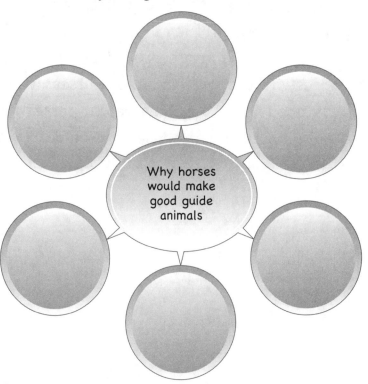

Why horses would make good guide animals

2. In the paragraph, the word *instinct* means

    a. trying very hard to understand something.

    b. taking an action in answer to a sound or command.

    c. feeling or ability that one is born with.

    d. running after an animal or person.

3. In the paragraph, the word *perform* means

    a. run after; chase.

    b. obey; listen to.

    c. hurry; go fast.

    d. do; carry out.

Lesson 33: Hearing Ear Dogs

Many articles have headings. A heading tells what a section is going to be about. It gives the main idea of the section. The heading for paragraph 2 in the following article is "What Hearing Ear Dogs Do." The section under that heading tells what hearing ear dogs do. If you know what a section is going to be about, then it is easier to understand that section. In fact, good readers turn headings into questions. For the heading "What Hearing Ear Dogs Do," they would ask, "What do hearing ear dogs do?" Then they read to answer that question.

Read the article. Turn the headings into questions to help you understand this article. Then answer the questions that follow it.

Hearing Ear Dogs

1   The smoke alarm goes off, but Tyrique (TIE-reek) doesn't hear it. Tyrique lost his hearing twenty years ago when he was just four years old. A light attached to the smoke alarm starts flashing. Tyrique doesn't see it. He is sound asleep. But Candy hears it. Candy is a hearing ear dog. Candy dashes to Tyrique and begins tugging on his pajamas. Smelling smoke, Tyrique leaps out of bed. The house is on fire. Because of Candy, Tyrique is able to get out of the house in time.

What Hearing Ear Dogs Do

2   You can probably guess what hearing ear dogs do. They help people who have hearing difficulties. Hearing ear dogs are sometimes known as signal dogs. The dogs are trained to let their owners know when certain sounds are heard. The dogs can be trained to <u>respond</u> to certain sounds such as a smoke detector, a doorbell, a phone ringing,

a baby crying, a car horn, or a fire truck siren. They can even be trained to alert their owners when someone calls the owner's name or when someone is trying to break into the owner's home.

Dogs That Make Good Hearing Ear Dogs

3   Not every dog can be a hearing ear dog. Hearing ear dogs need to be lively and alert. Dogs that just like to lie around might not pay attention to sounds or might not run to their owners when they hear the sounds. Hearing ear dogs must also be friendly. A dog that doesn't like to be around people wouldn't make a good hearing ear dog.

Training Hearing Ear Dogs

4   Hearing ear dogs are trained in steps. At first the dogs are trained to be around people. They have to get accustomed to being in crowds and going to stores and restaurants and other places where their owners go. Hearing ear dogs also learn to obey commands. They must learn to sit, stop, and come to their owners when told to do so. Then comes the hard part of their training. They are trained to alert their trainers to certain sounds.

5   When the dog hears one of the special sounds, it goes to its trainer and touches its trainer with its paw. It then leads the trainer to the sound. If the sound is one of danger, the dog lies down in front of its trainer after touching its trainer with its paw. This part of the training takes about four months.

6   Rewards are used to teach hearing ear dogs to let their trainers know when they hear certain sound. The trainer rings a doorbell or makes another special sound. The trainer shows the dog how to touch him with its paw. The dog is then given a reward. The reward could be a dog biscuit or a pat and some praise.

7   During the third part of the training, the deaf person and the hearing ear dog work together. The dog learns to run to the deaf person instead of the trainer when it hears certain sounds.

> *Turning Lives Around*
>
> 8 Owners of hearing ear dogs say getting their dogs has turned their lives around. Barry, an owner of a hearing ear dog named Meg, explains, "I feel that Meg has done so much for me. I could not imagine life without her. She has changed my life completely. She has become my ears. It is almost unbelievable that one so small can give so much. She has never let me down and is always there for me."

1. Paragraph 2 is mostly about

   a. who needs hearing ear dogs.

   b. how to care for hearing ear dogs.

   c. how hearing ear dogs help people.

   d. how to get a hearing ear dog.

2. Paragraph 3 is mostly about

   a. what kinds of dogs make good hearing ear dogs.

   b. where trainers get good hearing ear dogs.

   c. why dogs like to help people.

   d. where people can go to get hearing ear dogs.

3. Write the missing steps in the boxes:

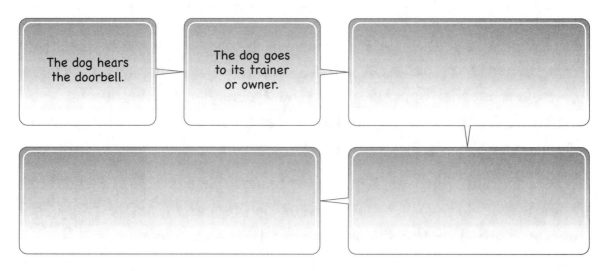

The dog hears the doorbell.

The dog goes to its trainer or owner.

4. How old is Tyrique now? *Hint:* Sometimes you have to use two facts from an article to answer a question.

    a. 4

    b. 14

    c. 20

    d. 24

5. For which of these sounds would a hearing ear dog lie down in front of its owner?

    a. Doorbell

    b. Telephone

    c. Smoke alarm

    d. Alarm clock

6. In paragraph 2, the word *respond* means

    a. try very hard to understand something.

    b. take an action in answer to a sound or command.

    c. listen to very carefully.

    d. run after an animal or person.

7. In paragraph 4, the word *accustomed* means

    a. find out about.

    b. be unhappy with.

    c. rest for a while.

    d. is used to something.

Lesson 34 ▸ Paws for Reading

Objectives: Students use a frame to complete a summary, identify main ideas and details, and use context clues.

Introduction: Have students read the title of the article in the Student Pages. Discuss possible meanings for the title and possible predictions. Call students' attention to the play on words: paws (pause) for reading. Have students predict what the article is about and what it will tell them. Have students read the selection to see how their predictions played out. For English learners, discuss the italicized expression in the following sentence: "This *gives them a chance* to be with a dog for an hour or so."

Guided and independent practice: Discuss students' predictions and their responses. Discuss why students might become anxious when reading aloud and what the benefits are of reading to a dog. Discuss, too, how they might feel about participating in a program such as Paws for Reading.

Lesson 34: Paws for Reading

Read the article, and answer the questions that follow it.

Paws for Reading

1 Some dogs help children with their reading. Dog owners bring their specially trained dogs to the library or the school. Children read their favorite book to the dogs. The children also talk to the dogs and pet them. The dogs enjoy the attention.

2 The children like reading to dogs because the dogs don't notice if the children get a word or two wrong. When they read to other people, the children sometimes get <u>anxious</u>. They are afraid that they will make a mistake. There is a second <u>benefit</u>. Most of the children who read to dogs don't have dogs of their own. This gives them a chance to be with a dog for an hour or so.

3 The program is called Paws for Reading. Children like the program. As one student explained, "I love to read, and I also really love animals."

---

1. Finish writing the summary by filling in the frame. Include only the most important information. Leave out any unnecessary words.

In Paws for Reading, dogs help students become better readers by

_____

_____.

Students like reading to dogs because

_____

_____ .

2. What is paragraph 2 mostly about?

   a. Why dogs like to be read to

   b. Why the students like to be read to

   c. Why the students like Paws for Reading

   d. Why the program is called "Paws for Reading"

3. Dogs like the program mainly because they like

   a. to hear good stories.

   b. to help students become better readers.

   c. being talked to and patted.

   d. to go places.

4. In paragraph 2, the word *anxious* means

   a. angry or cross.

   b. worried or afraid.

   c. late or not on time.

   d. brave; not afraid.

5. In paragraph 2, the word *benefit* means

   a. a short time or not long.

   b. a good or helpful thing.

   c. happy or pleased.

   d. done or finished.

Objectives: Students use a graphic organizer to summarize, compose a summary, identify main ideas and details, and use context clues.

Introduction: Have students read the title of the article in the Student Pages. Discuss how monkeys might help disabled people. Have students read the headings to find out what kinds of information the article will be giving them. Have students read the selection and use the headings to guide their reading. Encourage students to turn the headings into questions and then read to answer the questions. For English learners, discuss the figures of speech italicized in the following sentences: "Capuchin monkeys are *good with their hands*. Dr. Willard thought that what her friend needed was a *pair of hands to help him out.*"

Guided and independent practice: Discuss students' responses. Discuss with the class the characteristics of the best summaries written by students. Help students who are still having difficulty composing summaries. Discuss with students how they used the headings to guide their comprehension. Discuss how monkeys help people who are paralyzed and approximately how many commands a trained monkey can respond to. Have students compare having a monkey helper with having a dog as a helper.

Assessment: Note students' ability to use a web to summarize. If they have difficulty, model the process, and provide more practice. Also note students' overall performance on this and previous activities in this unit. Have they mastered key skills? If not, provide additional instruction and practice.

Extension: Additional information about Helping Hands monkeys is available at www.monkeyhelpers.org.

Lesson 35: Using Monkeys to Help Disabled People

Read the article, and answer the questions that follow it.

Using Monkeys to Help Disabled People

1 Helping a friend gave Dr. Mary Jane Willard an idea for using monkeys to help disabled people. Dr. Willard was helping a friend get out of a car. The friend was <u>paralyzed.</u> The friend had been injured in an accident and could not move from the shoulders down. Dr. Willard thought that what her friend needed was a pair of hands to help him out. "Why not train monkeys to help disabled people?" she thought to herself. Later she decided to start training capuchin (kap-YOU-shin) monkeys.

Why Capuchin Monkeys Can Be Good Helpers

2 Capuchin monkeys are a good choice for helping disabled people. Capuchin monkeys are smart and easy to train. Many circuses have trained capuchin monkeys to do tricks. Capuchin monkeys are small. They are only about 12 to 22 inches long. Because they are small, they don't eat much, and they aren't as likely to hurt a disabled person. Capuchin monkeys also live a long time. They live for thirty to forty years. Best of all, capuchin monkeys are good with their hands. They can pick up things.

3 Dr. Willard and a friend, Judi Zazula, started Helping Hands in 1979. Helping Hands trains monkeys to help disabled people. Training a monkey takes two years. Helping Hands places about twelve monkeys a year in homes throughout the United States. One of their helper

monkeys has been helping a disabled man for twenty-five years. The helper monkey has become part of his family.

Raising Helping Hands Monkeys

4   Before capuchin monkeys can be trained, they have to live with people. As soon as they are old enough to leave their mothers, the monkeys are placed in homes for about five years. The monkeys' keepers are specially chosen. They must enjoy animals and must not mind a little monkey business. Monkeys are cute animals, but they are very playful animals and can get into a lot of mischief. Monkey raisers need to be willing to spend a lot of time with the monkeys. The monkeys need to learn to trust and get along with humans.

Helping Disabled People

5   After they have been trained, capuchin monkeys are placed with disabled people. The monkeys can turn lights on and off. They can get their owners a drink or a snack. The monkeys take the lids off the containers and place the food in front of their owners. They learn to put a straw in a cup if that is how the person drinks. They can also microwave food, clean up spills, and put things in the trash. They can put a CD in a CD player or a DVD in a DVD player. They can bring their owner a book and turn the pages. They can pick up dropped objects and give them to the disabled person. The monkeys can carry out <u>approximately</u> fifty commands.

Greatest Job in the World

6   Do the monkeys mind working as helpers? The monkeys get food and a home. They also get rewards. After doing a job, they get a cracker, juice, or some other treat. Most important of all, they get lots of attention and a lot of love. If they could speak, they would probably say, "This is a lot better than being in a zoo or a circus! For a monkey, this is the greatest job in the world."

1. Fill in details from paragraph 2 that tell why capuchin monkeys can be good helpers.

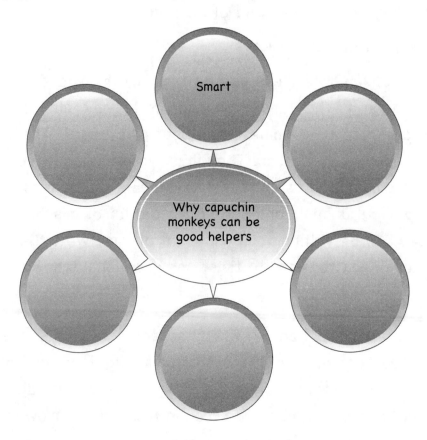

2. Now use the web to help you summarize the paragraph. Begin with a topic sentence.

_____

_____

_____

_____

_____

_____

_____

3. Fill in details from paragraph 5 that tell about ways in which capuchin monkeys can help disabled people.

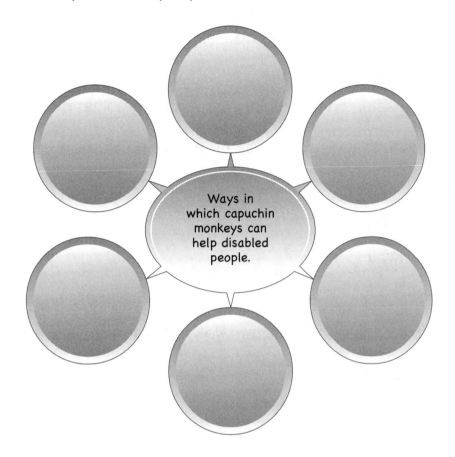

Ways in which capuchin monkeys can help disabled people.

4. Paragraph 2 is mainly about

a. why capuchin monkeys make good helpers for the disabled.

b. how capuchin monkeys help the disabled.

c. how capuchin monkeys got their name.

d. why capuchin monkeys are easy to train.

5. According to paragraph 4, it is important for young capuchin monkeys to spend a lot of time with people because the monkeys

a. need time to play.

b. get lonely.

c. need to learn to trust people.

d. get into trouble if no one is watching them.

6. What question does paragraph 5 answer?

    a. Are the monkeys hard to care for?

    b. What jobs can the monkeys do?

    c. How strong are the monkeys?

    d. What do disabled people think about having helper monkeys?

7. In paragraph 1, the word *paralyzed* means

    a. not able to move.

    b. not feeling well.

    c. living far away.

    d. being in a hospital.

8. In paragraph 5, the word *approximately* means

    a. about; nearly; not exactly.

    b. difficult; hard; taking a lot of work.

    c. asking for help; asking for food or money.

    d. important; needing to be done.

Dogs That Help People Who Are Sick, Sad, or Lonely

Objectives: Students identify main ideas and details, supply details, summarize, and use context clues.

Introduction: Have students read the title of the article in the Student Pages. Discuss how dogs might help people who are sick, sad, or lonely. Have students read the headings to find out what kinds of information the article will be giving them. Have students read the selection and use the headings to guide their reading.

Guided and independent practice: Discuss students' responses. Discuss with the class the characteristics of the best summaries written by students. Help students who are still having difficulty composing summaries. Discuss with students how they used the headings to guide their comprehension. Discuss what happened when doctors investigated the idea that dogs could help sick people feel better and also how dogs demonstrate that they could be good therapy dogs. To help students make connections, talk over experiences that they might have had in which a dog or other pet helped them to feel better when they were sick or sad or lonely.

Lesson 36: Dogs That Help People Who Are Sick, Sad, or Lonely

Read the article, and answer the questions that follow it.

Dogs That Help People Who are Sick, Sad, or Lonely

1 Each day the chaplain (CHAP-lin) at the hospital where Elaine Smith worked as a nurse visited patients. A chaplain is a priest, minister, or rabbi (RAB-eye) who works in a hospital or school, or in the army. On his visits, the chaplain brought along his dog, a golden labrador (LAB-ruh-door) retriever (ree-TREE-ver). Smith noticed that the patients smiled at the dog, talked to it, and petted it. After the chaplain and his dog left, the sick people seemed to feel a little better. They seemed calmer and less worried. Smith believed that having visits by dogs would help sick people get well. At the time she was working in England. When she came back home to the United States, she put her idea into action. She started Therapy (THAIR-uh-pea) Dogs International in 1976. The dogs are called therapy dogs because they help people get better. *Therapy* means "to help a sick person get better." She and a group of friends who owned dogs began visiting hospitals and homes for older people. They also got other dog owners to join. And they started telling hospitals and homes for older people about therapy dogs. Meanwhile, doctors <u>investigated</u> the idea that dogs could help sick people get well.

Helping Sick People

2 The doctors found that when dogs are around, people feel calmer. Their hearts beat a little slower. Seeing and touching a

dog makes them forget about being sick. They feel a little less lonely. They feel more like talking. Seeing a dog might remind them of a time when they had a dog of their own. They start talking about happy times. Dogs have a way of turning sad faces into happy faces. Therapy dogs help older people who have just been sitting around become more active. They want to take the dog for a walk or play with the dog.

Passing the Test

3   Dogs must pass a test before they can become therapy dogs. They must show that they are friendly around strangers and can sit still while being petted or brushed. They must also <u>demonstrate</u> that they can walk by the owner's side, come when called, and sit when told to do so. They must be able to go into crowded places without getting nervous. And, hardest of all, they must pass by food without stopping to eat it. They must also pass by other dogs that they might meet without chasing them or fighting or playing with them. Only well-trained dogs with good manners can become therapy dogs.

4   Therapy dogs also have to be healthy. They must have all of their shots. And they need to have a checkup by the vet at least once a year.

5   Therapy Dogs International started out with just a few dogs. Now more than 10,000 volunteers and more than 15,000 dogs belong to Therapy Dogs International. Volunteers like taking therapy dogs to homes for older people and hospitals. As one volunteer explained, "I think it is the greatest thing to make someone happy and allow them to tell me stories about their old friends."

1. What question does paragraph 2 answer?

   a. What kinds of dogs help sick people?

   b. In what ways do dogs help sick people feel better?

   c. What do sick people like to think about?

   d. How do doctors help sick people get better?

2. What question does paragraph 3 answer?

   a. What kinds of things must dogs be able to do to be chosen to become therapy dogs?

   b. What are some of the ways in which therapy dogs help sick people?

   c. How are therapy dogs trained so that they can help sick people feel better?

   d. Where can therapy dogs be found?

3. In paragraph 1, the word *investigated* means

   a. assisted or gave help with.

   b. looked into or tried to find out about.

   c. talked about to others or asked about.

   d. took notes on or wrote about.

4. In paragraph 3, the word *demonstrate* means

   a. listen to or obey.

   b. show or prove.

   c. hurry up or go quickly.

   d. look for or go after.

5. How do therapy dogs help sick people feel better? Fill in details in this web from paragraph 2 that will help you answer this question.

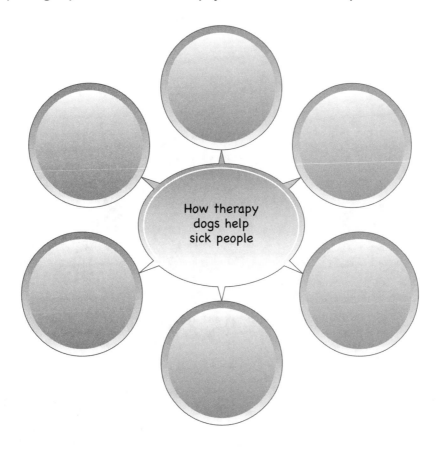

6. Now use the web to help you summarize the paragraph. Begin with a topic sentence.

_____

_____

_____

_____

_____

_____

7. What must dogs be able to do to pass a test to become a therapy dog? Fill in the web with details from paragraph 3 that will help you answer this question.

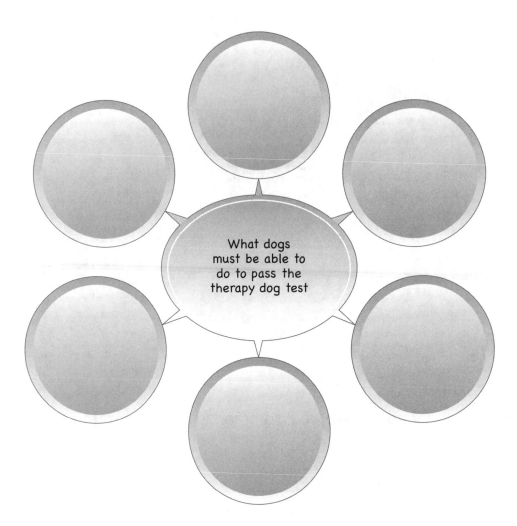

What dogs must be able to do to pass the therapy dog test

Lesson 36 Dogs That Help People Who Are Sick, Sad, or Lonely

Lesson 37   Assistance Dogs

Objectives: Students identify main ideas and details, create a title, summarize, and use context clues.

Introduction: Have students read the title of the article in the Student Pages. Discuss the meaning of the word *assistance.* Talk over what kinds of assistance or help dogs might give. Have students read the headings to find out what kinds of information the article will be giving them. Have students read the selection and use the headings to guide their reading. Encourage students to turn the headings into questions. For English learners, discuss the figures of speech that are in italics in the following sentences: *"A light bulb went off in her head.* The students *go off on their own* and start assistance dog centers in their towns and cities."

Guided and independent practice: Discuss students' responses. Discuss how Bonnie Bergin got her idea for assistance dogs and how Abdul aided Kerrill Knaus. Discuss, too, how Bonnie Bergin proved that people who said that training dogs to assist people who are disabled was a ridiculous idea were wrong. Discuss with students how they used the headings to guide their comprehension. Have students tell what they think Kerrill Knaus might be doing now. Tell students that Kerrill Knaus is still disabled and still uses a wheelchair but that she and her sister started a group that arranges for disabled people to take horseback rides.

Assessment: Note students' overall performance on this and previous exercises in this unit. Have they mastered key skills? If not, provide additional instruction and practice.

Extension: For more information about Bonnie Bergin and assistance dogs, students can visit the Bergin University of Canine Studies' Web site at http://www.berginU.org/.

Lesson 37: Assistance Dogs

Read the article, and answer the questions that follow it.

Assistance Dogs

1   While traveling in far-off countries, Bonnie Bergin noticed that people who couldn't walk used animals to <u>aid</u> them. They used donkeys and burros (BUR-rohz) to help them get around. The animals carried clothing, pots and pans and food, and other things that could be sold. The donkeys and burros helped the disabled people earn a living. A light bulb went off in Bonnie Bergin's head. She had an idea: "Why not get animals to aid disabled people in the United States?" Of course, there aren't many donkeys or burros in the United States. But there are lots of dogs in the United States. Bonnie Bergin took her idea home with her. In 1975 she started training dogs that would help disabled people.

The First Assistance Dog

2   People told Bonnie Bergin that training dogs to help disabled people was a <u>ridiculous</u> idea. They said that it would never work. But that didn't stop her. The first dog that Bonnie trained was Abdul (ab-DOOL). Bonnie Bergin spent two years training Abdul. Bonnie trained Abdul to help Kerrill Knaus (nows).

3   Kerrill Knaus has very weak muscles. She can't use her legs and has difficulty using her arms. Abdul learned to carry books, food, and other things for her. He carried them in two bags that were strapped around his back and stomach. If Kerrill dropped something, Abdul picked it up with his teeth. Abdul turned on lights and opened

doors for Kerrill and even pushed elevator buttons with his paws. Abdul became Kerrill Knaus's hands and legs.

4   Abdul helped Kerrill Knaus for more than a dozen years. He was honored as the most outstanding dog in America. Abdul proved that dogs could help people.

Assistance Dog Institute

5   In 1991 Bonnie Bergin started the Assistance Dog Institute. Besides raising and training dogs, the Assistance Dog Institute, now known as the Bergin University of Canine Studies, teaches students how to raise and train assistance dogs. The students go off on their own and start assistance dog centers in their towns and cities. Bonnie Bergin has helped others set up more than 150 centers for training assistance dogs. Hundreds of assistance dogs have been trained. And it all started with an idea and a dog by the name of Abdul.

1. Show the main things that happened in this article. Fill in the boxes with missing happenings.

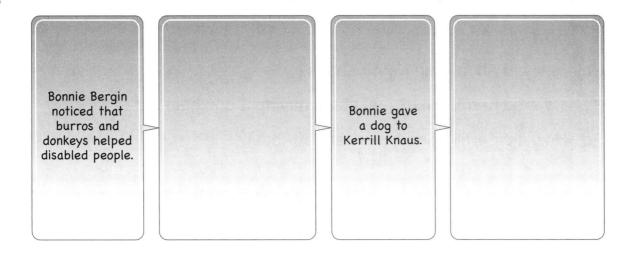

Bonnie Bergin noticed that burros and donkeys helped disabled people.

Bonnie gave a dog to Kerrill Knaus.

2. Now use the boxes in the chart to help you summarize the paragraph. Begin with a topic sentence. The topic sentence should tell the main thing that Bonnie Bergin did.

_____

_____

_____

_____

_____

3. What is paragraph 1 mostly about?

   a. How donkeys and burros help people

   b. Why Bonnie Bergin was in a far-off country

   c. How Bonnie Bergin got an idea for helping disabled people

   d. What kind of a person Bonnie Bergin is

4. What question does paragraph 3 answer?

   a. How was Abdul trained?

   b. How did Abdul help Kerrill Knaus?

   c. How did Kerrill Knaus feel about having a dog help her?

   d. How did Kerrill Knaus take care of Abdul?

5. According to paragraph 4, for how many years did Abdul help Kerrill Knaus?

    a. More than twelve

    b. More than fourteen

    c. More than sixteen

    d. More than eighteen

6. In paragraph 1, the word *aid* means

    a. watch.

    b. call.

    c. chase.

    d. help.

7. In paragraph 2, the word *ridiculous* means

    a. costing a lot of money.

    b. foolish.

    c. kind.

    d. difficult.

End-of-Theme Reflection

Discuss the Student Pages for the end-of-theme reflection. Ask students to list the service animals that they have read about in this unit. Discuss with students what they learned about service animals. Ask which service animals they like best and which they thought were most useful. Have them tell what the service animals had in common and in what ways they differed. Discuss also the people who started service animal groups.

Discuss with students what they have learned about summarizing. Ask them to give examples of times when they have used summarizing. Explain that their summaries might have been oral: they might have told about some information they learned or a story they read. Or their summary might have been silent or just a whisper. They might have summarized after reading an article or a section of an article. Or they might have written a summary. They might have written a paragraph as a summary or created a web or other graphic organizer as a summary.

In order for students to be able to transfer the skills they learned in this unit, it is essential that they practice applying those skills to their textbooks and other full-length materials. Suggested books are listed below. Have available copies of the suggested books, and encourage students to read them. Readability levels are given for each book. The first level listed is provided by Accelerated Reading (AR) and the second by Lexile Framework. All are on a grade 3 to 4 level. However, readability formulas do not measure concept load, background needed to read a book, or interest level. You might want to examine the books and use your professional judgment as to whether the books are appropriate for your students.

McDaniel, Melissa. (2005). *Guide Dogs*. **4.1, 730**

McGinty, Alice B. (1999). *Guide Dogs Seeing for People Who Can't*. **3.9, 790**

Moore, Eva. (1996). *Buddy: The First Seeing Eye Dog*. **3.8, 600**

Murray, Julie. (2009). *Service Animals*. **3.8**

Murray, Julie. (2009). *Therapy Animals*. **4**

Nichols, Catherine. (2007). *Therapy Horses*. **4.9**

Osofsky, Audrey. (1992). *My Buddy*. **Very easy reading. 3.0, 500**

Tagliaferro, Linda. (2005). *Service Dogs*. **3.9, 690**

Tagliaferro, Linda. (2005). *Therapy Dogs*. **4.3, 770**

Encourage students to apply their skills to the books. Using one of the books as a model, show students how they might use chapter titles and headings to help them determine the main ideas that they will be reading about. You might demonstrate how most chapter titles and chapter heads can be turned into questions, which readers then answer when they come to the end of the chapter or section. Encourage students to summarize their reading by telling the three to five most important facts they learned. Encourage the use of graphic organizers to highlight essential information. Students might also share their books with partners or in small groups. Students might wish to pursue a particular aspect of service animals. Instead of or along with reading the books, students might consult one of the Web sites listed in the Extension sections of the lessons. Web sites tend to be more difficult than books; however, Web site text can be read by a text-to-speech feature available on most computers.

What did you learn about summarizing? How have you used what you have learned? Write your answer on the lines.

_____

_____

What did you learn about animals that help people? What are some ways in which animals help people? Write your answer on the lines.

_____

_____

Do you know anyone who has a service dog or who has been helped by an animal in some way? Write your answer on the lines.

_____

_____

Which of the animals that you read about do you think is most useful? Give reasons for your choice. Write your answer on the lines.

_____

_____

What else would you like to know about service dogs and other animals that help people? Here is where you can go to find more information about service dogs and other animals that help people:

McDaniel, Melissa. (2005). *Guide Dogs*. New York: Bearport. Guide dogs help their owners cross streets, go shopping, and even escape from fires.

McGinty, Alice B. (1999). *Guide Dogs Seeing for People Who Can't*. New York: Rosen. Tells how Freedom, a Seeing Eye dog, was raised and trained.

Moore, Eva. (1996) *Buddy: The First Seeing Eye Dog*. New York: Scholastic. Tells how the first Seeing Eye dog was raised and how it helped its owner.

Murray, Julie. (2009). *Service Animals*. Edina, MN: ABDO. Tells how service animals are trained and how they help people.

Murray, Julie. (2009). *Therapy Animals*. Edina, MN: ABDO. Tells how therapy animals are chosen, how they are trained, and how they help people.

Nichols, Catherine. (2007). *Therapy Horses*. New York: Bearport. Explains how therapy horses are trained and how they help people who have disabilities.

Osofsky, Audrey. (1992). *My Buddy*. New York: Holt. A boy in a wheelchair tells how his dog helps him.

Tagliaferro, Linda. (2005). *Service Dogs*. New York: Bearport. Tells how service dogs help people.

Tagliaferro, Linda. (2005). *Therapy Dogs*. New York: Bearport. Tells how therapy dogs help people.

Inferring, which includes predicting and concluding, is an essential comprehension skill and lends itself to instruction. When taught to infer and provided practice, struggling readers do just as well as average readers (Hansen & Pearson, 1982). Inferences differ in their complexity. Some require putting together several pieces of information. Often they require combining background knowledge with information in the article being read. Making inferences is dependent on understanding the details in a selection and so builds on the previous units.

To develop the ability to infer, predict, and conclude, this unit provides the following activities:

- Selecting from a list of feeling and character trait words

- Inferring, predicting, and concluding

- Supporting inferences, predictions, and conclusions

- Using answer organizers

- Using frames

Introducing Inferring

Explain to students that an important reasoning skill is the ability to make inferences: guesses or conclusions that we draw from details. Stress with students the importance of basing inferences on details or other information. Model the process of making inferences. Think aloud as you make inferences so that students gain insight into the cognitive processes involved.

One effective technique for having students develop a sense of making inferences is through the use of pictures. By using pictures, students aren't hampered by a lack of adequate decoding skills or unknown vocabulary. The pictures might be drawn from a text that students are about to read. From a picture of a person, they might infer the person's age, where the person is, what the person might be doing, what the person is thinking, whether the person is rich or poor, and so forth. Stress the need to use features of the illustration and their own background of experience and reasoning to make plausible inferences. Once students feel comfortable with making inferences from pictures, have them base their inferences on sentences (Yuill & Oakhill 1991). Invite students to read the following sentences and, for each sentence, ask the students: What might you infer from this sentence? What leads you to make that inference? (Do not ask, "Why did you make that inference?" The use of *why* suggests that students are being judged.) Invite students to make as many inferences as they can.

> Alexia asked the teacher if she could choose a book about sports instead of one about animals.

> Henry's feet hurt, but he kept on walking.

Students might infer that Alexia is a girl because Alexia is a girl's name. They might also infer that Alexia is in school because she asked the teacher if she could switch books. And they might infer that she would rather read about sports than animals.

Continue with the exercise for the following sentences:

> Jamal was surprised to find that no one else had come to school.

> Reggie made sure that he had two sharpened pencils.

> Before leaving the house, Anna checked to be sure that the dog next door was chained up.

> Mirabella packed an extra sandwich just in case.

Macro cloze also provides excellent reinforcement for making inferences. In macro cloze, students supply a missing sentence. They use the first and third sentences to infer the content of the middle sentence as in the following examples.

Liftoff was supposed to be at six o'clock in the morning.

_____

The spaceship didn't take off until just a few minutes after noon.

I was getting ready to watch my favorite show.

_____

I decided to study my spelling words instead.

I heard a scream for help.

_____

I wish the people in the next apartment would turn down their TV.

Theme > People Helping People

Objectives: Students make and support inferences.

Introduction: The foundational cognitive skills for making inferences are using one or more details and one's own experience and knowledge and reasoning ability to draw a conclusion. Explain to students that we make inferences about people based on what they do and say and what other people say about them. For instance, your friend has three pet cats, two goldfish, a dog, and a parakeet. What inference might you make about your friend? Explain that you have another friend who gave up her vacation to help build houses for people who lost their homes in a storm. What might you infer about that person? Explain to students that they will be reading about a person by the name of Dan West who traveled from the United States to Spain. Show Spain on a map. Invite students to read the brief paragraph about Dan West in the Student Pages for this lesson. Tell them to notice the kinds of things that Dan West does and then to make an inference about the kind of person he is.

Guided and independent practice: Have students check their responses with the sample responses after the selection. Discuss their responses, especially the support they provided for their inferences. Have students read the title of the second article and predict what this one will tell them about Dan West. Have students read the selection to see how their predictions played out. Explain to students that they can change their predictions if they don't work out. Discuss students' responses. Explain to students that they can pick different characteristics, but they should be able to support the characteristic that they choose.

Extension: Provide added practice if needed. As you read to students and as they discuss selections they have read, prompt them to make inferences. As they make inferences about characters in stories or causes or effects in their content-area reading, encourage them to provide support by citing details.

This series of articles will tell you about people who help others. You will also be making inferences.

Lesson 38: Dan West

Making Inferences

Writers don't tell us everything. They expect their readers to use their thoughts and experiences to add to the information the author has provided. For instance, if the writer said that Maria had helped a neighbor carry her groceries and taken care of a pet for a friend and loaned someone at school a pen, the writer would not have to tell readers that Maria was kind. Readers could tell that from Maria's actions. Using clues and hints that the author gives you is known as inferring. Inferring is sometimes called "reading between the lines." Inferring is one of the most important reading skills.

Read the following paragraph about Dan West. What can you infer about him? What kind of a person does he seem to be? Write your inferences in the box after the paragraph. Support your answer with information from the paragraph.

Dan West

In the 1930s Dan West was giving out cups of milk to poor children in Spain. At the time, there was a war going on there. Dan West didn't live in Spain, but he had traveled there when he heard about the suffering of the children.

Write your answer on the line. Some words that tell about a person are: *kind, caring, loving, selfish, unselfish, hard working, brave, cheerful, mean.*	Dan West seems to be a _____ person.
Give one example that shows what kind of a person Dan West was.	
Tell what Dan West did when he went to Spain.	Dan West went to Spain and _____.
Now finish your answer by writing a sentence that tells what the example shows.	_____ shows that Dan West was a _____ person.

Did you infer that Dan West was a kind person? The paragraph didn't tell you that, but it did say that he had traveled to Spain when he heard about the suffering of the children. And the paragraph said that he was giving out cups of milk to poor children. These are the things that a kind person would do.

Read the following paragraph and see what else you can infer about Dan West. How do you think Dan West was feeling? Write your answer on the lines. Be sure to support your answer with information from the paragraph.

What Happens Next?

Dan could not stay in Spain much longer. Soon he would have to return to his home in the United States. Dan wondered what would happen when he left. Where would the children get milk when he wasn't around? What would happen to them? He thought about the children during the day. At night he would wake up and think of them some more. He tried to think of some plan to help the children when he wasn't there. But no plan came to mind.

Tell how Dan West was feeling. Some feeling words are: *sad, nervous, worried, happy, anxious, hopeless, angry, joyful, disappointed, calm, upset, afraid, lonely.*	Dan West was feeling _____.
Now support your answer by using information from the paragraph that shows how Dan West was feeling.	He _____ _____.

Did you infer that Dan West was worried, or sad, or upset? The paragraph didn't tell you that, but it did say that day and night, he tried to think of some plan to help the children, but no plan came to mind.

Lesson 39 ▶ Not a Cup But a Cow

Objectives: Students make and support inferences and use context clues.

Introduction: Have students read the article title in the Student Pages and predict what the article will tell them. Have students read the selection to see how their predictions played out. Explain to students that they can change their predictions if they don't work out.

Guided and independent practice: Discuss students' responses. Discuss what a slogan is and why the slogan "Not a Cup But a Cow" is a good one. Discuss what having a cow will provide for families. For English language learners, discuss the expression: "A big *smile broke across* Dan West's face."

Lesson 40 ▶ Getting Started

Objectives: Students support inferences and use context clues.

Introduction: Have students read the title of the article in the Student Pages and predict what the article will tell them. Have students read the selection to see how their predictions played out. Explain to students that they can change their predictions if they don't work out. Also introduce the strategy of using phonetic respellings. Explain that phonetic respellings put a word into syllables and show how each syllable should be pronounced. Inform students that dictionaries use phonetic respellings and that hard-to-pronounce words in this book also have phonetic respellings. Have students note the phonetic respelling of *heifers* in the article. Have them use the phonetic respelling to pronounce the word.

Guided and independent practice: Discuss students' responses. Discuss why donating a heifer is a good idea and why families would appreciate getting a heifer.

Assessment: Note students' ability to make inferences and provide support for those inferences. Provide corrective instruction if needed.

Lesson 39: Not a Cup But a Cow

Read the article, and answer the questions that follow it.

> ### Not a Cup But a Cow
>
> Then one day Dan West got an idea. Instead of giving children a cup of milk, why not give their families a cow? Then the children would have milk every day. And the mothers and fathers would feel better because they would be feeding their own families. Dan West had children of his own. He knew how important it is for parents to be able to <u>provide</u> food for their children. Dan West's <u>slogan</u> became "Not a cup, but a cow." A big smile broke across Dan West's face.

1. How was Dan West feeling after he thought of a plan? Write your answer on the line.

Dan West was feeling _____.

2. Now support your answer by using information from the paragraph. There is a detail in the paragraph that shows how Dan West was feeling after he thought of a plan. Write that on the lines.

_____

_____

_____

_____

3. Why was Dan West's plan a good one? The story tells what Dan West's plan was, but it doesn't say that the plan was a good one. You have to infer that the plan is a good one. If your inference is correct, you should be able to support it with reasons from the paragraph. Write down two reasons that the plan seems to be a good one.

Dan West's plan was a good one for the following reasons.

First,

_____

_____.

Second,

_____

_____.

4. In the paragraph, the word *provide* means

   a. cook or heat.

   b. give or supply.

   c. think about.

   d. plan for.

5. In the paragraph, the word *slogan* means a word or phrase that

   a. warns others to be careful.

   b. tells what a group plans to do.

   c. has been taken from a song.

   d. hides the truth.

Lesson 40: Getting Started

Read the following article, and answer the questions that follow.

Getting Started

1   Dan West decided that he would give away heifers (HEF-erz). He started Heifer International. Heifers are young female cows that give milk when they are grown. Then West had another idea. <u>Donating</u> a heifer would help one family. But there were lots of families that needed help. He decided that a family that was given a heifer would be asked to give away a heifer calf when their heifer grew a little older and had calves of her own. Then that family would give away a heifer calf when its heifer grew up and had calves. And the next family would give away a heifer and the next and the next.

2   As it turned out, families <u>appreciated</u> being helped when they were in need. They thanked Heifer International. But helping others gave them a different kind of feeling. It made them feel proud.

Credit: Heifer International.

1. What information in the article leads you to infer that Dan West planned carefully so that he could help as many families as possible? Answer the question by filling in the frame:

Dan West planned carefully so that he could help as many families as possible. Each family that was given a heifer was asked to

_____

_____

_____.

2. Why is it a good idea to ask each family that is given a heifer to later give a calf away? Use information from the article and your own ideas to

help you answer the question. Give two reasons. For the first reason, think how getting a heifer calf helps a family. For the second reason, think how you might feel if you were able to help someone in need.

Reason 1:

_____

_____

_____

Reason 2:

_____

_____

_____

3. In paragraph 1, the word *donating* means

   a. calling to.

   b. raising up.

   c. giving away.

   d. returning to.

4. In paragraph 2, the word *appreciated* means

   a. was thankful for.

   b. worked hard for.

   c. talked about.

   d. put in a safe place.

Lesson 41 ▸ A Big Dream

Objectives: Students support inferences and use context clues.

Introduction: Invite students to turn the title of the article in the Student Pages into a question and then read the article to answer their question. Explain that if the question doesn't work out, they can change the question.

Guided and independent practice: Discuss students' responses. Discuss what Dan West did when he arrived home and why his friends agreed to help him. Write model constructed responses on the board, and have students compare their responses with the models. Encourage students to tell about big dreams that they might have.

Lesson 42 ▸ Not Just Cows

Objectives: Students make and support inferences and use context clues.

Introduction: Invite students to use the title of the article in the Student Pages to make a prediction about what the article will tell. Have them read the article to see how their predictions play out.

Guided and independent practice: Discuss students' responses. Write examples of constructed responses on the board, and have students compare their responses with the examples. Discuss the kinds of animals that are currently being donated and the kinds of animals that produce wool. Discuss which animals students might choose to receive. Talk over reasons for their choices.

Assessment: Note students' overall performance on this and previous exercises in this unit. Have they mastered key skills? If not, provide additional instruction and practice.

Lesson 41: A Big Dream

Read the following paragraph, and answer the questions that follow it.

A Big Dream

When Dan West <u>arrived</u> home, he told friends and neighbors about his idea. He explained his plan to help poor people feed themselves. He told the people gathered to "dream no small dream." Dan West was out to change the world. He wanted to put an end to hunger. He wanted to help poor families all over the world feed themselves. Many of his friends <u>agreed</u> to help out. The first heifers were given away in 1944. Dan West passed away years later in 1971. But his idea lives on. Heifer International (IN-ter-NASH-uh-nuhl) has helped more than 9 million families in 125 countries.

1. What was big about Dan West's dream? Write your answer on the lines.

_____

_____

_____

_____

2. How do you know that he followed his dream? Use information from the paragraph to support your answer. Answer the question by filling in this frame:

Dan West followed his dream. His dream was to

_____

_____,

so he started Heifer International. Heifer International has helped

_____

_____.

3. In the paragraph, the word *arrived* means

    a. hurried up.

    b. felt lost.

    c. got to a place.

    d. was late.

4. In the paragraph, the word *agreed* means

    a. said yes.

    b. spoke softly.

    c. thought about.

    d. put away.

Lesson 42: Not Just Cows

Read the article, and answer the questions that follow it.

Not Just Cows

1 In some countries, people drink goat's milk instead of cow's milk, so Heifer International began giving away goats, too. Over the years, many kinds of animals have been added to the list of donated animals. <u>Currently</u>, Heifer International gives away heifers, goats, chickens, rabbits, llamas, water buffalo, pigs, sheep, bees, and other animals that will help people feed their families.

2 Some animals do more than provide food. Water buffalo are strong and can do work. They can pull a plow or carry heavy loads of food to market. Owners of water buffalo can make extra money by renting out the water buffalo to other farmers who need help with the plowing or carrying goods. Llamas can also carry heavy packs. Llamas can live high in the mountains and walk on steep trails. Llamas, sheep, and goats <u>produce</u> wool. Their wool can be used to make warm clothing and can be sold.

Credit: Heifer International.

1. What makes you think that Heifer International discovered that different people had different needs? Use information from the paragraphs to support your answer.

_____

_____

_____

_____

2. In paragraph 1, the word *currently* means

    a. now.   c. in the meantime.

    b. soon.   d. many years ago.

3. In paragraph 2, the word *produce* means

    a. find in a far-off place.   c. make or supply.

    b. sell at a low price.   d. make money from.

4. If you were raising animals to help your family, which animal would you most like to receive? Explain why. Fill in the frame with your answer.

The animal I would most like to receive is a

_____.

I have two reasons for wanting to receive a

_____.

First,

_____

_____.

Second,

_____

_____.

Lesson 43 ▶ Helping Families

Objectives: Students support inferences and use context clues.

Introduction: Invite students to turn the title of the paragraph in the Student Pages into a question, and then read the paragraph to answer the question. Remind them to use phonetic respellings and context clues.

Guided and independent practice: Discuss students' responses. Discuss how Heifer International trains families who are being given animals about how to take care of them. Discuss what kinds of shelters families might provide for the animals they receive. Write model constructed responses on the board, and have students compare their responses with the models. Discuss why building self-reliance is important. To help students make connections, discuss with them an experience they have had that has made them self-reliant. You might begin the discussion by describing an experience you have had that made you more self-reliant. Also discuss the response to question 5. Talk over why "Helping People Help Themselves and Others" is a good slogan for Heifer International. Since this question takes in all of the previous articles about Heifer International as well, encourage students to draw support from articles previously read.

Extension: Have students visit the Web site for Heifer International at http://www .heifer.org to find out more about this organization. The site includes a number of brief videos. Also obtain, if possible, the video *Beatrice's Goat* (CBS Broadcasting), originally broadcast on *60 Minutes*. The video shows Beatrice, who, because her family was given a goat, was able to attend school and, ultimately, college.

Lesson 43: Helping Families

Read the paragraph, and answer the questions that follow it.

Helping Families

Heifer International doesn't just give animals away. It wants the families to be self-reliant (rih-LIE-ent). Self-reliant means that people can do things for themselves. They don't have to depend on others. Heifer International <u>trains</u> the families who will be receiving the animals. They teach the families how to feed and care for the animals. And they make sure that the animals have proper <u>shelter</u>. The family might build a shed or a hutch for the animals they are to receive. They might also plant grass for the animals to eat.

1. What makes you think that many of the people who are given animals might not know how to care for them? Use information from the article to support your answer.

_____

_____

_____

_____

2. How do you know that Heifer International wants the animals it gives away to have good care? Fill in the frame. Use information from the article to support your answer.

Heifer International wants the animals it gives away to have good care. Heifer International teaches families

_____

_____ .

Heifer International makes sure that

_____ .

3. In the paragraph, the word *trains* means

   a. give enough food to.

   b. help to care for.

   c. give things that are needed.

   d. teach how to do something.

4. In the paragraph, the word *shelter* means

   a. straw or blankets used to keep animals warm.

   b. a place that keeps people or animals out of the rain and cold.

   c. a building that is far away from the city.

   d. a spot deep in the forest or in the middle of a field.

5. Why is "Helping People Help Themselves and Others" a good slogan for Heifer International? Support your answer with information from the paragraphs you just read or any of the other paragraphs about Dan West and Heifer International.

_____

_____

_____

_____

Introducing Predicting

In this next series of lessons, the focus is on predicting. Predicting is a highly effective strategy that combines the activation and application of prior knowledge, reasoning skills, and text knowledge. Predicting is sometimes known as *forward inferencing* because readers are inferring what might happen. Because it involves inferring about unknown events, predicting is the most difficult of the inferring strategies. So that predictions aren't just guesses, students should base their predictions on clues provided by titles, headings, illustrations, and whatever text they have read. They should also use their background knowledge to make predictions. They can use their background knowledge to hypothesize what is likely to happen, especially if the situation in the text is one with which they are familiar. When discussing students' predictions, ask them to tell what led them to make their predictions. For fiction pieces, students typically predict what will happen next. For nonfiction, students predict what the author will tell them about a topic or what they will learn by reading a piece of text.

Predicting is closely related to previewing. When previewing, students analyze the title, illustrations, headings, story introduction, or summary as a basis for making predictions. Flexibility is an important element in predicting. Students need to be able to modify their predictions on the basis of new information that they acquire as they read the text. Predicting is an ongoing strategy. Students continue to predict as they read a selection (Gunning, 2010). To introduce predicting, think aloud as you model the process of making a prediction.

Lesson 44 ▶ Young Helper

Objectives: Students make and support inferences, make and support predictions, and use context clues.

Introduction: Invite students to turn the title of the article in the Student Pages into a question and then read the article to answer the question. Remind them to use phonetic respellings and context clues. Tell students to stop after answering the first two questions, make a prediction, and then continue reading.

Guided and independent practice: Discuss students' responses. Write model constructed responses on the board, and have students compare their responses with the models. Discuss with students what going to the library and getting information about child labor and getting the teacher's permission to speak to the class about child labor shows us about the kind of person Craig is. Discuss with students what they predict Craig might do next. Encourage students to use information from the article and their own background knowledge and experience with the way people act.

Lesson 45 ▶ Starting Free the Children

Objectives: Students evaluate predictions, support inferences, and use context clues.

Introduction: Explain that the paragraph in this lesson will tell what Craig did. Invite students to turn the title into a question, then read to answer the question, and see how their predictions play out.

Guided and independent practice: Discuss students' responses. Discuss how Craig got volunteers to raise money to construct a school. Write model constructed responses on the board, and have students compare their responses with the models. Discuss with students what they predict Craig might do next.

Lesson 44: Young Helper

Read the paragraph, and then answer the questions that follow it.

Young Helper

You don't have to be old to help others. In April 1995, when he was just twelve years old, Craig Kielburger (KILE-bur-ger) was looking for the comics section in the newspaper. A story about a boy by the name of Iqbal Masih (IK-bow [like cow] muh-SEE) caught his eye. Iqbal Masih, who lived in Pakistan, had been forced to work long days in a factory that made rugs. He had worked twelve-hour days, six days a week from the time he was four years old until he escaped. His job was to tie tiny knots in the rugs. The article shocked Craig. Iqbal Masih was the same age as Craig. Craig couldn't imagine what it was like to work all day six days a week and never have a chance to attend school or play. Craig ripped the article out of the newspaper and put it in his backpack. But he couldn't get Iqbal Masih out of his mind. Riding the bus to school, he took the article out of his backpack and read it over and over again. After school, he went to the library and got as much information as he could find on child <u>labor</u>. The next day, with the teacher's <u>permission</u>, he told the class about Iqbal Masih and about the millions of children who were forced to work in factories and mines.

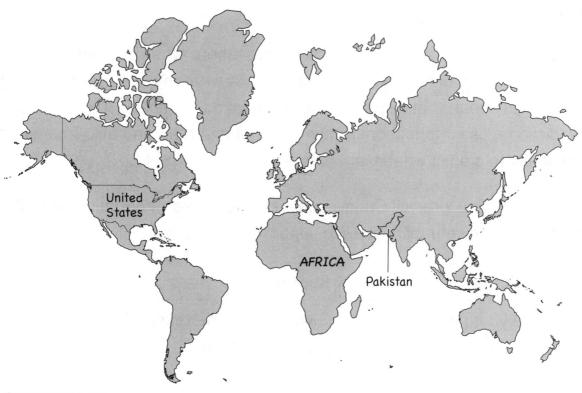

1. How did Craig feel after he read the article?

_____

_____

Use information from the paragraph to support your answer. Write two details that show how Craig felt after he read the article.

Detail 1:

_____

_____

Detail 2:

_____

_____

Making Predictions

So far, you have been making inferences about what has already happened. You can also make inferences about what might happen. Making inferences about what might happen is known as *predicting.* To make good predictions, use information from what you have read and also from what you know to predict what might happen.

2. What do you predict Craig might do next? Use information from the paragraph and your own ideas to support your answer.

Prediction	Support
Write your prediction below:	Give at least one reason for your prediction below:

3. In the paragraph, the word *labor* means

    a. schooling.

    b. work.

    c. being poor.

    d. living far away.

4. In the paragraph, the word *permission* means

    a. talk to and listen to.

    b. stay in a place.

    c. allowing or letting do.

    d. helping with for a while.

Lesson 45: Starting Free the Children

Read the paragraph, and answer the questions that follow it.

Starting Free the Children

Talking about the problem of child labor wasn't enough for Craig. He wanted to do something about it. He asked for volunteers to form a group that would find out more about child labor. Craig and eleven other students formed a group they called "Free the Children." One of the first things Free the Children did was to raise money to build a school for poor children. It cost approximately $7,000 to build a school. Craig and the other members of Free the Children held bake sales and garage sales to raise <u>funds.</u> They collected money from other kids and from adults. Free the Children collected enough money to <u>construct</u> a school in Pakistan. Pakistan was where Iqbal Masih had lived.

1. How did your prediction about what Craig might do turn out? What did Craig do? Write your answer on the lines.

_____

_____

_____

_____

2. What leads you to infer that Craig is the kind of person who likes to take action? Use information from the article to support your answer.

Inference	Information from the Paragraph That Supports the Inference
Craig is the kind of person who likes to take action.	

3. What makes you think that Free the Children worked hard to raise money? Use information from the article to support your answer.

Inference	Information from the Paragraph That Supports the Inference
Free the Children worked hard to raise money.	

4. In the paragraph, the word *funds* means

   a. something that is necessary or important.

   b. materials used in building.

   c. plans for future projects.

   d. money set aside for a special purpose.

5. In the paragraph, the word *construct* means

   a. fix.

   b. build.

   c. find.

   d. paint.

Lesson 46 ▶ The Growth of Free the Children

Objectives: Students support inferences, supply supporting details, and use context clues.

Introduction: Invite students to turn the title of the article in the Student Pages into a question and then read the article to answer the question. Remind students to fill in the blank circles in the web. For English learners, discuss the italicized expressions in the following sentences: "Meanwhile, Free the Children *began to spread* to other schools. They also *raised money* to help them."

Guided and independent practice: Discuss students' responses. Discuss the meanings of *chapters* and *supports* according to the way they are used in the article. Remind students that some words have several meanings and that you need to see how the word is used in order to determine the correct meaning. Write model constructed responses on the board, and have students compare their responses with the models.

Assessment: Note students' ability to use context clues. If necessary, review the process by doing a think-aloud in which you show how you use context clues. Provide guided practice.

Lesson 47 ▶ Helping with Health

Objectives: Students support inferences, supply supporting details, and use context clues.

Introduction: Invite students to turn the title of the article in the Student Pages into a question and then read the article to answer the question. Remind students to fill in the blank circles in the web in question 1.

Guided and independent practice: Discuss students' responses. Discuss why it was important for Free the Children to send medical supplies and why Free the Children urged sporting goods companies to stop purchasing balls that children had sewn in factories. Write model constructed responses on the board, and have students compare their responses with the models.

Lesson 46: The Growth of Free the Children

Read the article, and answer the questions that follow it.

The Growth of Free the Children

1   Later Craig traveled to Asia to see for himself how children in Pakistan, India, and other countries were forced to work. One of the things he learned is that millions of children around the world have never been to school. With the help of an author, he wrote a book about his trip and the work of Free the Children. His book is called *Free the Children*. He was just fifteen years old when his book was published.

2   Meanwhile, Free the Children began to spread to other schools. Today there are 750 Free the Children <u>chapters</u> in schools in Canada and the United States. The children in these chapters learn about ways they can help poor children in other countries. They also raise money to help them. With the help of thousands of young people and lots of adults, Free the Children has built more than five hundred schools.

3   Free the Children also helps parents of poor children find ways to make money. If parents make enough money to <u>support</u> their children, the children won't have to be sent to work. Free the Children donates farm animals for the families and tools for farming. They also supply sewing machines, machines that polish gems, and other small machines that can be used to earn money.

Credit: Photo courtesy of Free the Children, www.freethechildren.com.

1. What leads you to infer that Free the Children has raised a lot of money? Use information from the article to support your answer. Pick at least one detail that would show that Free the Children must have raised a lot of money.

Write a sentence that states your inference.	Free the Children _____ _____ _____
Write a sentence or two to support your inference. Tell what Free the Children did that shows that the people in the group must have raised a lot money.	Free the Children _____ _____ _____ _____ _____ _____

Copyright © 2010 by John Wiley & Sons, Inc.

2. Fill in the blank circles to show how Free the Children helps parents make money:

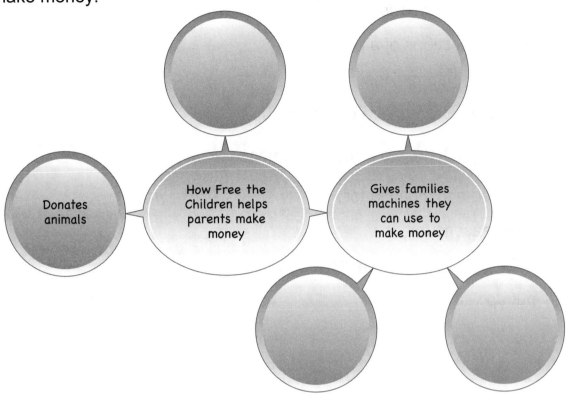

Donates animals

How Free the Children helps parents make money

Gives families machines they can use to make money

3. How do you know that Free the Children helps people help themselves? Use information from the web above and the article to help you answer the question. Write your answer on the lines.

_____

_____

_____

_____

_____

_____

_____

4. In paragraph 2, the word *chapters* means

    a. lists of laws or rules.

    b. parts or sections of a book.

    c. events or happenings.

    d. branches or parts of a club or group.

5. In paragraph 3, the word *support* means

    a. get food and clothing for.

    b. give reasons for.

    c. hold up or keep from falling down.

    d. put up with.

Lesson 47: Helping with Health

Read the article, and answer the questions that follow it.

Helping with Health

1 Of course, schools don't help much if children are too sick to attend. Free the Children also sends health supplies to poor people. And it helps them keep their water clean so diseases aren't spread. Free the Children trains health workers so they can visit villages that don't have doctors or nurses.

2 Free the Children also wrote letters to leaders in Canada, the United States, and other countries. They asked government leaders not to buy products that children had made. Some countries now put a special mark on rugs that were made by adults, not by children. Sporting goods companies in the United States stopped purchasing soccer balls that were sewn by children when Free the Children urged them to do so.

---

1. Fill in the blank circles to show how Free the Children helps poor countries improve the health of their people:

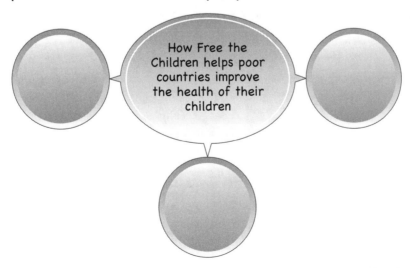

How Free the Children helps poor countries improve the health of their children

2. Why do you think Free the Children asked people not to buy products made by children? (Think about what would happen if people stopped buying rugs and other products made by children.) Write your answer on the lines.

_____

_____

_____

3. In paragraph 1, the word *supplies* means

    a. money and gold.

    b. bandages, medicines, and other needed things.

    c. planes, trains, ships, and cars.

    d. tents and huts and other buildings that can be put up fast.

4. In paragraph 2, the word *purchasing* means

    a. buying.

    b. borrowing.

    c. making.

    d. hiding.

Lesson 48 ▶ Youth in Action

Objectives: Students support a main idea, make and support inferences, and use context clues.

Introduction: Invite students to turn the title of the article in the Student Pages into a question and then read the article to answer the question.

Guided and independent practice: Discuss students' responses. Also discuss why the program for helping others is called "Youth in Action." Discuss why Youth in Action was established and some of the ways in which young people can make a positive difference.

Extension: Students can visit the Free the Children Web site at www.freethechildren .com to learn more about the organization and the kinds of activities sponsored by Youth in Action.

Lesson 49 ▶ Saint of the Gutters

Objectives: Students support inferences and use context clues.

Introduction: Invite students to turn the title of the article in the Student Pages into a question and then read the article to answer the question. They might turn the heading into the questions: "Who is the 'Saint of the Gutters'?" or "Why is someone called 'The Saint of the Gutters'?" Remind students to use the phonetic respelling that appears in the paragraph.

Guided and independent practice: Discuss students' responses. Discuss why Mother Teresa moved to a distant country and chose to live in poverty. Write model constructed responses on the board, and have students compare their responses with the models. Discuss where Albania is and show Albania and India on the map in the Student Pages.

Lesson 48: Youth in Action

Read the article, and answer the questions that follow it.

Youth in Action

1   When they saw the good things that Free the Children had done, lots of young people wanted to take action. But they weren't sure how. Craig and his brother Marc started Youth in Action groups. They also <u>established</u> a number of programs that Youth in Action groups could take part in. Their programs include raising money for schools, food, and clean water for people in poor countries. Craig and his brother also work with schools to help them teach their students about ways of making the world a better place for all people.

2   Craig has spent more than half his life helping others. Free the Children has assisted more than 1 million people. But maybe the most important thing Craig has done is to show young people that they can make a <u>positive</u> difference.

1. What makes you think that Craig is the kind of person who will keep on thinking of new ways to help people in need? Use information from the article to support your answer.

Inference	Information from the Article That Supports the Inference
Craig is the kind of person who will keep on thinking of new ways to help people in need.	

2. In paragraph 1, the word *established* means

   a. started.

   b. taught.

   c. thanked.

   d. wanted.

3. In paragraph 2, the word *positive* means

   a. sure about something; not having any doubts.

   b. doing something good; having good results or effects.

   c. not looking back; not having regrets.

   d. more than enough; beyond what is needed.

Lesson 49: Saint of the Gutters

Read the paragraph, and answer the questions that follow it.

Saint of the Gutters

As a young girl growing up in Albania, Agnes Bojaxhiu (bah-YAHZ-hee-oh) had no idea that one day she would become one of the most famous people in the world. Her dream was to become a missionary (MISH-uh-nair-ee). She wanted to help people living in <u>distant</u> lands. Agnes's dream came true. She became a missionary in far-off India. She took the name Sister Teresa. She taught geography in a girls' high school and later became the school's principal. Then on September 10, 1946, while riding on a train, she had a strange feeling. She felt that she was being called to help the poor. "I was to give up all and work with the poorest of the poor," she said. "I was to live among them." In order to help the people living in <u>poverty</u>, Sister Teresa believed that she had to live the way they did. As she explained, "How can you truly know the poor unless you live like them? If they complain about the food, we can say that we eat the same." Sister Teresa wore a piece of clothing known as a *sari* (SAR-ee). It was made of rough cloth and was white with a blue edging. Sister Teresa owned just two saris and a pair of sandals.

Credit: Art Explosion.

Copyright © 2010 by John Wiley & Sons, Inc.

1. How do you know that Sister Teresa lived the way the poor did? Give two examples from the article.

Example 1:

_____

_____

Example 2:

_____

_____

Lesson 49 **Saint of the Gutters**   213

2. In the paragraph, the word *distant* means

   a. tall.

   b. having many people.

   c. far away.

   d. very large.

3. In the paragraph, the word *poverty* means

   a. not clean.

   b. sickly.

   c. not doing well.

   d. being poor.

Lesson 50 ▶ Helping the Poorest of the Poor

Objectives: Students support inferences and use context clues.

Introduction: Invite students to turn the title of the article in the Student Pages into a question and then read the article to answer the question. They might turn the heading into the question: "How were the poorest of the poor helped?"

Guided and independent practice: Discuss students' responses. Discuss what Mother Teresa might have said in order to persuade others to join the Missionaries of Charity. What did the Missionaries of Charity do to lessen the sorrow of the poor? Write model constructed responses on the board, and have students compare their responses with the models. Discuss where Calcutta is, and show it on a map. Explain that Calcutta is now called *Kolkata*.

Lesson 51 ▶ The Most Admired Person in the World

Objectives: Students support inferences and use context clues.

Introduction: Discuss the meaning of *admire*. Invite students to turn the title of the article in the Student Pages into a question and then read the article to answer the question. They might turn the heading into the question: "Why was Mother Teresa the most admired person in the world?" Remind students that they can change the question they create if it doesn't work out.

Guided and independent practice: Discuss students' responses. Discuss why Mother Teresa wanted to cancel the dinner that was being given in her honor. Discuss, too, how she treated the poor with love, care, and dignity. Write model constructed responses on the board, and have students compare their responses with the models. To foster the making of connections, discuss with students people whom they admire, the positive characteristics these people have, and ways in which they are like Mother Teresa.

Assessment: Note students' overall performance on this and previous exercises in this unit. Have they mastered key skills? If not, provide additional instruction and practice.

Lesson 50: Helping the Poorest of the Poor

Read the article, and answer the questions that follow it.

Helping the Poorest of the Poor

1   To answer the call to help others, Sister Teresa started living with and taking care of the poorest of the poor in Calcutta, India. Calcutta is now known as Kolkata (KOHL-kuh-tah) and is one of the poorest cities in the world. She also <u>persuaded</u> others to help out and started a group called the "Missionaries of Charity." Sister Teresa and the other missionaries would go through the streets of Calcutta and seek people who needed help. Often they would discover very sick people lying in the gutter. They had been abandoned there because no one would care for them. The missionaries picked them up and carried them to a hospital or to the missionaries' home. They took care of people no one else would care for. They bandaged their wounds and fed them and gave them a clean bed to lie in. With their love and caring, they eased the loneliness and <u>sorrow</u> of the people who had been abandoned. Sister Teresa came to be called the "Saint of the Gutters."

2   Sister Teresa also started a school for the children who lived in the poorest parts of Calcutta and a home for children whose parents had died or were unable to take care of them. Many of these children were wandering the streets. The children called this loving woman who took care of them "Mother Teresa."

1. How do you know that Mother Teresa and the Missionaries of Charity were very kind people? Use information from the article to support your answer.

Inference	Information from the Article That Supports the Inference
Mother Teresa and the Missionaries of Charity were very kind people.	_____ _____ _____ _____ _____

2. What makes you think that the city of Calcutta did not take good care of its poor? Give two reasons using information from the article to support your answer.

Reason 1:

_____

_____

Reason 2:

_____

_____

3. In paragraph 1, the word *persuaded* means

  a. talked about to others.

  b. convinced.

  c. listened to or told about.

  d. asked for or questioned.

4. In paragraph 1, the word *sorrow* means

  a. sadness.

  b. sickness.

  c. problems.

  d. pains.

Lesson 51: The Most Admired Person in the World

Read the article, and answer the questions that follow it.

The Most Admired Person in the World

1 As the years passed, Mother Teresa and the Missionaries of Charity started homes for the poor in a number of countries. People began talking about the wonderful work that Mother Teresa and the Missionaries of Charity were doing. When people were asked what person they admired above all others, most said "Mother Teresa."

2 In 1979, Mother Teresa was awarded the Nobel Peace Prize. This is the world's highest prize. It is given to the person who has done the most to bring peace to the world. Mother Teresa was given a medal and $190,000. What did she do with the money? She used it to help the poor, of course. There was also a dinner to be held in her honor. She asked the Nobel committee to <u>cancel</u> the dinner and use the money to feed the poor. "That money will feed four hundred children for a year," she explained.

3 In 1997, Mother Teresa passed away. More than fifteen thousand people came to her funeral. Famous people and world leaders attended. And so did thousands of poor people. Mother Teresa had fed them, given them a place to sleep, and had helped heal their wounds. But more important, she had treated them with love, caring, and <u>dignity.</u> They would miss her.

1. How do you know that helping the poor was just about the most important thing to Mother Teresa? Give two reasons, using information from the article to support your answer.

Reason 1:

_____

_____

Reason 2:

_____

_____

2. What makes you think that the dinner for Mother Teresa would have been very costly? Use information from the article to support your answer.

_____

_____

_____

3. Why do you think Mother Teresa was the most admired person in the world? You can use information from all the paragraphs about Mother Teresa to support your answer.

_____

_____

_____

_____

4. In paragraph 2, the word *cancel* means

    a. plan carefully; make a plan for the future.

    b. pay for with cash or check; make a trade for.

    c. decide who the guests will be and where they will sit.

    d. stop a dinner, party, or other event; put an end to.

5. In paragraph 3, the word *dignity* means

    a. smiles and laughter.

    b. smoothness.

    c. respect and proper attention.

    d. quickness and speed.

Lesson 52 — Craig Kielburger and Mother Teresa

Objectives: Students make and support inferences and use context clues.

Introduction: Invite students to read the title of the article in the Student Pages and then read the article to find out how Mother Teresa inspired Craig Kielburger. For English learners, discuss the italicized expression in the following sentence: "She had this incredible power about her because she *had such a big heart.*"

Guided and independent practice: Discuss students' responses. Discuss how when Craig met Mother Teresa, she still had an incredible power even though she was old and frail. Write model constructed responses on the board, and have students compare their responses with the models. Discuss with students ways in which they might make the world a better place. Explain that these can be small actions or deeds.

Lesson 53 — The Meeting

Objectives: Students make and support inferences and use context clues.

Introduction: Invite students to read the title of the article in the Student Pages and then read the article to find out about how Brandon seemed to feel about the meeting.

Guided and independent practice: Discuss students' responses. Discuss how Brandon's mother thought it was essential for children in the home to have books to read in their spare time. Discuss with students how they might have felt if they had been in Brandon's place.

Lesson 52: Craig Kielburger and Mother Teresa

Read the article, and answer the questions that follow it.

Craig Kielburger and Mother Teresa

While still a teenager, Craig Kielburger met Mother Teresa. Mother Teresa was old and <u>frail</u> but still helping the poor. Speaking of that meeting, Craig said, "Of all the well-known people I've met, the person who inspired me the most would be Mother Teresa. She had this <u>incredible</u> power about her . . . because she had such a big heart. I asked her how she kept her hope in the face of so much poverty, and she said, 'We must always realize that we can do no great things, only small things with great love.'" Remembering Mother Teresa's words, Craig Kielburger has a message for young people all around the world: "You have the spirit of Mother Teresa . . . inside you. No matter what your gifts, no matter what your talents, kids can help change the world."

1. Why do you think Mother Teresa inspired Craig Kielburger? Use information from the article to support your answer.

_____

_____

_____

2. What did Mother Teresa mean when she said, "We must always realize that we can do no great things, only small things with great love"?

_____

_____

_____

_____

_____

3. In the paragraph, the word *frail* means

   a. weakened or not in good health.

   b. having lived a long time.

   c. having a difficult time remembering.

   d. moving very slowly.

4. In the paragraph, the word *incredible* means

   a. not easily seen.

   b. difficult to understand.

   c. very bright or shiny.

   d. surprising; hard to believe.

Lesson 53: The Meeting

Read the paragraph, and answer the questions that follow it.

The Meeting

Brandon Keefe hoped the meeting would be over soon. His mother had taken him to work that day. Brandon's mother, Robin Keefe, worked at a home for children whose parents could not take care of them. At the meeting, Brandon's mom and other people who worked at the home discussed the need for a library at the home. They wanted a collection of books that the children could read in their <u>spare</u> time. They thought it was <u>essential</u> for young people to have good books to read. Brandon, who was just eight years old at the time, was sitting in a corner playing a handheld video game that he had brought with him. The more the people talked, the more he wiggled.

1. How was Brandon feeling? Use information from the paragraph to help you answer the question.

Brandon seemed to be feeling

_____.

First, he

_____

_____.

Second,

_____

_____.

2. In the paragraph, the word *spare* means

    a. soon.

    b. late.

    c. extra.

    d. long.

3. In the paragraph, the word *essential* means

    a. very important or needed.

    b. costing a lot of money.

    c. taking a long time.

    d. not easily found.

Lesson 54 ▸ The Next Day

Objectives: Students make and support predictions, support inferences, and use context clues.

Introduction: Explain to students that they will be asked to make a prediction about halfway through the article in the Student Pages. Remind them that predictions are based on the information that they have read plus their background knowledge. For English learners, discuss the italicized expression in this sentence: "Brandon's *hand shot up into the air.*"

Guided and independent practice: Discuss students' predictions and their responses to the other questions. Discuss with students why they might have been surprised that Brandon suggested that the class collect books for the home where his mom worked. Discuss why Brandon urged the other third graders to help collect books that would appeal to the children in the home.

Assessment: Note students' ability to make and support predictions. If necessary, provide additional instruction and practice.

Lesson 55 ▸ BookEnds

Objectives: Students support inferences and use context clues.

Introduction: Encourage students to predict what will happen as a result of the book drive.

Guided and independent practice: Discuss students' predictions and responses to the other questions contained in the Student Pages. Discuss how people were generous and donated money to buy shelves and chairs. Discuss, too, how BookEnds locates homes, hospitals, and recreation centers that need books.

Extension: Encourage students to visit the BookEnds Web site at http://www.bookends .org to find out more about it.

Lesson 54: The Next Day

Read the article, and answer the questions that follow it.

The Next Day

1 The next day at school, Brandon's teacher said that the class was going to work on a community service project. In a community service project, students do something to help others. She asked the class if anyone had any good ideas for a service project. Brandon's hand shot up into the air.

1. What do you predict Brandon will say? Use information from this article or the one before it to help you answer the question.

Prediction	Information from the Paragraphs That Support the Prediction
I predict that Brandon will	

> 2 "The home where my mom works needs books," Brandon explained. "Everybody has books that they've outgrown," he continued. "Why not give the ones we've already read to kids who need them?" he <u>urged</u>. The other students thought that was a fine idea. So did the teacher. Brandon organized a book drive to collect books that were new or slightly used that would <u>appeal</u> to young people.

2. How do you know that Brandon listened to what was being said at his mother's meeting? Use information from this article or the one before it to help you answer the question.

Inference	Information from the Article That Supports the Inference
Brandon listened to what was being said at his mother's meeting.	_____ _____ _____ _____

3. In paragraph 2, the word *urged* means

   a. mumbled quietly.

   b. ask for strongly.

   c. yelled at angrily.

   d. whispered softly.

4. In paragraph 2, the word *appeal* means

   a. give information to.

   b. be close to.

   c. interesting to.

   d. having a lot of hard words.

Lesson 55: BookEnds

Read the article, and answer the questions that follow it.

> ### BookEnds
>
> Brandon and his helpers collected 847 books. People were very <u>generous</u>. They also donated money to buy shelves, chairs, and tables. The home got its library. Seeing how much the library meant to the children in the home, Robin Keefe and Brandon started BookEnds. BookEnds <u>locates</u> group homes, hospitals, schools, recreation centers, and after-school programs that need books. Some places don't have any books. Some places don't have enough books, or their books are old. BookEnds then helps students organize book drives. So far, BookEnds has helped more than 100,000 young people donate more than 1 million books.

1. What makes you think that lots of young people think that giving away books is a good idea? Use information from the article to support your answer.

_____

_____

_____

_____

2. In the paragraph, the word *generous* means

    a. able to work hard.

    b. being friendly toward others.

    c. willing to share with others.

    d. being calm and peaceful.

3. In the paragraph, the word *locates* means

    a. walks toward.

    b. leaves early.

    c. finds.

    d. takes care of.

Introducing Concluding

Concluding is a type of inferring that generally entails considering a number of pieces of information before drawing a conclusion about them. A typical difficulty that students experience with drawing conclusions is not considering all the facts or pieces of information. Another is not considering that several conclusions might be drawn from a set of facts. Students need lots of practice in considering all the evidence when drawing a conclusion and drawing the most logical conclusions.

Lesson 56 ▶ Conclusions

Objective: Students draw conclusions.

Introduction: Explain to students that conclusions are another kind of inference. A selection usually has a number of facts or other pieces of information that lead to the conclusion. Read and discuss with students the explanatory paragraph at the top of the page of the article in the Student Pages. Discuss why it is possible to conclude that Mother Teresa cared deeply for the poor.

Guided and independent practice: Have students read the examples and draw a conclusion. Have students compare their conclusion with the conclusion provided.

Extension: Provide additional lists of facts or other details, and have students draw conclusions from them. During class discussions, encourage students to draw conclusions. Emphasize that the conclusions should be well thought out and should be based on the facts or other details.

Lesson 57 ▶ Need for Clean Water

Objectives: Students support conclusions, make and support predictions, and use context clues.

Introduction: Explain that events in the article in the Student Pages take place in Canada and Uganda, a country in Africa. Point out Africa and Uganda on a map. Point out Canada on the map in the Student Pages for the lesson, and note the distance between Canada and Uganda. Invite students to read the title of the article and then read to find out about the need for clean water and what Ryan planned to do about it.

Guided and independent practice: Discuss students' responses. Discuss what the water was like that Jimmy was drinking—that it was filthy and had a bad odor.

Assessment: Note students' ability to draw and provide support for conclusions. Are they able to transfer the skill to content and outside reading? Provide corrective instruction if necessary.

Lesson 56: Conclusions

Read the paragraph, and answer the question that follows it.

Conclusions

One kind of an inference is called a "conclusion." In a conclusion, you put a number of facts or ideas together. For instance, while you were reading about Mother Teresa, you learned that she cared for the poorest of the poor, started schools for poor children, and started homes for poor children and homes for other poor people who were sick and had been left on the streets. You also learned that she gave away her prize money to the poor, and asked that the money set aside for a dinner to honor her be used to feed the poor. From all this you can come to the conclusion that Mother Teresa cared deeply about the poor.

Read the sentences below. What conclusion can you draw from all of them together? Write your conclusion on the lines.

- Aubyn Burnside was nine years old when she started Suitcases for Kids. Suitcases for Kids collects suitcases and backpacks for kids who are going to camp, moving from one foster home to another, or going to a hospital but don't have a suitcase or backpack to carry their things.

- Melvin Colbert was eleven years old when he noticed cars speeding through his neighborhood. He got the town to build a bike path to the park so kids wouldn't have to ride their bikes on dangerous streets.

- Hannah Taylor was only five years old when she started the Lady-bug Foundation. The Ladybug Foundation helps find places for the homeless to live. Hannah has collected more than $5,000 to help the homeless.

- When he was thirteen years old, Jeffrey Lambin visited his brother in the hospital and noticed that he had nothing to do but watch TV. Jeffrey started Kids Karts. Kids Karts are loaded with toys, games, and books and are wheeled around to sick kids in hospitals.

- Jason Crowe was nine years old when he started a newspaper for kids in order to raise money to help fight cancer.

My conclusion is that

_____

_____

_____

_____

Did you conclude that young people can help others? If so, you are correct. The sentences tell about five young people who helped others.

Lesson 57: Need for Clean Water

Read the paragraphs, and answer the questions that follow them.

Need for Clean Water

1   How far do you have to go to get a drink of water? Chances are that clean, fresh water is just a few steps away. But for Jimmy Akana of Uganda (you-GAN-duh), a country in Africa, getting water meant walking to the nearest well, which was three miles away. And the water was not clean. It was a dirty brown color and smelled bad. But Jimmy would get so thirsty that he would drink the water even though it looked <u>filthy</u> and had a bad <u>odor</u>. The smelly water could have made Jimmy sick. Disease-carrying germs live in dirty water. Dirty water is a leading cause of sickness in many countries.

2   When he heard about the need for clean water in Africa, Ryan Hreljac (HURL-jack) of Canada decided to do something about it. He was only six years old, but he didn't let that stop him. His teacher told Ryan's class that for just seventy dollars, a well could be dug in Africa. Ryan began doing small jobs around the house and for neighbors to earn the money. He washed windows. That earned him two dollars. He cleaned his neighbor's yard. That earned him another two dollars. He vacuumed for a dollar. At last, after four months of doing chores, Ryan had saved up seventy dollars. Ryan's mom drove him to the office of Watercan. Watercan is an organization that builds wells for poor people all around the world. The people at Watercan had bad news for Ryan: his seventy dollars would buy only a hand pump.

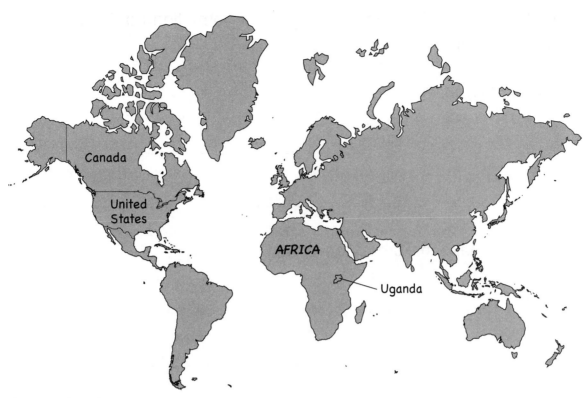

Credit: Art Explosion.

1. What leads you to conclude that Ryan is hard working? Use information from the article to support your answer. Give at least three examples.

Example 1:

_____

_____

Example 2:

_____

_____

Example 3:

_____

_____

2. What do you predict Ryan will do? Use information from the article to support your answer.

I predict that Ryan will

_____

_____ .

The reason I make this prediction is that

_____

_____ .

3. In paragraph 1, the word *filthy* means

    a. very warm.

    b. very rough.

    c. very sick.

    d. very dirty.

4. In paragraph 1, the word *odor* means

    a. sound.

    b. smell.

    c. taste.

    d. feeling.

Lesson 58 ▶ A Well for Jimmy's Village

Objectives: Students make predictions, support inferences, and use context clues.

Introduction: Invite students to read the title of the article in the Student Pages, turn the title into a question, and read the article to answer the question. Remind students that if the question doesn't seem to be working out, they can change the question.

Guided and independent practice: Discuss students' responses. Also discuss how Ryan was able to accumulate $2,000 and why he requested that the well be located near a school.

Lesson 59 ▶ Pen Pals

Objectives: Students support conclusions and use context clues.

Introduction: Invite students to read the title of the article in the Student Pages. Discuss what pen pals are. Have students predict who the pen pals might be and what they might tell each other. Have students read the selection to see how their predictions work out.

Guided and independent practice: Discuss students' responses. Also discuss what the boys told each other. Discuss why Ryan traveled to Uganda and how the people of Uganda showed Ryan how grateful they were by having a celebration in his honor.

Extension: Have students trace Ryan's trip from Canada to Uganda.

Lesson 58: A Well for Jimmy's Village

Read the paragraph, and answer the questions that follow it.

A Well for Jimmy's Village

When Ryan heard that he didn't have enough money for a well, he said, "I'll just have to do more chores." Word of Ryan's efforts to get a well built in Africa began to spread. Newspapers and TV shows did stories about Ryan. A ninety-year-old woman sent Ryan a check for $25. Other kids sent him their spending money. Businesspeople sent in checks. People invited Ryan to come and speak to them about the need for wells. Over the months, with the help of many generous people, Ryan <u>accumulated</u> the $2,000 needed to dig a new well. Ryan asked that the new well be located near a school. His <u>request</u> was granted. It was decided to build the well near Angola Primary School in the village of Agweo in Uganda. Uganda is in the eastern part of Africa. The village of Agweo is where Jimmy Akana lives.

1. How did your prediction turn out? What did Ryan do when he learned that the $70 he collected would buy only a hand pump?

_____

_____

_____

2. How do you know that Ryan isn't the kind of person who gives up easily? Use information from the article to support your answer. Begin your answer by saying what kind of person Ryan is. Then support that statement.

_____

_____

_____

_____

_____

3. In the paragraph, the word *accumulated* means

   a. gathered or collected over a period of time.

   b. counted every day.

   c. belonged to or owned by others.

   d. shared with people in need.

4. In the paragraph, the word *request* means

   a. a bill that has to be paid.

   b. something that is asked for.

   c. something that happened far away.

   d. needing something.

Lesson 59: Pen Pals

Read the paragraphs, and answer the questions that follow them.

Pen Pals

1 After the well was built, Ryan began writing letters to the students at the Angola Primary School. Jimmy and Ryan became pen pals. In their letters, the boys wrote about the food they ate and their homes and what their countries were like. Ryan was surprised to hear that Jimmy lived in a house made of grass. Jimmy was surprised to learn that Ryan played a sport called ice hockey. Ice hockey wasn't played in Uganda. Jimmy tried to imagine what it would be like to skate on ice.

2 Ryan wanted to see the well that he had worked so hard for, and he wanted to meet his pen pal. Ryan traveled to Uganda and met Jimmy in person. The people of the village wanted to thank Ryan for the wonderful clean water that his well was bringing them. The people of the village lined up in two long rows as Ryan walked down the road to the well. They clapped as Ryan passed and called his name, "Ryan! Ryan!" Later the people of the village had a big <u>celebration</u>. They sang and danced and had lots of food to eat. Holding a celebration was their way of showing Ryan how <u>grateful</u> they were for all that he had done for them.

1. What leads you to conclude that the people of the village thought highly of Ryan? Use information from the article to support your answer. Give two examples.

Example 1:

_____

_____

Example 2:

_____

_____

2. In paragraph 2, the word *celebration* means

    a. a long trip to a distant country.

    b. a special party to honor someone or something.

    c. ways of helping people in need.

    d. people helping each other.

3. In paragraph 2, the word *grateful* means

    a. helpful.

    b. thankful.

    c. careful.

    d. hopeful.

Lesson 60   School Visit

Objectives: Students support conclusions, make and support predictions, and use context clues.

Introduction: Invite students to read the title of the article in the Student Pages, create a question based on the title, and read the article to answer the question.

Guided and independent practice: Discuss students' responses. Also discuss how the students and the headmaster showed that they were appreciative. Discuss, too, what the headmaster proclaimed.

Lesson 61   Brothers

Objective: Students support inferences and use context clues.

Introduction: Invite students to read the title of the article in the Student Pages, create a question based on the title, and read the article to answer the question. Remind students that if the question doesn't seem to be working out, they can change it.

Guided and independent practice: Discuss students' responses. Also discuss why Jimmy's life was in grave danger and how having Jimmy accompany Ryan on tours would help to raise money.

Extension: To learn more about Ryan and Jimmy, arrange for students to visit the Web site for Ryan's Well Foundation at http://www.ryanswell.ca.

Lesson 60: School Visit

Read the article, and answer the questions that follow it.

School Visit

1   The next day Ryan visited Jimmy's school. The students thanked him once more. They were very <u>appreciative</u>. They also explained that they were following his example. Although they didn't have much, they shared with others. The students had decided they would spend five days each year assisting older people or people who were sick. The students in Uganda taught Ryan a lesson. As he explains, "In Uganda, they learned that you can help others no matter who you are. If everyone thought that way and did something nice every day for someone else, the world would be a much better place."

2   The headmaster of the school in Uganda set aside a special day to honor Ryan. From that time on, July 27, the day of Ryan's visit, would be known as Ryan's Day. "Ryan is our son and brother," the headmaster <u>proclaimed</u>. Both Jimmy and Ryan were sad when it came time for Ryan to leave.

1. What leads you to conclude that Uganda is a poor country? Use information from this article or previous (PREE-vee-uhs) articles to support your answer. (Previous means "coming before.") Give two examples.

Reason 1:

_____

_____

Reason 2:

_____

_____

2. What do you predict will become of Ryan and Jimmy's friendship? Support your prediction with information from the article.

Prediction	Support
I predict that Ryan and Jimmy's friendship will _____ _____ _____ _____	Give at least one reason for your prediction. _____ _____ _____ _____

3. In paragraph 1, the word *appreciative* means

    a. wanting more.

    b. being happy.

    c. able to help others.

    d. thankful.

4. In paragraph 2, the word *proclaimed* means

    a. listened carefully to all that was said.

    b. announced to a group of people; declared.

    c. planned ahead of time for a special event.

    d. decided after thinking about something for a long time.

Lesson 61: Brothers

Read the article, and answer the questions that follow it.

Brothers

Jimmy Akana never knew his parents. He was raised by an aunt. There was a war in Uganda. Jimmy's parents might have been killed or captured in the war. A few years after Ryan's visit, the war came to Jimmy's village. Rebel soldiers dragged Jimmy out of his home and were going to force him to join their army. But Jimmy escaped. Still, his life was in <u>grave</u> danger. Ryan's parents invited Jimmy to come to Canada, where Ryan and his family lived. Ryan had started Ryan's Well Foundation. The foundation raises money to build more wells. Jimmy could <u>accompany</u> Ryan on speaking tours to raise money for wells. After all, who knew better about the need for wells and clean water than Jimmy did? In 2003, Jimmy became one of the family. He now lives with the Hreljacs in Canada. He and Ryan have become brothers.

1. What makes you think that Ryan's parents were worried about Jimmy's safety? Use information from the article to support your answer.

_____

_____

_____

2. What kind of people are Ryan's parents? Use information from the article to support your answer. First tell what kind of people Ryan's parents are. Then support your statement.

_____

_____

_____

_____

_____

_____

3. In the paragraph, the word *grave* means

    a. hopeless.

    b. serious.

    c. hidden.

    d. lasting.

4. In the paragraph, the word *accompany* means

    a. go or travel with.

    b. talk to or with.

    c. carry heavy bags.

    d. write letters to.

Lesson 62 ▶ **Greg's Plan**

Objectives: Students support conclusions and inferences and use context clues.

Introduction: Ask students if they have ever been lost. Discuss how they got lost and how they felt when they were lost. Ask them to tell how they found their way or were found after being lost. Have students read the first sentence of the article in the Student Pages. Being lost helped Greg Mortenson find himself. Ask students to tell what it means *to find yourself*. Explain that this is a figure of speech and that one of its meanings is to find your purpose in life. Have students read this true story about Greg Mortenson, a mountain climber. Have them read to find out how Greg found himself.

Guided and independent practice: Discuss how Greg became lost and how he found himself. Also discuss students' written responses to the questions contained in the Student Pages. Discuss why Greg was exhausted and why he was in mourning. Encourage students to predict what Greg will do next.

Lesson 62: Greg's Plan

Read the article, and answer the questions that follow it.

Greg's Plan

1 Being lost helped Greg Mortenson find himself. Weak from months spent trying to climb K-2, one of the highest mountains in the world, Greg was on his way down to the valley below but had wandered away from his guide and had taken a wrong turn. So exhausted from the climbing that he was barely able to stand, Greg was helped by the generous people of Korphe. Although very poor, they shared what they had with Greg. They fed him and saw to it that he got plenty of rest. They also located his guide, who led Greg to the valley below.

2 Greg found that he missed the people of Korphe. They had been kind and friendly. He had felt a deep sense of peace with them. Greg decided to return. Still weak and thin, Greg spent several weeks getting his strength back. Greg was a nurse. After regaining some of his strength, he helped many of Korphe's sick people. Getting to the nearest doctor meant a two-day walk.

3 One day Greg asked the headman, Haji Ali (HAJ-ee ah-lee), if he could see the village's school. Haji Ali gave him a sad look but agreed to take him to the school. Greg was shocked by what he saw. There was no school building. There were no pencils or paper. The students wrote in the dirt with sticks or with muddy water on pieces of slate. The teacher came only three days a week. The other two days he taught at a school in another village. Even

though the teacher was paid only a dollar a day, the people were too poor to pay him to teach for a full week.

4   Greg felt as though his heart was being torn out. He knew that he had to do something. His younger sister, Christa, had died a few months before. Greg was still <u>mourning</u> her loss. In her memory he had planned to place her necklace on the top of K-2. But he had failed to reach the top of K-2. Now he had a better plan. He turned to Haji Ali and announced, "I am going to build you a school." The school would be in his sister Christa's memory.

Credit: Image courtesy Central Asia Institute.

1. What leads you to conclude that Greg Mortenson likes to help people? Use information from the article to support your answer. Give two examples.

Example 1:

_____

_____

Example 2:

_____

_____

2. Why didn't the people in the village get to see a doctor very often?

_____

_____

3. In paragraph 1, the word *exhausted* means

   a. hungry; not having enough to eat.

   b. sad; not happy.

   c. worried; not calm.

   d. very tired; worn out.

4. In paragraph 4, the word *mourning* means

   a. quiet; soft.

   b. willing to help others; willing to share.

   c. quiet; not talking very much.

   d. showing sadness or sorrow.

Lesson 63 ▶ Finding His Life's Work

Objectives: Students draw and support conclusions.

Introduction: Briefly review what Greg had promised to do. Discuss what steps need to be taken in order to build a school. Review students' predictions as to what Greg will do next. Have students read to see how their predictions play out. Remind students that they might have to modify predictions as they read. Also discuss students' responses to the questions in the practice lesson.

Guided and independent practice: Discuss students' predictions and how they might have had to modify them. Also discuss students' responses to the questions in the Student Pages. Have students calculate how much in dollars the children contributed. Discuss why it might be a good idea to ask children to donate pennies rather than dollars.

Assessment: Note students' overall performance on this and previous exercises in this unit. Have they mastered key skills, especially drawing and supporting conclusions? If not, provide additional instruction and practice.

Extension: Have students view film clips at Pennies for Peace at http://www .penniesforpeace.org. The film clips retell Mortenson's story and also talk about having students around the world collect pennies to build schools for children in Pakistan and Afghanistan. The site also includes curriculum materials.

Lesson 63: Finding His Life's Work

Read the article, and answer the questions that follow it.

Finding His Life's Work

1   Back home in the United States, Greg began making his promise come true. His first job was to collect money. He figured that he needed more than $12,000. He sent out hundreds of letters explaining his plan to build a badly needed school. Out of 560 letters, he got just 1 reply. Tom Brokaw, a TV news announcer, sent him $100. But Greg also got help from school children. Greg's mother was the principal of a school. She invited Greg to tell the students about his plans. The students <u>contributed</u> 62,400 pennies. That helped, but Greg still needed more money. Then Greg learned that a wealthy inventor was interested in his idea. The inventor had climbed the mountains near the school where the village of Korphe was located. Nervously, Greg called the inventor and asked for his help. The inventor sent Greg a check for $12,000, but warned Greg not to waste the money. Greg sold his car and just about everything else that he owned, bought an airline ticket, and headed back to Korphe. Greg felt so happy and proud when he returned to Korphe and told Haji Ali that he had purchased supplies for the school that he had promised to build. But Haji explained that there was a problem. They would need to build a bridge to get the supplies up the mountainside to the village.

2   Now Greg needed $10,000 for the bridge. He called the wealthy inventor again. The inventor sent him another check. He asked Greg to bring him a photo of the school as soon as it was finished.

Months later, the 280-foot bridge held up by strong steel cables was finished. Work on the school was finally begun a few months later. Greg was in a hurry to get the school built. He became impatient with the workers. Then one day, Haji Ali invited Greg to his home and explained: "You must respect our ways. The first time you share tea, you are a stranger. The second time you share tea, you are an honored guest. The third time you share a cup of tea, you become family. Doctor Greg, you must take time to share three cups of tea."

3   Greg listened. As he explained later, "That day, Haji Ali taught me the most important lesson I've ever learned in my life. He taught me that I had more to learn from the people I work with than I could ever hope to teach them."

4   A few weeks later, the school was completed. But Greg's work was just beginning. Other villages needed schools. Since that time, Greg has raised money for seventy-seven schools that educate 30,000 children in Pakistan and Afghanistan. Becoming lost helped him to find his life's work.

Credit: Image courtesy Central Asia Institute.

1. What leads you to conclude that Greg Mortenson keeps on trying even when problems arise? Use information from the article to support your answer. Give two examples.

Example 1:

_____

_____

Example 2:

_____

_____

2. What makes you think that Greg didn't have much money of his own? Give at least one reason. Use information from the article.

_____

_____

3. In paragraph 1, the word *contributed* means

   a. thought about for a long time.

   b. counted quickly but carefully.

   c. gave money or help along with others.

   d. wanted very badly.

4. In paragraph 4, the word *educate* means

   a. talk to in a friendly way; ask questions about.

   b. give help to; help with a problem.

   c. lead from one place to another; find.

   d. teach; build the knowledge and skills of.

End-of-Theme Reflection

Discuss the end-of-theme reflection on the Student Pages. Discuss with students what they have learned about inferring, predicting, and concluding. Ask students to list the people that they read about in this unit. Invite them to draw conclusions about the people they read about. Have them tell what the people had in common. Discuss with students what they learned about people helping people. Ask which people they like best and which they thought were most helpful.

Have available copies of the suggested books and encourage students to read them. Readabilities, provided by Accelerated Reading (AR) and Lexile Framework, are posted. However, readability formulas do not measure concept load, background needed to read a book, or interest level. You might want to examine the books and use your professional judgment as to whether they are appropriate for your students.

Hover, Susan Bame. (1995). *Faith the Cow*. **1.9**

McBrier, Page. (2001). *Beatrice's Goat*. **4, 640**

Miller, Jennifer. (2009). *Mother Teresa*. **4.5, 660**

Mortenson, Greg. (2009). *Listen to the Wind: The Story of Dr. Greg and the Three Cups of Tea*. **4.6, 740**

Schrock, Jan West. (2008). *Give a Goat*. **4, 810**

Shoveller, Herb. (2006). *Ryan and Jimmy and the Well in Africa That Brought Them Together*. **5.6, 810**

Thompson, Sarah L. (2009). *Three Cups of Tea: One Man's Journey to Change the World … One Child at a Time (The Young Reader's Edition)*. **6.3, 910**

Weiss, E. (2008). *Mother Teresa: A Life of Kindness*. **3.6, 640**

Woronoff, Kristen. (2002). *Mother Teresa: Helper of the Poor*. **4.5**

Encourage students to apply their skills to the books they read. Using one of the books as a model, show students how they might use chapter titles and headings to help them determine the main ideas that they will be reading about. You might demonstrate how most chapter titles and chapter heads can be turned into questions, which readers then answer when they come to the end of the chapter or section. Encourage students to summarize their reading by telling the three to five most important facts they learned. Encourage, too, the use of graphic organizers to highlight essential information. Students might also share their books with partners or in small groups. Students might wish to find out more about people helping people. Instead of or along with reading the books, students might consult one of the Web sites listed in the Extension sections of the lessons. Web sites tend to be more difficult than books; however, Web site text can be read by a text-to-speech feature available on most computers.

What did you learn about making inferences and drawing conclusions? How might you use these skills and strategies in reading that you do in school and out of school? Write your answer on the lines.

_____

_____

_____

_____

What did you learn about people helping people? What are some ways that the people you read about helped others? Write your answer on the lines.

_____

_____

_____

_____

Think of all the people that you read about: Dan West, Craig Kielburger, Brandon Keefe, Ryan Hreljac, Greg Mortenson, and Mother Teresa. Which person did you admire most? Give reasons for your choice. Write your answer on the lines.

_____

_____

_____

_____

_____

_____

_____

Would you like to find out more about people helping people? Here are some books where you can get more information.

Hover, Susan Bame. (1995). *Faith the Cow*. Laguna Niguel, CA: FaithQuest. Tells the story of the first cow that was given away by Heifer International.

McBrier, Page. (2001). *Beatrice's Goat*. New York: Atheneum. The gift of a goat from Heifer International helps to make Beatrice's dream come true.

Miller, Jennifer. (2009). *Mother Teresa*. North Minneapolis, MN: Lerner Publications. Tells the story of Mother Teresa's life and how she helped the poor.

Mortenson, Greg. (2009). *Listen to the Wind: The Story of Dr. Greg and the Three Cups of Tea*. New York: Dial. Children in a village in Pakistan tell how a stranger built a bridge and a school for them after the people of the village came to his aid.

Schrock, Jan West. (2008). *Give a Goat*. Gardiner, ME: Tilbury House. Hearing the book *Beatrice's Goat* read aloud, a fifth-grade class decides to raise money to buy a goat. This true story was written by Dan West's daughter.

Shoveller, Herb. (2006). *Ryan and Jimmy and the Well in Africa That Brought Them Together*. Tonawanda, NY: Kids Can Press. Tells how a well helped the two boys meet and how Jimmy became part of Ryan's family.

Thompson, Sarah L. (2009). *Three Cups of Tea: One Man's Journey to Change the World … One Child at a Time (The Young Reader's Edition)*. New York: Dial. Tells how Greg Mortenson became lost and ill while climbing a mountain but was aided by the people in a small village in Pakistan. In return, he devoted his life to building schools for the children of that village and other villages.

Weiss, E. (2008). *Mother Teresa: A Life of Kindness*. Eden Prairie, MN: Bellwether Media. Focuses on Mother Teresa's work with the poor.

Woronoff, Kristen. (2002). *Mother Teresa: Helper of the Poor*. Farmington Hills, MI: Gale. Tells about Mother Teresa's early years and how she helped the poor.

UNIT 4

> **Facts and Opinions**

Unit Four develops the ability to discriminate between facts and opinions and reviews previously taught skills and strategies. It also explores the theme of inventions. The ability to identify statements as fact or opinion is a simplification of the sophisticated skill of classifying statements as being empirical, analytical, attitudinal, or value.

Facts can be verified by empirical or analytical means as accurate or inaccurate by counting, measuring, weighing, touching, hearing, observing, or analyzing—for example, "The car weighs 3,500 pounds" or "The car is metallic silver in color." An analytical statement is one that can be verified by analyzing the statement and, if necessary, checking with some sort of reference. For instance, "There are twelve in a dozen" and "A year has fifty-two weeks" are analytical statements.

Opinions are statements that express an attitude or a value and cannot be proved. The terms *fact* and *opinion* are imperfect descriptions. The word *fact* suggests something that can be proved with objective evidence and suggests something that is true. For example, "Years ago astronomers calculated that we are moving around the center of the Milky Way at about 500,000 miles an hour" is an empirical, or factual, statement. It can be proved by measuring the speed of the Earth's movement. However, more recent calculations estimate the speed as being 600,000 miles an hour. The first statement does not become an opinion because it was proved to be inaccurate. It does not become an attitude or a statement of feeling; the statement is still empirical.

An empirical statement is one that can be proved to be accurate or inaccurate. An attitude or value (opinion) statement cannot be proved. It can be strongly held, defended, explained, and rationalized, but there is no objective way that the statement can be proved right or wrong. As used in this unit, the word *fact* refers to a statement that can be proved correct or incorrect. It does not include the secondary meaning of the word, which indicates that a statement is true.

Theme ➤ Inventions

Lesson 64 ▸ Facts and Opinions

Objectives: Students identify statements as being a fact or opinion. For fact statements, students tell how the fact might be verified as being correct or incorrect.

Introduction: To introduce the concept of factual and opinion statements, have students tell whether the following statements are facts or opinions and, if facts, how they might be proved:

We have twenty-five students in our class.

There are twelve boys.

There are thirteen girls.

Our classroom is the best in the school.

Our classroom is the largest in the school.

It is raining today.

Rainy days are best for learning.

Guided and independent practice: Once students have caught onto the concept of verification as the element that differentiates between factual and opinion statements, have them read and discuss the explanation of facts and opinions at the top of the Student Pages for this lesson. Discuss how two statements differ and why one is a fact and one an opinion. Discuss the concept of verifying statements as being an indicator of whether a statement is a fact or an opinion. Have students complete the Student Pages for the lesson. Discuss students' responses. Emphasize the importance of verifying factual statements.

Extension: As the opportunity presents itself, discuss whether statements are opinions or facts. Note that in some instances, information is presented as being factual when it is actually an opinion. Also present the concept of backing up opinions with facts or evidence. For instance, when students form opinions about characters in stories or real people in history texts, encourage them to provide support for their judgments. Explain that although you can't prove opinions, you can, in many instances, provide support for them.

Did you know that some inventors were close to your age? In fact, one of the inventors of TV thought of the idea when he was just fourteen years old. As you read about inventors young and old, you'll be learning how to tell the difference between a fact and an opinion. You will also be reviewing main ideas and details, summarizing, inferences, predictions, and conclusions.

Lesson 64: Facts and Opinions

To see how facts and opinions differ, read the two sentences below. Which one is fact? Which one is an opinion?

> The largest passenger plane can carry more than 550 people.
>
> Flying on passenger planes is fun.

The first sentence is a factual statement. Factual statements can be proved correct or incorrect. You can prove factual statements by counting, measuring, weighing, touching, hearing, or observing. The first sentence can be proved by counting all the people on the plane. If the plane is full and you count all the people and they total more than 550, then you have proved the statement to be correct. But suppose the total was only 549. Then you have proved the statement incorrect. The first sentence is still a factual statement. A statement does not have to be true or correct to be factual. You only have to be able to prove that it is right or wrong. The second statement, "Flying on passenger planes is fun," is an opinion. An opinion is what you believe or how you feel about something. Some people enjoy flying, and others do not. Some people might even think that flying is boring. Opinions cannot be proved. There is nothing about an opinion that can be counted, measured, weighed, touched, heard, or observed.

Read the following statements about an inventor by the name of Charles Zimmerman. Underline <u>fact</u> if the statement can be proved in some way and <u>opinion</u> if it is simply someone's opinion. If the statement is factual, then on the line, tell how it could be proved: say whether a person would mainly count, measure, weigh, touch, listen, or observe to prove each factual statement. The first two have been done for you.

_____

fact   <u>opinion</u>   1. Charles Zimmerman built one of the   _____
                           strangest planes of all times.

<u>fact</u>   opinion   2. In 1933 Charles Zimmerman began   <u>observe</u>
                           working on a round plane.

fact   opinion   3. His idea for a round plane was excellent.   _____

fact   opinion   4. He worked on the round plane for eight   _____
                           years.

fact   opinion   5. Zimmerman tested his round plane in a   _____
                           wind tunnel.

fact   opinion   6. The round plane flew for the first time in   _____
                           1942.

fact   opinion   7. Zimmerman's round plane was amazing. _____

fact   opinion   8. It could fly as fast as 500 miles an hour. _____

fact   opinion   9. It could fly as slow as 40 miles an hour. _____

fact   opinion   10. Planes with regular wings will stall if _____
                         they fly that slowly.

fact   opinion   11. Zimmerman's round plane was flown _____
                         more than 100 times.

fact   opinion   12. The round plane was powered by _____
                         propellers.

fact   opinion   13. Work was stopped on the plane after jet _____
                         engines were invented.

fact   opinion   14. Zimmerman should have kept working _____
                         on his plane.

fact   opinion   15. It is too bad that he stopped working _____
                         on it.

fact   opinion   16. Building round planes was a good idea. _____

Lesson 65 ▶ A Sticky Invention

Objectives: Students identify details, support conclusions, use context clues, and note facts and opinions.

Introduction: Have students read the title of the article in the Student Pages and predict what the article might be about. Have students read the article and see how their predictions play out.

Guided and independent practice: Have students complete and discuss their responses. Since this is the first time they have selected a fact and an opinion from an article, discuss their selections. Emphasize that factual statements can be proved correct or incorrect. Also discuss why sticky notes were easy to remove and what the company did to get people accustomed to using them. Also have students discuss how they use sticky notes.

Lesson 66 ▶ A Frozen Invention

Objectives: Students identify details, support conclusions, use context clues, and note facts and opinions.

Introduction: Have students read the title of the article in the Student Pages and predict what the article might be about. Have students read the article and see how their predictions play out.

Guided and independent practice: Have students complete and discuss their responses. To reinforce vocabulary, have students explain why Epperson obtained a patent on his delicious frozen treat. Discuss with students their favorite Popsicle flavors.

Lesson 65: A Sticky Invention

Read the article, and answer the questions that follow it.

A Sticky Invention

1   Singing led to a small invention that has been a big help to millions of people. Art Fry sang in a choir (kwire). He wanted a way to mark the songs the choir was going to sing. He wanted a piece of paper that was sticky enough so that it would stick to the page, but he didn't want it to stick so tightly that he couldn't <u>remove</u> it without damaging the page. Fry worked for a company that made glue. One of its workers had made a glue that was sticky but not too strong and could be used over and over again. Fry coated the top of small pieces of paper with the glue. He stuck these to pages of his notebook. The sticky pieces of paper did a good job of marking Fry's place. People at Art Fry's company soon found that these sticky notes could be more than just bookmarks. People found that they were good for writing little notes.

2   At first, the sticky notes didn't sell very well. So the company that made them started giving some away. People weren't <u>accustomed</u> to sticking notes on books or papers. Once people saw how useful the sticky notes were, they started buying and using them.

3   Office workers began using them to mark important places in their company's reports and to write notes to each other. Then teachers and students started using these handy sticky notes. Students used them to mark a favorite part in a story or to write notes about a story. The students could make notes and mark passages without writing in their books.

4   Chances are you have used these sticky notes. Millions of pads of sticky notes are sold each year. Can you guess the name of Art Fry's invention? If you said "Post-it® Notes," you are right. Post-it® Notes are a great invention.

5   Although Art Fry invented the sticky notes, he couldn't have created them without the help of Spencer Silver's glue. Silver had been trying to make a glue that was extra strong. Instead he created glue that was extra weak. It was so weak that if you used it to stick one piece of paper onto another piece of paper, you could easily remove the stuck-on piece of paper. The good thing about the weak glue was that it didn't seem to dry up. You could use it over and over again. Because the new glue stayed sticky, Silver thought that there might be uses for it, but he couldn't think of what they might be. Art Fry was the one who found uses for Silver's weak glue.

1. What led Art Fry to invent sticky notes?

   a. He wanted to find a use for the company's new glue.

   b. He wanted a way to mark his place in a songbook.

   c. He wanted to help his friend out.

   d. He wanted to become rich and famous.

2. According to paragraph 1, what extra use did the people at Fry's company discover for sticky notes?

    a. Repairing torn books

    b. Writing notes

    c. Making drawings

    d. Putting notices on bulletin boards

3. Why did the company give away a lot of sticky notes?

    a. They had a lot of sticky notes left over and wanted to get rid of them.

    b. The sticky notes were getting too old to use.

    c. They believed that if people saw how useful they were, they would buy them.

    d. Giving away sticky notes was the company's way of advertising other products that the company made.

4. In paragraph 1, the word *remove* means

    a. take away.

    b. stick to.

    c. fall off.

    d. clean up.

5. In paragraph 2, the word *accustomed* means

    a. helped with.

    b. thought about.

    c. worked hard.

    d. used to.

6. Using information from the story, support the following conclusion: Sticky notes were created by people working together. Write your answer in the box.

Conclusion	Supporting Details
Sticky notes were created by people working together.	

7. Write one fact and one opinion in paragraph 4.

Fact:

_____

_____

Opinion:

_____

_____

Lesson 66: A Frozen Invention

Read the article, and answer the questions that follow it.

A Frozen Invention

1 You don't have to be old to be an inventor. Frank Epperson invented the Popsicle® when he was just eleven years old. One night in 1905, Frank mixed a drink of soda water and fruit-flavored powder. He left the mixture outside. It was very cold that night, and the soda froze. Frozen in the middle of the soda was a stick that Frank had used to stir the soda. Using the stirring stick as a handle, Frank pulled the frozen soda out of the glass and licked it. It tasted good. In fact, it was <u>delicious</u>.

2 When he grew up, Frank Epperson sold land and houses for a living. By 1921 he had a wife and five children to support. But Frank never forgot the frozen treat that he had discovered. Frank had always been interested in machines. As a boy, he had helped his father with machines that his father used in his shop. Now Frank built a machine that could be used to freeze the soda water to make the frozen treats. He couldn't freeze the treats in the regular way. The treats had to be frozen very quickly. If frozen slowly, the sugar and flavoring would sink to the bottom, so the top half of the frozen treat would taste like water and the bottom half would be extra sweet. Frank's quick-freezing machine worked fine. He was soon making and selling the frozen treats in seven flavors. He named the frozen ice on a stick Ep-Sicles. His children didn't think that was a very good name for the frozen flavored

ice on a stick. They called the frozen treats "Pop's sicles." The name was later changed to "Popsicles®." In 1924 Frank <u>obtained</u> a patent for his frozen treat. A patent is a government promise that says only the inventor can make, sell, or use his or her invention for a certain amount of time. In the United States, a patent lasts for twenty years.

3 During the late 1920s and the 1930s, the United States went through hard times. Many people lost their jobs. Twin ice pops with two sticks were created. They cost just five cents and two kids could share them.

4 Today Popsicles are still being sold. In fact, about 1 billion are sold each year. Popsicles® come in thirty flavors. The most popular flavor is orange. However, the best-tasting flavor is strawberry.

1. Paragraph 1 tells mainly

   a. How Popsicles® are made.

   b. How Frank Epperson discovered Popsicles®.

   c. What happens when it gets cold.

   d. How people lived years ago.

2. Why did the Popsicles® have to be frozen quickly?

   a. So they could be made in a hurry

   b. So that they taste right

   c. So that many Popsicles® could be made in a little bit of time

   d. So that different flavors could be made

3. What is the most popular Popsicle® flavor?

    a. Lemon

    b. Raspberry

    c. Orange

    d. Grape

4. Twin Popsicles® were invented mainly because

    a. people could buy treats for two kids for just five cents.

    b. they would last longer.

    c. one could be saved to be eaten later.

    d. people would buy more of them.

5. Popsicles® were first sold in the

    a. 1920s.

    b. 1930s.

    c. 1940s.

    d. 1950s.

6. In paragraph 1, the word *delicious* means

    a. cold.

    b. hard to hold onto.

    c. good tasting.

    d. large.

7. In paragraph 2, the word *obtained* means

    a. lost.

    b. got.

    c. made.

    d. learned.

8. What support is there in paragraph 4 for the conclusion that Popsicles®
are a favorite treat?

_____

_____

9. What support is there in paragraph 4 for the conclusion that not everyone
likes the same flavor?

_____

_____

10. Write one fact and one opinion that are in paragraph 4.

Fact:

_____

_____

Opinion:

_____

_____

Lesson 67 ▶ An Invention for a Cold Day

Objectives: Students identify details and main ideas, make inferences, support conclusions, use context clues, summarize, and identify facts and opinions.

Introduction: Have students read the title of the article in the Student Pages and predict what invention the article is describing. Have students read the article and see how their predictions play out.

Guided and independent practice: Have students complete and discuss their responses. To reinforce vocabulary, have students discuss how earmuffs are protectors for ears on frigid days. Also ask them to tell what kind of protectors people wear when they are riding a bike or skateboarding.

Lesson 68 ▶ Young Inventors

Objectives: Students identify details, use context clues, draw and support conclusions, and note facts and opinions.

Introduction: Invite students to turn the title of the article in the Student Pages into a question and then read the article to answer the question. Remind students to modify the question if it doesn't work out.

Guided and independent practice: Discuss students' responses. Have students tell which of the young inventors had the most important invention and which had the most surprising invention. To reinforce vocabulary, have students tell how old Braille was when he devised a system of writing for people who are blind and how Epperson developed the Popsicle. (Students might need to refer back to Lesson 66.)

Assessment: Note students' overall performance on this and previous exercises in this unit. Are they able to discriminate between a fact and an opinion and explain why a statement is a fact or an opinion? If necessary, provide additional instruction.

Lesson 67: An Invention for a Cold Day

Read the article, and answer the questions that follow it.

An Invention for a Cold Day

1   It was a bitter cold day in Maine in 1873 as fifteen-year-old Chester Greenwood was trying out a new pair of ice skates. A <u>frigid</u> wind was whipping across the ice and freezing his ears. He wrapped his head in a scarf, but the scarf was uncomfortable. Besides, the wool was itchy and the scarf kept on slipping. Chester had an idea. He would make a covering for his ears. He bent two pieces of wire so that they would fit over his ears. Then he joined the pieces of wire so that they would fit over his head. After he returned home, he asked his grandmother to sew pieces of fur over the outside of the earpieces and velvet over the insides. He adjusted the wires so that each ear was covered with the fur piece. Later, Chester used a steel band instead of wire. The band could be adjusted so that the pieces of fur and velvet would fit over the ears.

2   Maine is a cold state. People in Maine thought that Chester's invention was a good idea. He called his invention "ear <u>protectors</u>." Later they came to be called "earmuffs." Chester set up a factory in Farmington, Maine, to make earmuffs. In 1883 his factory turned out 30,000 earmuffs. By 1936 the factory was making 400,000 earmuffs a year.

3   Chester patented the invention in 1877 when he was just eighteen years old. Although earmuffs are his most famous invention, it wasn't his only invention. He invented a steel-toothed rake, a spark plug for cars, a mousetrap, a new kind of rubber band, a hook for lifting doughnuts out of boiling oil, and a whistling tea kettle. Chester Greenwood was named as one of America's fifteen most outstanding inventors.

4   Making earmuffs gave jobs to hundreds of people in and around Farmington, Maine. Even today Farmington is known as the earmuff capital of the world. Each December there is a Chester Greenwood Parade in Farmington. Everyone in the parade wears earmuffs. The parade is a lot of fun. And the state of Maine set aside December 21 as Chester Greenwood Day. Chester Greenwood passed away in 1937, but his invention lives on.

1. How old was Chester Greenwood when he invented earmuffs?

    a. 13

    b. 15

    c. 18

    d. 21

2. In paragraph 1, the word *frigid* means

    a. very windy.

    b. very cold.

    c. very dark.

    d. very late.

3. In paragraph 2, the word *protector* means something that

    a. is made of thick fur.

    b. keeps a person or thing from harm.

    c. is made by hand.

    d. has never been made before.

4. How do you know that as time went on, a greater number of people bought earmuffs?

_____

_____

_____

5. What makes you think that the people of Farmington, Maine, haven't forgotten Chester Greenwood even though he died in 1937?

_____

_____

_____

6. Why do you think the Chester Greenwood Parade is held in December rather than in June or July?

_____

_____

_____

7. Using information from the story, support the following conclusion: Chester Greenwood was an outstanding inventor. Write your answer in the box.

Conclusion	Supporting Details
Chester Greenwood was an outstanding inventor.	

8. Imagine that you are Chester Greenwood, and this is the day that you thought up the idea for earmuffs. Write a paragraph that could have appeared in your journal that day.

_____

_____

_____

_____

_____

9. Write one fact and one opinion included in paragraph 4.

Fact:

_____

_____

Opinion:

_____

_____

Lesson 68: Young Inventors

Read the article, and answer the questions that follow it.

Young Inventors

Chester Greenwood was just fifteen years old when he invented earmuffs. Over the years, thousands of earmuffs made in his factory were sold. Louis Braille was the same age as Chester Greenwood when he <u>devised</u> braille. Braille is a way of writing that uses raised marks so that blind people can read with their fingertips. Philo Farnsworth was just fourteen years old when he got an idea for transmitting and receiving moving pictures. His idea was used in the invention of television. Television is one of the world's most important inventions. Margaret Knight was just twelve years old when she got an idea for making machines that spun cotton more safely. Frank Epperson was just eleven years old when he created a frozen fruit juice treat. He <u>developed</u> the frozen fruit juice treat into the Popsicle®.

1. How old was Braille when he invented a system of writing for the blind?

    a. 13

    b. 14

    c. 15

    d. 16

2. Which conclusion can be supported with information in the story?

    a. Young people can be inventors.

    b. It takes many years to develop an invention.

    c. Inventions change the way we live.

    d. Inventions help solve problems.

3. List at least three details to support the conclusion sentence you have chosen in question 2. Write your answer in the boxes.

Conclusion	Supporting Details

4. In the paragraph, the word *devised* means

    a. figured out and made.

    b. remembered and talked about.

    c. thought about and questioned.

    d. helped with.

5. In the paragraph, the word *developed* means

    a. forgot about.

    b. tried to do.

    c. changed; made into.

    d. fixed something that tastes good.

6. Write one fact and one opinion included in the paragraph.

Fact:

_____

_____

Opinion:

_____

_____

Lesson 69 ▶ A Walk in a Field

Objectives: Students make predictions, use context clues, draw and support conclusions, and note facts and opinions.

Introduction: In this lesson and Lessons 70 to 72, students make predictions after reading each segment of text. As with other strategies, review predicting by describing it and explaining its value. Then model the process of predicting. Read the article title aloud and discuss possible predictions. You might say that since this unit is about inventions, you predict that a person got an idea for an invention while walking in the field.

Guided and independent practice: Read the first paragraph with students, and encourage them to make predictions on the basis of what they have read. Then have students complete and discuss their responses. Also talk about the fabric that Velcro is made of and why Velcro® is said to be versatile. You might discuss students' experiences with Velcro®. And you might see how many examples of Velcro® or a similar device you can find.

Lesson 70 ▶ A Time-Saving Invention

Objectives: Students make and evaluate predictions, draw and support conclusions, use context clues, and distinguish between facts and opinions.

Introduction: Read the title of the article in the Student Pages. Then discuss possible predictions.

Guided and independent practice: Invite students to read the first paragraph, and then encourage them to make predictions on the basis of the title and what they have read. Have students complete and discuss their responses. Discuss the two additional predictions that students were asked to make. Discuss with students how their predictions played out and how they might have modified them. To reinforce vocabulary, have students discuss why Rohwedder added a stapling machine after he assembled a machine that would slice bread and why it was fortunate that Rohwedder gave up on the idea of using staples. To foster making connections, discuss with students whether they know someone like Rohwedder—someone who had to overcome difficulties. Discuss how that person's experience is similar to that of Rohwedder's.

285

Lesson 69: A Walk in a Field

More About Predicting

When making predictions, we use facts and other details to tell what might happen in the future. For instance, weather scientists use information about wind, temperature, amount of moisture in the air, and other details to predict the weather. As they read, good readers use titles, headings, pictures, and what they already know to predict what will happen next or what the author will tell them. As they read and get more information, good readers might change their predictions or make new ones. In this lesson and Lessons 70 to 72, you will be stopping in the middle of the article to make a prediction and then continuing to read to see how your prediction worked out.

Read the article, and answer the questions that follow it.

A Walk in a Field

1   If it hadn't been for a dog and a walk in a field, we might not have a handy device that millions of people use. In 1948 George de Mestral took his dog for a walk in a field. When de Mestral got home, he noticed that both he and the dog had burrs attached to them. Burrs are round balls of seeds that grow on wild bushes. De Mestral wondered how the burrs had become attached to him and his dog and why they didn't fall off. He had to pull hard on the burrs to get them off the dog and his clothes. De Mestral took a look at one of the burrs under a microscope. The burrs had thousands of tiny hooks. The hooks had become attached to the threads of his clothes and his dog's hair.

What do you predict will happen next? Write your prediction on the lines.

_____

_____

_____

_____

2   As he thought about how the burrs had attached themselves, an idea for a new type of fastener began to form in de Mestral's mind. He imagined a fastener that would have two parts. One part would have lots of tiny wire-like hooks. The other part would have lots of tiny cottony circles or loops. The hooks would fit into the loops, and would be a fastener. But the hooks and loops would be easily fastened and unfastened, so that the fastener could be used over and over again. He figured his invention would be easier to use than buttons, or snaps, or zippers, or shoelaces.

Was your prediction after paragraph 1 correct, or did you have to change it? Can you predict the invention that de Mestral was working on? Write your prediction on the lines.

_____

_____

_____

_____

3   De Mestral got help for his invention from a cloth maker. Even so, it took three years for de Mestral to get his invention to work. De Mestral and the cloth maker tried different kinds of <u>fabric</u>. And they tried different ways of lining up the hooks and the loops. At last, de Mestral found that a fabric known as nylon worked best. De Mestral called his invention "Velcro." The word *Velcro* came from the French word *velour*, which means "velvet," and the French word *crochet*, which means "hook." De Mestral got a patent for Velcro® in 1952.

Was your prediction after paragraph 2 correct, or did you have to change it? What do you predict will happen now that Velcro has been invented? Write your prediction on the lines.

_____

_____

_____

4   With the help of a friend, de Mestral set up a company to make and sell Velcro® fasteners. At first people weren't very interested in Velcro®. Some didn't think it would work. Others didn't like the way it looked. And some didn't like the ripping sound it made when they unfastened it. But over the years, people came to see that Velcro® worked well. They got used to the ripping sound and the way it looked.

5   Over the years, hundreds of uses have been found for this <u>versatile</u> fastener. Today the hook-and-loop fastener that de Mestral invented is sold around the world and is found on hundreds of products. Velcro® is a wonderful invention.

> **6** Since a patent lasts for only twenty years, other companies also now make the fasteners that de Mestral invented. But the companies can't use the Velcro® name. Instead, they call their fasteners "hook-and-loop fasteners." The name Velcro® has become a brand name. Velcro® is the name of a brand of hook-and-loop fasteners.

1. The reader can conclude from paragraph 4 that

   a. it took a while for Velcro® to become popular.

   b. Velcro® was a big success from the start.

   c. Velcro® is not as popular as it once was.

   d. most people have never heard of Velcro®.

2. What do you think was the most important thing to de Mestral?

   a. Making money

   b. Becoming famous

   c. Getting Velcro® to work right

   d. Finding new uses for Velcro®

3. In paragraph 3, the word *fabric* means

   a. cloth.

   b. metal.

   c. bits of plastic.

   d. coat or jacket.

4. In paragraph 5, the word *versatile* means

   a. does not wear out for a long time.

   b. can be made by machines.

   c. does not cost much money.

   d. can be used in many ways.

5. How do you know that it wasn't easy to get Velcro® to work right?

_____

_____

6. What makes you think that de Mestral was a curious person? Use details from the story to support your answer.

Conclusion	Supporting Details
De Mestral was a curious person.	

7. Write one fact and one opinion included in paragraph 5.

Fact:

_____

_____

Opinion:

_____

_____

Lesson 70: A Time-Saving Invention

Read the article, and answer the questions that follow it.

A Time-Saving Invention

1   Otto Rohwedder sold rings and watches for a living, but his main interest was bread. In the early 1900s, bread was not sliced. If you wanted a piece of bread, you had to cut a piece off the loaf.

What do you predict this article will tell you? Write your prediction on the lines.

_____

_____

_____

_____

---

2   Otto Rohwedder figured he could make life a little easier if he invented a machine that sliced bread. Bakers laughed at Rohwedder's idea. "The bread will go stale!" they warned. The bakers were right. When bread is exposed to air, it does get stale. The crust on unsliced bread keeps the air out and so keeps the inside of the loaf from getting stale.

What do you predict Rohwedder did to solve the problem of stale bread? Write your prediction on the lines.

_____

_____

_____

_____

3   Despite the warnings of the bakers, Rohwedder continued working on his invention. After he <u>assembled</u> a machine that sliced bread, he added a stapling machine. After the bread was sliced, it was stapled back together again so that air would not get in. The staples were made of metal, so that made eating the bread dangerous. If you forgot to take the staples out and ate one by mistake, that could hurt your insides. <u>Fortunately</u>, Rohwedder had the good sense to give up on the stapling idea. He invented a machine that would wrap the bread in waxed paper. The wrapping would keep the bread from getting stale.

4   As he was working on his invention, Rohwedder ran into two problems that nearly put an end to his machine.

What do you predict those problems might be? Write your prediction on the lines.

_____

_____

5   In 1915 Otto Rohwedder's doctor told him that he had a serious illness and had just one year to live. The doctor was wrong: Rohwedder lived for another forty-five years. In 1917 Rohwedder's workshop burned down. All his work was destroyed. Rohwedder rebuilt his workshop and his slicing machine. It took him another eleven years, but at last, in 1928, his bread-slicing machine was finished and it worked. On July 6, 1928, sliced bread went on sale in Chillicothe, Missouri. It was a great day for bread lovers.

1. If the author added another paragraph to the end of the story, it would most likely describe

    a. how much sliced bread cost.

    b. what happened when sliced bread went on sale.

    c. what kind of package sliced bread was put in.

    d. how many different kinds of sliced bread there were.

2. The reader can conclude from paragraph 3 that Rohwedder

    a. was willing to turn to a new idea when an idea didn't work out.

    b. knew exactly what he was doing most of the time.

    c. let people talk him out of things even when he thought the people were wrong.

    d. was a very stubborn person.

3. In paragraph 3, the word *assembled* means

    a. cleaned up.   c. threw away.

    b. put together.   d. shut down.

4. In paragraph 3, the word *fortunately* means

    a. closely; close by.   c. quickly; very fast.

    b. soon; not too long.   d. luckily; by good luck.

5. Which of the following is an opinion?

    a. It took Rohwedder more than twenty years to invent a bread slicing machine.

    b. Sliced bread went on sale on July 6, 1928.

    c. Sliced bread was first sold in Chillicothe, Missouri.

    d. July 6, 1928, was a great day for bread lovers.

6. Write two details from the story that the author included to show that Rohwedder didn't give up easily.

Characteristic	Supporting Details
Rohwedder didn't give up easily.	

Lesson 71 ▶ The Letter That Changed a Life

Objectives: Students make predictions, identify details, distinguish between facts and opinions, use context clues, and support inferences.

Introduction: Read the title of the article in the Student Pages aloud, and discuss possible predictions. Discuss how a letter might change someone's life. For English learners, discuss the italicized expression in the following sentence: "He was looking for *a new start in life.*"

Guided and independent practice: Have students read the first portion of the article and then reconsider their predictions, if necessary, when they are asked to write a prediction. Have students finish reading and complete the Student Pages. Discuss their responses and how their predictions played out. To reinforce vocabulary, have students tell why being durable was important to people buying jeans and why Strauss probably became a wealthy man. Discuss the fact that jeans are more popular now than ever before.

Lesson 72 ▶ The X-Y Position Indicator

Objectives: Students make predictions, identify and support main ideas, distinguish between facts and opinions, use context clues, and create a title.

Introduction: Read the title of the article in the Student Pages aloud, and discuss the meanings of *position* and *indicator*. Then discuss possible predictions.

Guided and independent practice: Invite students to read the first paragraph of the article, and then encourage them to modify their original predictions on the basis of what they have read. Have students complete and discuss their responses. Discuss the importance of the mouse. To reinforce vocabulary, discuss what kind of surface the mouse works on and how it tracks movement.

Assessment: Note students' overall performance on this and previous exercises in this unit. Have they mastered key skills? Are they able to discriminate between a fact and an opinion and explain why a statement is a fact or an opinion? How are they doing with previously taught skills: inferring, predicting, noting the main idea, and using context? Provide additional instruction and practice as needed.

Lesson 71: The Letter That Changed a Life

Read the article, and answer the questions that follow it.

The Letter That Changed a Life

1   A letter changed Levi Strauss's life. In 1849 gold was discovered in California. Thousands of people rushed to California in hopes of finding gold and becoming <u>wealthy.</u> The people hoping to find gold were foolish and greedy. One of those who headed for California was Levi Strauss. Levi Strauss wasn't looking for gold. Levi Strauss was a clever, hard-working man. He was looking for a new start in life. Up to this time, Levi Strauss had worked for his two brothers in New York City. The brothers sold clothes and blankets and other goods. Levi Strauss planned to set up a similar business in California.

2   Over the years, Strauss's business grew. In 1872 he got a letter from one of his customers, a tailor in Nevada. The tailor, Jacob Davis, had an idea for making better work pants. The pockets on work pants often tore. Jacob Davis added metal rivets to the pockets. Rivets are pieces of metal used to join things together. The rivets worked well, and the miners liked them. Davis didn't have enough money to get a patent for his invention. He also needed help making the pants. In his letter, Davis said that if they worked together, the two of them "could make a very large amount of money."

What do you predict Strauss will do? Write your prediction on the lines.

_____

_____

3   Strauss could see that riveted work pants were a good idea. He agreed to help Davis. The two decided to make the pants. They decided to use denim cloth because it is a strong cloth that doesn't tear easily and is long lasting. At first, the riveted denims were called "dungarees." *Dungarees* is a word from the Hindi language of India that means "rough cloth." Because they were tough and <u>durable</u>, dungarees were worn by thousands of farmers, miners, builders, and other workers. Later, dungarees came to be called "jeans." "Jeans" is a better name for the pants than "dungarees."

1. If the author added another paragraph to the end of the story, it would most likely describe

    a. how jeans came to be popular for all-around wear and not just for work.

    b. how the rivets were changed.

    c. what Strauss's growing-up years were like.

    d. what happened when an earthquake hit San Francisco.

2. Why did Strauss move to California?

    a. To hunt for gold

    b. To get away from his brothers

    c. To start a business

    d. To meet his business partner

3. What was Jacob Davis's idea?

    a. To add rivets to work pants

    b. To use a cheaper cloth

    c. To use a lighter cloth

    d. To use cloth that was easy to wash

4. Why did the men decide to use denim cloth?

    a. It was cheap.

    b. It looked good.

    c. It was strong.

    d. It was easy to get.

5. Which of the following statements is a fact?

    a. The people hoping to find gold were foolish and greedy.

    b. Levi Strauss was a clever, hard-working man.

    c. Dungarees were worn by thousands of workers.

    d. "Jeans" is a better name for the pants than "dungarees."

6. In paragraph 1, the word *wealthy* means

    a. smart.

    b. famous.

    c. rich

    d. happy.

7. In paragraph 3, the word *durable* means

    a. costing just a little bit of money.

    b. easy to take care of.

    c. easy to make.

    d. lasting for a long time.

8. What makes you think that Davis didn't have much money? Use information from the article to answer this question.

_____

_____

_____

_____

9. What makes you think that Davis's idea for a new kind of work pants was a good one? Use information from the article to answer this question.

_____

_____

_____

_____

Lesson 72: The X-Y Position Indicator

Read the article, and answer the questions that follow it.

The X-Y Position Indicator

1   Chances are you never heard of the X-Y position indicator, but you have probably used one and might even use it every day. The X-Y is not big. It fits in your hand. It is moved on a flat <u>surface</u>. Inside the X-Y are two little wheels. When the X-Y is moved, one wheel <u>tracks</u> the left-right movement on a computer screen. The other wheel tracks the up-down position. Using the X-Y, you can move to any position on the computer screen.

What do you predict the X-Y is?

_____

_____

2   What did you predict that the X-Y is? It's called a mouse. "Mouse" is a great name for the X-Y. It got its name because it has the shape of a mouse's body, and the wire attached to it looks a bit like a tail. Today many computers have a cordless mouse. But not long ago, the mouse had to be attached to the computer with a cord.

3 The first personal computers did not have a mouse. The keyboard was used to give the computer all its commands. If you wanted to move across or up or down the computer screen, you had to use the arrow keys.

4 A scientist by the name of Douglas Englehart invented the mouse in 1964, but it took a while for his invention to be used. It wasn't used much until the 1970s. People finally began to realize that the mouse made computers much easier to use. Today it's hard to imagine operating a computer without the help of the mouse.

1. If the author added another paragraph to the end of the story, it would most likely describe

    a. how the mouse changed the way computers were used.

    b. how the cost of computers went down.

    c. how Englehart got the idea for the mouse.

    d. who gave the mouse its name.

2. Paragraph 2 tells mainly

    a. how the mouse works.

    b. how the mouse got its name.

    c. why the mouse was invented.

    d. when the mouse was first used.

3. Which of the following statements is an opinion?

    a. The first computers did not have a mouse.

    b. A scientist by the name of Douglas Englehart invented the mouse in 1964.

    c. At first the mouse was called the "X-Y position indicator."

    d. "Mouse" is a better name than "X-Y position indicator."

4. In paragraph 1, the word *surface* means

    a. outside or top part of.

    b. long part of.

    c. a rough part of.

    d. the hidden part of.

5. In paragraph 1, the word *tracks* means

    a. follows a path or trail made by something; follows the movement of.

    b. learns about; finds out about.

    c. supplies energy to; supplies power to.

    d. holds onto tightly for a time; places a hold on for a while.

6. The title of this story is "The X-Y Position Indicator." What could be another title for it? Explain your answer with information from the story.

_____

_____

_____

_____

_____

_____

_____

End-of-Theme Reflection

Discuss what students learned in this unit about distinguishing between facts and opinions. Ask students to list the inventions that they read about. Discuss with students how these inventions helped make life easier or better or changed our lives in some ways. Discuss with students which invention, in their opinion, was most important. Also discuss which inventor, in their opinion, was their favorite. Discuss the main characteristics that the inventors shared and examples of those characteristics.

In order for skills learned in this unit to transfer, it is essential that students apply the skills to their textbooks or other full-length materials. Suggested books are listed below. Have available copies of the suggested books, and encourage students to read them. Readability levels provided by Accelerated Reading (AR) and Lexile Framework are listed. Most are on a grade 4 to 5 level. However, readability formulas do not measure concept load, background needed to read a book, or interest level. You might want to examine the books and use your professional judgment as to whether the books are appropriate for your students.

Barretta, Gene. (2006). *Now and Ben: The Modern Inventions of Benjamin Franklin.* **5.1, 910**

Bingham, Caroline. (2004). *Invention.* **5.6**

Jones, Charlotte Foltz. (1997). *Accidents May Happen: Fifty Inventions Discovered by Mistake.* **6.9**

Krensky, Stephen. (2008). *A Man for All Seasons: The Life of George Washington Carver.* **5.4**

McCully, Emily Arnold. (2006). *Marvelous Mattie: How Margaret E. Knight Became an Inventor.* **4.2, 720**

Rossi, Anne. (2005). *Bright Ideas: The Age of Inventions in the United States, 1870–1910.* **5.4**

Wyckoff, Edwin. (2008). *The Teen Who Invented Television: Philo T. Farnsworth and His Awesome Invention.* **4.5**

Encourage students to apply their skills when they read books. Using one of the books in the list as a model, show students how they might use chapter titles and headings to help them determine the main ideas that they will be reading about. You might demonstrate how most chapter titles and chapter heads can be turned into questions, which readers then answer when they come to the end of the chapter or section.

Encourage students to summarize their reading by telling the main facts about the inventor or invention that they are reading about. They might focus on how the invention came to be created and its importance. They might also note statements that are factual and statements that are opinions. Encourage, too, the use of graphic organizers to highlight essential information. Students might create a time line to highlight the main events in an inventor's life. Instead of or along with reading the books, students might consult one of the following Web sites:

National Gallery for America's Young Inventors

> http://www.nmoe.org/gallery/i96.htm

Zoom Inventors and Inventions

> www.enchantedlearning.com/inventors/

Kennesaw State University Educational Technology Center: Inventors/Inventions (has links to a number of sites)

> http://edtech.kennesaw.edu/web/inventor.html

What did you learn about the differences between facts and opinions?
How can you tell if a statement is factual? Write your answers on the lines.

_____

_____

_____

_____

_____

How have you used your ability to tell the difference between facts and
opinions? How might you use it in the future? Write your answers on the
lines.

_____

_____

_____

_____

_____

What did you learn about inventions and inventors? Write your answer on the lines.

_____

_____

_____

_____

_____

Which invention was most important? Give reasons for your choice. Write your answer on the lines.

_____

_____

_____

_____

_____

Would you like to find out more about inventors and their inventions? Here are some books where you can get more information.

Barretta, Gene. (2006). *Now and Ben: The Modern Inventions of Benjamin Franklin*. New York: Holt. Shows and tells about Ben Franklin's many inventions and how some are still in use.

Bingham, Caroline. (2004). *Invention.* New York: DK. Uses many photos and drawings to explain how new inventions come into being and to give a history of inventions.

Jones, Charlotte Foltz. (1997). *Accidents May Happen: Fifty Inventions Discovered by Mistake*. New York: Delacorte. Explains how plastic, paper, raisins, and forty-seven other inventions were discovered by accident.

Krensky, Stephen. (2008). *A Man for All Seasons: The Life of George Washington Carver.* New York: Amistad. Carver, born a slave and orphaned at an early age, became an outstanding plant scientist.

McCully, Emily Arnold. (2006). *Marvelous Mattie: How Margaret E. Knight Became an Inventor*. New York: Farrar Straus Giroux. Explains how Margaret Knight came to invent a machine to make square paper bags.

Rossi, Anne. (2005). *Bright Ideas: The Age of Inventions in the United States, 1870–1910.* Washington, DC: National Geographic. Highlights the creation of a number of key inventions.

Wyckoff, Edwin. (2008). *The Teen Who Invented Television: Philo T. Farnsworth and His Awesome Invention*. Berkeley Heights, NJ: Enslow. Tells the amazing story of the teenager whose ideas were used in the invention of television.

Comparing and contrasting are powerful abilities. Marzano, Gaddy, and Dean (2000) found that teaching comparing and classifying boosted students' performance on achievement tests by 45 percentile points. This represents a gain of about one and a half years. Nearly a century ago, Terman (1916), who developed the Stanford-Binet Intelligence Test, declared that comparing and contrasting were the most important cognitive abilities.

Introducing Comparing and Contrasting

Explain to students that comparing and contrasting are key skills. Discuss times in which they are called on to make comparisons and contrasts in school and out of school. Tell students that they will be using a graphic organizer called a *frame matrix* to help them make comparisons and contrasts. Tell students that at first they will be comparing animals, but then they will compare people and, after that, different ways of sleeping. Explain that the following words are often used to make comparisons: *compare, contrast, differ, different, differences, same, similar, similarities,* and *however.*

Theme A  Confusing Animals

Lesson 73 ▶ **African and Asian Elephants**

Objectives: Students make comparisons and contrasts and use context clues.

Introduction: Invite students to turn the title of the article in the Student Pages into a question and then read the article to answer the question. Since the articles in this unit involve making comparisons and contrasts, students might place the words *differ* and *same* or *similar* and *different* in the question they formulate. Their question for this lesson might be: "How are African and Asian elephants similar, and how are they different?" Remind students that they will be looking for differences and similarities and that they will be placing key differences and similarities in the frame matrix.

Guided and independent practice: Discuss students' responses in the Student Pages. Note that both African and Asian elephants are enormous, but African elephants are even larger than Asian elephants. Note, too, why the size of the ears differ. African elephants live mostly on the plains, where it is hotter than in the forests where Asian elephants live, and so they need bigger ears to cool themselves off. Fill out a sample frame matrix so students can see how to use it.

Extension: Incorporate compare-and-contrast questions in classroom discussions. Compare animals, events, characters, authors, favorite books, and other topics that are being discussed.

Have you ever wondered how frogs are different from toads, or how African elephants are different from Asian elephants, or how alligators are different from crocodiles? In this theme, you will be comparing these and other animals. Seeing how thing are alike and how they are different helps us to understand them better. To help you make comparisons, you will use a frame matrix. In a frame matrix, the things being compared are listed in a vertical (straight up and down) column. The categories in which they are being compared are listed in the horizontal (straight across) columns. Take a look at the frame matrix in question 1 in the Student Pages for African and Asian Elephants, which follows.

Lesson 73: African and Asian Elephants

Read the article, and answer the questions that follow it.

African and Asian Elephants

1 Take a close look at the pictures of the African and Asian elephants. How are the elephants alike? How are they different? African and Asian elephants look very similar. Both are very large animals. In fact, these <u>enormous</u> beasts are the biggest land animals on Earth. However, if you look at the picture, you can see that African elephants are bigger than Asian elephants. African elephants weigh up to 14,000 pounds or more and are about 12 feet high at the shoulder. Asian elephants weigh up to 12,000 pounds and are about 9 feet high at the shoulder. African elephants also have bigger ears.

2   Why do you think African elephants have bigger ears? African elephants are found mostly on the <u>plains</u>. It's hot on the plains. African elephants use their large ears to cool off. Asian elephants live mostly in the forests where it is cooler.

3   Asian elephants have more toes. An Asian elephant has five toes on the front foot. An African elephant has only four. An African elephant has two fingers at the tip of its trunk. An Asian elephant has just one. Both male and female African elephants have tusks, but only male Asian elephants have tusks. Asian elephants have two bumps on their forehead. African elephants have none.

African elephant

Asian elephant

1. Fill in the boxes in the frame matrix.

	African Elephants	Asian Elephants
Where they live		
Weight		
Height at shoulder		
Ears		
Trunks		
Tusks		
Toes		
Forehead		

2. In paragraph 1, the word *enormous* means

   a. alike; almost the same.

   b. very large.

   c. very dangerous

   d. living nearby.

3. In paragraph 2, the word *plains* means

   a. things that are not fancy.

   b. things that are easy to understand.

   c. flat pieces of land.

   d. things that are simple.

Lesson 74   Savanna and Forest Elephants

Objectives: Students make comparisons and contrasts and use context clues.

Introduction: Invite students to turn the title of the article in the Student Pages into a question and then read the article to answer the question. Since the articles in this unit involve making comparisons and contrasts, students might place the words *differ* and *same* or *similar* and *different* in the question they formulate. Their question for this lesson might be: "How are savanna and forest elephants similar, and how are they different?" Remind students that they will be looking for differences and similarities and that they will be placing key differences and similarities in the frame matrix.

Guided and independent practice: Discuss students' responses. Discuss why savanna and forest elephants differ.

Extension: Additional information about savanna and forest elephants can be found at Animal Corner at http://www.animalcorner.co.uk/rainforests/forestelephant.html.

Lesson 75   Dugongs and Manatees

Objectives: Students make comparisons and contrasts and use context clues.

Introduction: Invite students to turn the title of the article in the Student Pages into a question and then read the article to answer the question. Since the articles in this unit involve making comparisons and contrasts, students might place the words *differ* and *same* or *similar* and *different* in the question they formulate. Their question for this lesson might be: "How are dugongs and manatees similar, and how are they different?" Remind students that they will be looking for differences and similarities and that they will be placing key differences and similarities in the frame matrix.

Guided and independent practice: Discuss students' responses. Note that dugongs live in shallow water and have keen hearing but poor eyesight.

Extension: Additional information about manatees can be found at The Wild Ones Animal Index at http://www.thewildones.org/Animals/manatee.html.

Lesson 74: Savanna and Forest Elephants

Read the article, and answer the questions that follow it.

Savanna and Forest Elephants

At first it was thought that all African elephants were of the same type. But there are actually two types of elephants in Africa: savanna elephants and forest elephants. <u>Savanna</u> elephants live in the flat grasslands of Africa. The <u>habitat</u> of forest elephants is the forests of Africa. Both the savanna and the forest elephants are enormous. They have big ears, trunks, and tusks. But the forest elephant's ears are smaller and are rounder. However, savanna elephants are larger. A full-grown male savanna elephant weighs 14,000 pounds (6,350 kilograms). A full-grown male forest elephant weighs only about 10,000 pounds (4,536 kilograms). The tusks of two types of African elephants also differ. The tusks of savanna elephants are curved; the tusks of forest elephants are shorter and are straight. Can you think why this might be? Shorter, straighter tusks are better for pushing through the forest.

1. Fill in the boxes in the frame matrix with information from the article.

	Savanna Elephants	Forest Elephants
Where they live		
Size		
Ears		
Tusks		

2. In the paragraph, the word *savanna* means

   a. a large forest that has many wild animals.

   b. flat, treeless grasslands in hot parts of the world.

   c. swampy places that are hard to get to.

   d. hilly country in far-off lands.

3. In the paragraph, the word *habitat* means a

   a. place that is hard to find.

   b. far-off or distant place.

   c. place that is full of dangers.

   d. place where an animal lives.

Lesson 75: Dugongs and Manatees

Read the article, and answer the questions that follow it.

Dugongs and Manatees

Dugongs

1   Have you heard of an animal called a dugong? Dugongs are large sea animals. They can grow to be 10 feet (3 meters) long and weigh up to 900 pounds (408 kilograms). Dugongs like to live in warm, <u>shallow</u> water where sea grasses grow. They use their front flippers to push themselves through the water.

2   Dugongs are sometimes known as "sea cows." Like cows, they spend much of their time eating grass. But the grass they eat is under the sea.

3   Dugongs are mammals. This means that they need to breathe air. They can stay under water for only a few minutes.

4   Dugongs have poor eyesight but <u>keen</u> hearing. They find grasses with their whiskers. Whiskers cover their upper lip and their large snout. The whiskers are feelers that tell the dugongs what it is touching.

5   Dugongs take a long time to grow up. Some animals are full-grown a few months after they are born. But dugongs take sixteen or more years before they are ready to have babies. But that's okay. Dugongs live for seventy years or more. They are one of the longest-living mammals on Earth. They live just about as long as people do.

Manatees

6   Manatees are cousins to dugongs and are also large sea creatures. And they are also mammals. Manatees can be 12 feet (3.7 meters) long and weigh 1,500 pounds (680 kilograms) or more. Like dugongs, they are known as sea cows and eat sea plants. They also live in warm, shallow water and feed on the plants that grow at the bottom of streams, rivers, and canals. They use their front flippers to push themselves along the bottom of the waterway. Manatees eat a lot. They eat up to 100 pounds (45 kilograms) of plants a day. Manatees have good hearing and good eyesight.

7   Manatees grow up a little faster than dugongs and don't live quite as long. They live for only about sixty years.

1. Fill in the boxes in the frame matrix with information from the article.

	Dugongs	Manatees
Habitat (where they live)		
Size		
Senses		
Food		
Life expectancy (how long they live)		

2. In paragraph 1, the word *shallow* means

   a. near the shore.

   b. very smooth.

   c. full of salt.

   d. not deep.

3. In paragraph 4, the word *keen* means

   a. very smart; being able to learn quickly.

   b. wanting to do.

   c. very sharp; able to sense small differences.

   d. very lively; full of life.

Lesson 76 ▶ Alligators and Crocodiles

Objectives: Students make comparisons and contrasts and use context clues.

Introduction: Invite students to turn the title of the article in the Student Pages into a question and then read the article to answer the question. Since the articles in this unit involve making comparisons and contrasts, students might place the words *differ* and *same* or *similar* and *different* in the question they formulate. Their questions for the selection might be: "How are alligators and crocodiles similar, and how are they different?" Remind students that they will be looking for differences and similarities and that they will be placing key differences and similarities in the frame matrix.

Guided and independent practice: Discuss students' responses. Discuss how the snouts of alligators and crocodiles are different and whether alligators or crocodiles have teeth that protrude and are visible even when the jaws are closed.

Lesson 77 ▶ Squid and Octopuses

Objectives: Students make comparisons and contrasts and use context clues.

Introduction: Invite students to turn the title of the article in the Student Pages into a question and then read the article to answer the question. Since the articles in this unit involve making comparisons and contrasts, students place the words *differ* and *same* or *different* and *similar* in the question they formulate. Their questions for the selection might be: "How are squid and octopuses similar, and how are they different?" Remind students that they will be looking for differences and similarities and that they will be placing key differences and similarities in the frame matrix.

Guided and independent practice: Discuss students' responses. Discuss how squid and octopuses propel themselves through the water and which one has more tentacles.

Extension: Students can learn more about the giant squid at National Geographic's Web site at http://animals.nationalgeographic.com/animals/invertebrates/giant-squid .html.

Lesson 76: Alligators and Crocodiles

Read the article, and answer the questions that follow it.

Alligators and Crocodiles

1 Alligators and crocodiles have many similarities. Both have a long snout and rows of sharp teeth. Both use their long tails to swim through the water, and both can also run fast for short distances. Both eat a variety of creatures. They eat fish, birds, turtles, and other animals. Both live in warm places in or near the water, but crocodiles are more likely to be found in saltwater.

2 Crocodiles are shyer than alligators. They are more likely to hide from people. Alligators have a broad snout that is shaped like a U. Crocodiles have a narrow snout that is shaped like a V. Alligators are bluish. Crocodiles are green or a greenish brown. Both alligators and crocodiles have a very large fourth tooth. When its jaws are closed, the alligator's fourth tooth fits inside and is not <u>visible</u>. But the crocodile's fourth tooth <u>protrudes</u> and can be easily seen outside its jaws.

1. Fill in the boxes in the frame matrix with information from the article.

	Alligators	Crocodiles
Overall appearance		
Habitat		
Movement		
Food		
Snout		
Coloring		
Teeth		
Behavior		

2. In paragraph 2, the word *visible* means

    a. very dangerous.

    b. sharp and pointy.

    c. can be seen.

    d. frightening to look at.

3. In paragraph 2, the word *protrudes* means

    a. is sharp.

    b. sticks out.

    c. keeps other animals away.

    d. used in fights.

Lesson 77: Squid and Octopuses

Read the article, and answer the questions that follow it.

Squid and Octopuses

People often confuse squid and octopuses, and it's easy to see why. Both squid and octopuses live under water, and both have long armlike body parts known as <u>tentacles</u>. Both squid and octopuses have large eyes and sharp beaks. Both <u>propel</u> themselves through the water by squirting water out of a tube. Both can change color to match their surroundings and can squirt ink at their enemies. However, there are a number of differences between the two creatures. The squid has ten tentacles, and the octopus has just eight. Two of the squid's tentacles are extra-long. The octopus has a rounded body. The squid's body is bullet shaped and looks as if it has an arrowhead on the end of it. The squid has an inside shell that gives it its shape. The octopus has no inside shell. It has a tough covering known as a mantle.

1. Fill in the boxes in the frame matrix with information from the article.

	Squid	**Octopuses**
Habitat		
Overall appearance		
Movement		
Shell		
Defense		

2. In the paragraph, the word *tentacles* means

   a. finlike body parts on the sides of animals to guide them through the water.

   b. armlike body parts that grow around the mouth or head and are used to touch, hold, or move.

   c. mouth or beak of underwater animal used to crunch shells of animals.

   d. tubelike body part used to jet animals through the water suddenly and with great speed.

3. In the paragraph, the word *propel* means

   a. stay; rest in one spot.

   b. hold; get a handle on.

   c. move; push forward.

   d. finish; end.

Objectives: Students make comparisons and contrasts and use context clues.

Introduction: Invite students to turn the title of the article in the Student Pages into a question and then read the article to answer the question. Since the articles in this unit involve making comparisons and contrasts, students place the words *differ* and *same* or *different* and *similar* in the question they formulate. Their question for the selection in this lesson might be: "How are frogs and toads similar, and how are they different?" Remind students that they will be looking for differences and similarities and that they will be placing key differences and similarities in the frame matrix.

Guided and independent practice: Discuss students' responses. Discuss ways in which frogs and toads seem to be nearly identical and which one has dry skin and which has moist skin.

Assessment: Note students' overall performance on this and previous exercises in this unit. Have they mastered key skills? Are they able to compare and contrast? If not, provide additional instruction and practice.

Lesson 78: Frogs and Toads

Read the article, and answer the questions that follow it.

> ### Frogs and Toads
>
> Frogs and toads seem to be <u>identical</u> until you take a closer look. Both frogs and toads have big protruding eyes, long tongues, and strong back legs. With their long tongues, they can catch plenty of insects. With their strong back legs, they can hop on land or swim through the water. Both frogs and toads grow up in the water. However, toads are usually darker than frogs. Frogs have smooth, <u>moist</u> skin. Toads have dry, rough skin that is full of small bumps known as warts. But both frogs and toads have a poison on their skins that helps keep enemies away. Most toads live in fields or near the water, but most frogs live in or near the water.

1. Fill in the boxes in the frame matrix with information from the article.

	Frogs	**Toads**
Habitat		
Overall appearance		
Skin		
Movement		
Food		
Defense		

2. In the paragraph, the word *identical* means

   a. having large protruding eyes.

   b. living in the same place.

   c. easily frightened.

   d. exactly the same.

3. In the paragraph, the word *moist* means

   a. damp or wet.

   b. soaked or very wet.

   c. dry or rough.

   d. swampy or muddy.

End-of-Theme Reflection

Discuss with students what they have learned about comparing and contrasting and how they are using these skills. Students also discuss what they have learned about animals. Ask: "Which of the pairs of animals that you read about were most similar? What are the main ways in which you can tell them apart?" In order for skills learned in this unit to transfer, it is essential that students use the skills when they read their textbooks and other full-length materials. Although the brief articles that students have read so far are building background knowledge and reading skill, students need to apply these skills to full-length selections. Suggested books are listed below. Have available copies of the suggested books and encourage students to read them. Readability levels provided by Accelerated Reading (AR) and Lexile Framework are posted. Most are on a grade 4 to 5 level. However, readability formulas do not measure concept load, background needed to read a book, or interest level. You might want to examine the books and use your professional judgment as to whether the books are appropriate for your students.

Bish, Nic. (2008). *Frogs*. **3.7, 890**

Kalman, Bobbie. (2006). *Endangered Manatees*. **5.4**

Kalman, Bobbie. (2006). *Endangered Frogs*. **5.6**

Joubert, Beverly, and Joubert, Derek. (2008). *Face to Face with Elephants*. **5.5**

Markle, Sandra. (2004). *Crocodiles*. **5.5, 980**

Moffett, Mark. (2008). *Face to Face with Frogs*. **5.6**

Nicklin, Flip, and Nicklin, Linda. (2007). *Face to Face with Dolphins*. **5.2**

Simon, Seymour. (1999). *Crocodiles and Alligators*. **6.3, 1010**

Encourage students to apply their skills to books they read. Using one of the books as a model, show students how they might use chapter titles and headings to help them determine the main ideas that they will be reading about. You might demonstrate how most chapter titles and chapter heads can be turned into questions, which readers then answer when they come to the end of the chapter or section. Encourage students to summarize their reading by telling the three to five most important facts they learned. Encourage, too, the use of graphic organizers to highlight essential information. Students might also share their books with partners or in small groups. Students might wish to find out more about a particular animal or pair of animals. Instead of or along with reading the books, students might consult one of the Web sites listed in the Extension sections of the lessons or one the animal sites recommended by the American Library Association at http://www.ala.org/ala/aboutala/offices/library/alarecommends/recommendedwebsites.cfm. Web sites tend to be more difficult than books; however, Web site text can be read by a text-to-speech feature available on most computers.

What did you learn about comparing and contrasting? How have you used the skill of comparing and contrasting? Write your answers on the lines.

_____

_____

_____

_____

Think of all the animal pairs that you read about. Which pair was most interesting? Give reasons for your choice. Write your answer on the lines.

_____

_____

_____

_____

_____

_____

Here is where you can go to find out more about some of the animals that you read about:

Bish, Nic. (2008). *Frogs.* New York: Scholastic. Has outstanding photos of frogs and toads.

Kalman, Bobbie. (2006). *Endangered Manatees.* New York: Crabtree. Describes and compares manatees and tells why they are endangered and what might be done to save them.

Kalman, Bobbie. (2006). *Endangered Frogs.* New York: Crabtree. Describes frogs and toads and explains why they are endangered.

Joubert, Beverly, and Joubert, Derek. (2008). *Face to Face with Elephants.* Washington, DC: National Geographic. With photos and stories, the Jouberts show and tell what it is like to get up close to elephants.

Markle, Sandra. (2004). *Crocodiles.* Minneapolis, MN: Carolrhoda Books. Describes in detail the characteristics of and habits of the Nile crocodile. Has great photos.

Moffett, Mark. (2008). *Face to Face with Frogs.* Washington, DC: National Geographic. Photos show and text discusses a number of unusual frogs. Includes a discussion of the differences between frogs and toads.

Nicklin, Flip, and Nicklin, Linda. (2007). *Face to Face with Dolphins.* Washington, DC: National Geographic. With photos and stories, the authors show and tell what dolphins are like and how to get to know them better.

Simon, Seymour (1999). *Crocodiles and Alligators.* New York: HarperCollins. Full of interesting information about crocodiles and alligators.

Theme B > Famous People

The lessons in this theme look at pairs of famous people and provide additional practice with comparing and contrasting. Although each of the individuals described is unique, encourage students to note common characteristics.

Lesson 79   Champion Mistakes

Objectives: Students make comparisons and contrasts and use context clues.

Introduction: Invite students to turn the title of the article in the Student Pages into a question and then read the article to answer the question. Their question might be: "What were the champion mistakes?" Remind students that they will be looking for differences and similarities and that they will be placing key differences and similarities in the frame matrix.

Guided and independent practice: Discuss the champion mistakes and students' responses. Discuss which player was given lots of individual help and which was rejected by the Dodgers. Discuss how Mikan overcame his clumsiness. To foster making connections, ask students to tell about a time when they overcame an obstacle that was holding them back. Have them compare their situation with that of Mikan's.

Extension: Students can obtain additional information about Hank Aaron at the Milwaukee Braves Web site at http://mlb.mlb.com/atl/history/aaron.jsphttp://mlb.mlb.com/atl/history/aaron.jsp. Students can obtain additional information about George Mikan at the NBA Encyclopedia Web site at http://www.nba.com/history/players/mikan_bio.html.

In this theme, you will compare sports heroes and famous artists. You will also meet famous people who went to the same high school at the same time.

Lesson 79: Champion Mistakes

Read the article, and answer the questions that follow it.

Champion Mistakes

1   George Mikan was turned down for a basketball scholarship by Notre Dame University (NOH-ter dame YOO-nuh-ver-suh-tee) because the head coach thought the 6-foot 10-inch player was too clumsy. A university is a large college. An assistant coach, Ray Meyer, talked Mikan into applying to go to DePaul University. Mikan was accepted at DePaul and given <u>individual</u> help by Meyer, who had become the coach at DePaul. With Mikan's help, DePaul won the national championship in 1945. Later, as a professional basketball player, Mikan led the Minneapolis Lakers (the Lakers are now in Los Angeles) to five league titles. Mikan became known as one of basketball's greatest players.

2   Hank Aaron was <u>rejected</u> by the Brooklyn Dodgers baseball team. (The Dodgers later moved from Brooklyn to Los Angeles.) He was told that he was too small. Signed later by the Boston Braves, Hank Aaron set eleven records and hit 755 home runs. (The Braves moved to Milwaukee and then to Atlanta.) Hank Aaron became one of baseball's greatest hitters.

1. Fill in the boxes in the frame matrix with information from the article.

	Mikan	Aaron
Sport played		
Reason turned down		
Accomplishments		

2. In paragraph 1, the word *individual* means

    a. extra; more than given to others.

    b. for one person or by one person.

    c. carefully planned.

    d. not given fairly to all.

3. In paragraph 2, the word *rejected* means

    a. helped; given extra lessons.

    b. turned down; not accepted.

    c. sent to the right place.

    d. not being given needed help.

Lesson 80 ▶ Late Start

Objectives: Students make comparisons and contrasts and use context clues.

Introduction: Invite students to turn the title of the article in the Student Pages into a question and then read the article to answer the question. Their question might be: "Who got a late start, and what did the person do?" Remind students that they will be looking for differences and similarities and that they will be placing key differences and similarities in the frame matrix. For English learners, discuss the italicized expression in the following sentence: "When she was fifty years old, Clementine Hunter decided that she, too, could 'mark a picture' if *she put her mind to it*."

Guided and independent practice: Discuss students' responses. Discuss who encouraged Clementine Hunter and why her paintings were assembled and sent around the country. What special occasion was being celebrated? Have students tell what happened when Grandma Moses attempted to sew when she got older and how this led her to begin painting.

Extension: Students can obtain additional information about Clementine Hunter at http://www.clementinehunterartist.com/. Additional information about Grandma Moses can be found at Who2? at http://www.who2.com/grandmamoses.html.

Lesson 80: Late Start

Read the article, and answer the questions that follow it.

Late Start

1 Clementine Hunter worked as a cook at a plantation, which is a large farm. The plantation was in Louisiana (lew-ee-zee-ANN-uh). The plantation was a gathering place for artists. When she was fifty years old, Hunter decided that she, too, could "mark a picture" if she put her mind to it. Using some worn brushes and half-empty tubes of paint, Hunter painted an outdoor scene and showed it to one of the artists. Surprised by the beauty of the picture, the artist <u>encouraged</u> Hunter to paint more pictures. Hunter did just that. Often she painted all night long in her cabin and then reported for work at the plantation in the morning. At first, Hunter's colorful paintings sold for two or three dollars each. Later they sold for thousands of dollars. In 1955 she had a one-woman show at the New Orleans Museum of Art. She later had shows in museums across the country. In 1986, to honor Hunter's 100th birthday, the president of the United States telephoned her and some of her paintings were assembled in a show that traveled around the country. Hunter died in 1988 at the age of 102. She had created some five thousand paintings.

2 Grandma Moses didn't start painting until she was in her seventies. Grandma Moses was a housewife. She had taken care of her home and raised her family. Up until that time, she had sewn flowers and other designs on clothes, curtains, and table cloths. But

she was having trouble with her hands. Her hands got sore when she <u>attempted</u> to sew. So Grandma Moses began painting instead of sewing. At first she used regular house paint and old brushes. Many of her paintings showed farming scenes. Grandma Moses had lived all her life on a farm.

3 People liked her paintings. They were very colorful. In 1949 the president gave her an award in honor of her painting. Although she didn't start painting until late in life, Grandma Moses created hundreds of paintings. She lived to be 101.

1. Fill in the boxes in the frame matrix with information from the article.

	Clementine Hunter	Grandma Moses
Occupation (kind of work done)		
When she began painting		
Kinds of paintings		
Accomplishments		
Honors		
How long she lived		

2. In paragraph 1, the word *encouraged* means

    a. gave ideas that would help correct mistakes.

    b. explained very clearly how things should be done.

    c. explained a set of rules.

    d. said and did things that would make a person want to keep on trying.

3. In paragraph 2, the word *attempted* means

    a. gathered together.

    b. made to look their best.

    c. tried to do something.

    d. thought about for a while.

Lesson 81 ▶ Famous High School Students

Objectives: Students make comparisons and contrasts and use context clues.

Introduction: Invite students to turn the title of the article in the Student Pages into a question and then read the article to answer the question. Their question might be: "Who were the famous high school students, and what did they do?" Remind students that they will be looking for differences and similarities and that they will be placing key differences and similarities in a frame matrix.

Guided and independent practice: Discuss the famous high school students and their accomplishments and students' responses. Discuss who liked to recite poems and what effect this had on Dunbar. Discuss how Dunbar wrote his first poem at age six and wrote poems for the remainder of his life.

Extension: Students can obtain additional information about Dunbar and his poems at University of Dayton: Paul Laurence Dunbar at www.dunbarsite.org. Additional information about the Wright brothers can be found at the Wright Brothers Aeroplane Company at http://www.wright-brothers.org/.

Lesson 81: Famous High School Students

Read the article, and answer the questions that follow it.

Famous High School Students

1   The other students in Dayton High School in Dayton, Ohio, had no way of knowing it, but one day, two of their classmates would become famous throughout the world. Paul Dunbar would go on to become a famous poet. Orville Wright would become the first person to fly an airplane. Orville and his older brother, Wilbur, invented the first successful airplane. Orville was in Paul's class. Wilbur Wright had gone to high school in Indiana. All three boys were hard workers. Paul started a newspaper while he was still in school. The Wright brothers started a printing business. They printed Paul's newspaper. They also repaired bikes.

2   In some ways the boys were very different. Paul liked to work with words. His mother had learned poetry when she was a slave. She worked in the home of her owners, who often read poetry to their children. Paul's mother listened in. From the time he was a baby, Paul's mother <u>recited</u> poems and sang songs to him. Paul wrote his first poem at the age of six, and he continued to write poems for the <u>remainder</u> of his life. He wrote several books of poetry and became a famous poet. Orville and Wilbur liked to work with machines. They opened a bicycle shop, but spent much of their time working on machines that would fly. Finally, on December 13, 1903, Orville flew the flying machine that the brothers had built in their bicycle shop. It was the first flight of a heavier-than-air machine powered by a motor. It marked the start of the age of the airplane. It was too bad Paul Dunbar wasn't there to write a poem about that magical first flight.

1. Fill in the boxes in the frame matrix with information from the article.

	Dunbar	Wright Brothers
Work habits		
Interests		
Accomplishments		

2. Using information from the frame matrix, fill in the blanks in the frame paragraph.

The Wright brothers and Paul Dunbar were similar in at least one way. All three were

_____.

In later years, all three boys became

_____.

The Wright brothers

_____.

Paul Dunbar

_____.

Copyright © 2010 by John Wiley & Sons, Inc.

3. How were the Wright brothers and Paul Dunbar different? Give examples.

The Wright brothers were different from Paul Dunbar. Paul Dunbar liked to

_____.

He

_____.

The Wright brothers liked to

_____.

They

_____.

4. In paragraph 2, the word *recited* means

   a. wrote about or took notes on.

   b. listened to for a long time.

   c. said from memory or read aloud.

   d. watched over for a while.

5. In paragraph 2, the word *remainder* means

   a. best time; easiest time.

   b. change of seasons of the year.

   c. rooms; large spaces.

   d. rest of; part left over.

End-of-Theme Reflection

Discuss the end-of-theme reflection that appears on the Student Pages. Discuss the common characteristics that the famous people had, and have students tell which person they admire most and why. Discuss which famous people students would like to learn more about. Tell students that their choices are not limited to the people they have read about in this book. They can choose other famous people. Have available copies of the suggested books that follow, and encourage students to read them. Readability levels provided by Accelerated Reading (AR) and Lexile Framework are posted for the books in the following list. All are on a grade 4 to 5 level. However, readability formulas do not measure concept load, background needed to read a book, or interest level. You might want to examine the books and use your professional judgment as to whether the books are appropriate for your students.

Encyclopedia Britannica. (2004). *Remarkable People in History*. **No readability estimate available.**

Hudson, Wade (Ed.). (2003). *Poetry from the Masters: The Pioneers: An Introduction to African American Poets*. **4.7** (estimated by Follett Library Resources)

Kramer, Sydell. (1997). *Basketball's Greatest Players*. **4.2, 660**

Old, Wendie C. (2002). *To Fly: The Story of the Wright Brothers*. **5.4, 780**

Salas, Laura. (2006). *Phillis Wheatley: American Poet*. **4.6**

Venezia, Mike. (2003). *Grandma Moses*. **4.8, 940**

Whitehead, Kathy. (2008). *Art from the Heart: Folk Artist Clementine Hunter*. **5.3, 870**

Wyckoff, Edwin. (2008). *The Man Who Invented Basketball: James Naismith and His Amazing Game*. **4.3**

Encourage students to apply their skills to other books they read. Using one of the books as a model, show students how they might use chapter titles and headings to help them determine the main ideas that they will be reading about. You might demonstrate how most chapter titles and chapter heads can be turned into questions, which readers then answer when they come to the end of the chapter or section. Encourage students to summarize their reading by telling the three to five most important facts they learned about the person they were reading about. Encourage, too, the use of graphic organizers to highlight essential information. Students might create a time line to highlight key events in their subject's life or use a web to show key accomplishments. Students might also share their books with partners or in small groups. Students might also wish to find out more about a particular famous person. Instead of or along with reading the books, students might consult one of the Web sites listed in the Extension sections of the lessons. Web sites tend to be more difficult than books; however, Web site text can be read by text-to-speech feature available on most computers.

What did the famous people that you read about have in common? Which one do you admire most? Why? Tell about the person you admire most, and give reasons for your choice. Write your answer on the lines.

_____

_____

_____

_____

_____

_____

_____

_____

_____

_____

Would you like to learn more about famous people? Here are some books that you can read to find out more about famous people.

Encyclopedia Britannica. (2004). *Remarkable People in History*. Chicago: Author. Tells about the most important people from olden times and modern times.

Hudson, Wade (Ed.). (2003). *Poetry from the Masters: The Pioneers: An Introduction to African American Poets*. East Orange, NJ: Just Us Books. Contains thirty-six poems written by eleven African American poets. Also tells about the poets.

Kramer, Sydell. (1997). *Basketball's Greatest Players*. New York: Random House. Tells the stories of eleven famous basketball stars.

Old, Wendie C. (2002). *To Fly: The Story of the Wright Brothers*. New York: Clarion. Tells about the Wright brothers' early years and how they invented the airplane.

Salas, Laura. (2006). *Phillis Wheatley: American Poet*. Mankato, MN: Capstone Press. Tells the story of a slave whose poetry won her freedom.

Venezia, Mike. (2003). *Grandma Moses*. Danbury, CT: Children's Press. Tells how Grandma Moses became a famous painter.

Whitehead, Kathy. (2008). *Art from the Heart: Folk Artist Clementine Hunter*. New York: Putnam. Tells how Clementine Hunter overcame many difficulties to become a famous painter.

Wyckoff, Edwin. (2008). *The Man Who Invented Basketball: James Naismith and His Amazing Game*. Berkeley Heights, NJ: Enslow. Tells the story of the invention of basketball and how it became a popular sport.

Theme C > Sleep

This theme, which looks at sleep in animals and people, provides additional practice with comparing and contrasting. Practice is also provided in skills and strategies previously introduced.

Lesson 82 ▸ Two Kinds of Sleep

Objectives: Students make comparisons and contrasts, draw and support conclusions, and use context clues.

Introduction: Invite students to turn the title of the article in the Student Pages into a question and then read the article to answer the question. Their question might be: "What are the two kinds of sleep?" Remind students that they will be looking for differences and similarities and that they will be placing key differences and similarities in the frame matrix.

Guided and independent practice: Discuss students' responses. Have them identify the stages of sleep and contrast REM and non-REM sleep. Discuss which kind of sleep seems more restful.

Lesson 83 ▸ Half Asleep

Objectives: Students make comparisons and contrasts, explain why, and use context clues.

Introduction: Invite students to turn the title of the article in the Student Pages into a question and then read the article to answer the question. Their question might be: "What is meant by being half asleep?" Remind students that they will be looking for differences and similarities and that they will be placing key differences and similarities in the frame matrix.

Guided and independent practice: Discuss students' responses. Have them explain why a hippo needs to be able to cover its nostrils and why it has to ascend from the river bottom every thirty minutes.

The articles in this section will take you into the world of sleep. They will tell why we need to sleep and how sleep changes as we grow older. The articles will also tell you about some of the strange ways of sleeping that animals have. At the same time, you will be learning how to compare and contrast. You will also be practicing comprehension skills presented earlier.

Lesson 82: Two Kinds of Sleep

Read the article, and answer the questions that follow it.

Two Kinds of Sleep

Not all sleep is the same. There are two kinds of sleep. The first kind is called **R**apid **E**ye **M**ovement (REM) sleep. During REM sleep, our eyes <u>flicker</u>. They move up and down fast. During REM sleep, we dream. The other kind of sleep is non-REM sleep. During non-REM sleep, the eyes do not move <u>rapidly</u>. Our breathing slows down, and our hearts beat more slowly. We do little or no dreaming in non-REM sleep. During the night, we move back and forth between REM and non-REM sleep, but we spend most of our time in non-REM sleep. Someone who sleeps for eight hours spends about six hours in non-REM sleep and two hours in REM sleep.

1. Fill in the boxes in the frame matrix to show the main ways that REM and non-REM sleep differ.

Kind of Sleep	Eyes	Breathing	Heart Rate	Dreaming	Amount of During Sleep
REM					
Non-REM					

2. In what ways do REM and non-REM sleep differ? Answer the question by supporting the topic sentence. Use the frame matrix to get information for supporting the topic sentence.

REM and non-REM sleep differ in a number of ways.

_____

_____

_____

_____

3. Which kind of sleep seems more restful: REM or non-REM? Support your conclusion with information from the article.

_____

_____

_____

4. In the paragraph, the word *flicker* means

   a. change what is happening.

   b. move a short distance and stay there.

   c. look in front of and in back of.

   d. move lightly and quickly up and down or back and forth.

5. In the paragraph, the word *rapidly* means

   a. fast.

   b. carefully.

   c. strangely.

   d. at the same time.

Lesson 83: Half Asleep

Read the article, and answer the questions that follow it.

Half Asleep

1   Dolphins have a strange way of sleeping. Only half of a dolphin's brain sleeps at one time. Dolphins sleep under water. But dolphins are mammals. They need to breathe air. Luckily, they can go for thirty minutes without taking a breath. So they need to come up for air at least every half-hour. The half of the brain that is awake signals the dolphin's body when it is time to come to the surface for air. After the half of the brain that was sleeping gets enough rest, it wakes up, and the other half goes to sleep.

2   Hippos can sleep on land or in the water. When they go underwater, their ears close up and flaps of skin cover their <u>nostrils</u>, so water doesn't get up their noses. However, hippos are mammals, so they have to breathe. They, too, can stay under water for thirty minutes. Hippos' bodies rise from under the water when it is time to take in some air, and then their bodies go under the water again. The hippo's brain is also probably partly awake and signals the hippo that it's time to <u>ascend</u> to the surface for a breath of air.

1. Fill in the boxes in the frame matrix with information from the article.

	Kind of Animal	Where They Sleep	How Long They Can Stay Under Water	How They Get Air While Sleeping
Dolphin				
Hippo				

2. In what ways are hippos and dolphins alike? Answer the question by filling in the frame. Use the chart to get information for filling in the frame.

Dolphins and hippos are

_____.

Both sleep

_____.

Both can stay underwater for

_____.

They get air by

_____.

3. Why do dolphins and hippos need to breathe?

_____

_____

_____

4. In paragraph 2, the word *nostrils* means

    a. lips and teeth.

    b. smiles of happiness.

    c. openings at the end of the nose.

    d. faces when rising from the water.

5. In paragraph 2, the word *ascend* means

    a. swim slowly.

    b. go up.

    c. move away from.

    d. return to.

Lesson 84 ▸ Sleeping in Space

Objectives: Students make comparisons and contrasts, make inferences, and use context clues.

Introduction: Invite students to turn the title of the article in the Student Pages into a question and then read the article to answer the question. Their question might be, "How do astronauts sleep in space, or how is sleeping in space different from sleeping on Earth?" Remind students that they will be looking for differences and similarities and that they will be placing key differences and similarities in the frame matrix.

Guided and independent practice: Discuss students' responses. Discuss how the lack of gravity makes sleeping in space different from conditions where there is gravity. Also discuss how many hours of sleep most adults require.

Assessment: Note students' overall performance on this and previous exercises in this unit. Have they mastered key skills? Are they able to compare and contrast? If not, provide additional instruction and practice.

Extension: To obtain more information about sleeping in space, students might visit the NASA Web site, "Sleeping in Space," at http://spaceflight.nasa.gov/living/spacesleep/index.html.

Lesson 85 ▸ Our Changing Sleep Needs

Objectives: Students make comparisons and contrasts, identify details, supply supporting details, and use context clues.

Introduction: Invite students to turn the title of the article in the Student Pages into a question and then read the article to answer the question. Their question might be, "How do sleep needs change as people grow older?" or "Why do sleep needs change?" Remind students that they will be looking for differences and similarities and that they will be placing key differences and similarities in the frame matrix.

Guided and independent practice: Discuss students' responses. Have them explain why an older person's need for sleep might decrease. Also discuss whose sleep would most likely be interrupted by a loud noise: that of a teen or that of an older person.

Lesson 84: Sleeping in Space

Read the article, and answer the questions that follow it.

Sleeping in Space

1   Sleeping in space is different from sleeping on Earth. There is almost no <u>gravity</u> in space, so your body can float around. You don't need a soft bed because your body doesn't rest on the bed. It floats a little bit above it. You don't get tired of sleeping on your back or your side because you are really sleeping on air. Astronauts can sleep in special sleeping compartments, or they can sleep in sleeping bags. The sleeping bags are attached to the walls. Astronauts can <u>don</u> eyeshades to block out the light and earplugs to block out noise. That's something that some people on Earth do, too.

2   Astronauts are scheduled for eight hours of sleep every day. That's the same amount of sleep that most adults on Earth require. Astronaut Eileen Collins explains, "As far as sleeping, you can sleep anywhere you want in the orbiter. Usually you look for a place that's quiet. We talk among ourselves as to who's going to sleep where, and on both of my flights I <u>elected</u> to sleep in the middeck with my head close enough to the stairs so that I could go up to the flight deck immediately if there were a problem. I find that to be a rather quiet place. You've got the fans going. I sleep very well in space. We're scheduled for eight hours' sleep, although I don't usually sleep the whole time. I find it very easy to sleep in space. You don't have any pressure points. You don't have to roll around—going to your right side and then to your left side—sleeping in space is very comfortable." Eileen Collins is lucky. Most astronauts don't sleep well in space.

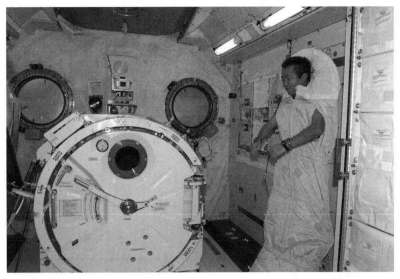

Credit: NASA

1. Fill in the boxes in the frame matrix to compare how people on Earth sleep with the way astronauts in space sleep.

	Where They Sleep	How They Sleep	How Long They Sleep	How They Can Block Out Noise and Light
People on Earth				
Astronauts				

2. In what ways are the sleep of astronauts in space and people on Earth different? In what ways are they the same? Answer the questions using the frame matrix in question 1 to fill out the frame.

Sleeping in space is different from on Earth. Because there is very little gravity in space, astronauts do not have to sleep

_____.

They can sleep

_____.

In some ways, sleeping in space is similar to sleeping on Earth. Both astronauts and people on Earth

_____

_____

_____.

3. Why do you think the sleeping bags are attached to the walls?

    a. So the astronauts won't fall down

    b. So the astronauts won't get lost

    c. So the astronauts won't float

    d. So the astronauts will be comfortable

4. In paragraph 1, the word *gravity* means the force that

    a. causes objects to move to the center of the Earth.

    b. powers spaceships as they move through space.

    c. makes it possible to travel in space.

    d. helps things grow.

5. In paragraph 1, the word *don* means

    a. need.

    b. find out.

    c. put on.

    d. talk about.

Lesson 85: Our Changing Sleep Needs

Read the article, and answer the questions that follow it.

Our Changing Sleep Needs

1   The amount of sleep that we need changes as we grow older. Newborn babies sleep almost 20 hours a day. By age two, children sleep about 14 or 15 hours a day. By age ten, the amount of sleep needed <u>decreases</u> to about 11 hours. Teens require about 9 or 10 hours of sleep. Young people are still growing. Sleep gives their bodies a chance to grow. Sleep also rests children's brains. Children's brains tire faster than the brains of grown-ups. Children are also more active than grown-ups. Some young people are on the move all day long. Their bodies need extra rest. Young people may not like to go to bed early, but sleep is good for them.

2   Adults need less sleep than children. They need about 8 hours of sleep. As people grow older, their biological clocks begin to change. Biological clocks are our bodies' sense of time. Biological clocks tell us when it is time to sleep and when it is time to be awake. Because of changes in their biological clocks, people who are in their sixties or older might not sleep as soundly as they did when they were younger. Their sleep is <u>interrupted</u>. They wake up more often during the night. They are also more easily awakened by noises. They become sleepier earlier in the evening and become wakeful earlier in the morning. Young people sleep more soundly. They often sleep straight through the night. And they are not easily awakened by loud noises. One group of ten-year-olds kept on sleeping even though a jet was taking off nearby.

1. Fill in the boxes in the frame matrix to show the main ways in which the sleep of ten-year-olds differs from the sleep of people in their sixties and older.

Group	Amount of Sleep Needed	How They Sleep	How Easily They Are Awakened
Ten-year-olds			
People in their sixties and older			

2. How does the sleep of ten-year-olds differ from the sleep of people in their sixties and older? Write your answer on the lines. Use the chart to get information for answering the question.

_____

_____

_____

_____

3. Why do older people go to bed earlier?

a. They have to get up early.

b. Their biological clocks change.

c. There isn't much to do after it gets dark.

d. They need more sleep than when they were younger.

4. Why should young people get plenty of sleep? Give at least three reasons from the article.

Young people should get plenty of sleep. First, sleeping

_____ .

Second,

_____ .

Finally,

_____ .

5. In paragraph 1, the word *decreases* means

  a. becomes less important.

  b. stays almost the same.

  c. grows less.

  d. becomes greater.

6. In paragraph 2, the word *interrupted* means

  a. having many bad dreams.

  b. lasting for a long time.

  c. not very sound or deep.

  d. broken up; broken in on.

Lesson 86 ▶ Night Sleepers and Day Sleepers

Objectives: Students make comparisons and contrasts, make and support inferences, supply supporting details, and use context clues.

Introduction: Invite students to turn the title of the article in the Student Pages into a question and then read the article to answer the question. Their question might be, "Which animals are night sleepers and which are day sleepers?" or "Why do some creatures sleep at night and some during the day?" Remind students that they will be looking for differences and similarities and that they will be placing key differences and similarities in the frame matrix.

Guided and independent practice: Discuss students' responses. Have them explain why some animals are nocturnal. Ask them to tell what nocturnal animals might be trying to avoid. Students might discuss whether their pets are diurnal, nocturnal, or crepuscular.

Lesson 87 ▶ Larks and Owls

Objectives: Students make comparisons and contrasts, draw and support conclusions, and use context clues.

Introduction: Invite students to turn the title into a question and then read to answer the question. Their question might be, "Who are larks and owls?" or "How do larks and owls differ in the way they sleep?" Remind students that they will be looking for differences and similarities and that they will be placing key differences and similarities in the frame matrix.

Guided and independent practice: Discuss students' responses. Have them explain when they get weary and whether they seem to be extreme larks or extreme owls or somewhere in between. You might take a poll to see how many larks, owls, and in-betweens are in your class.

Lesson 86: Night Sleepers and Day Sleepers

Read the article, and answer the questions that follow it.

Night Sleepers and Day Sleepers

1   Some animals are <u>nocturnal</u> (nok-TUR-nuhl). They sleep during the day and hunt for food at night. Raccoons, skunks, possums, owls, bats, rhinoceroses, tigers, and some other big cats are nocturnal. Nocturnal animals usually have sharp senses so they can find food in the dark and also <u>avoid</u> getting caught. Many desert animals are nocturnal. They sleep during the day while the hot sun is beating down on the desert. They come out at night after the sun has gone down. That's a better time to hunt for food. Other animals are diurnal (die-UR-nuhl). They sleep at night and are active during the day. Most birds are diurnal. It's easier for birds to find food in the daytime. People are diurnal.

2   A number of animals are crepuscular (krih-PUS-kih-ler). They are active at dusk, during that period of time when the sun is setting. Or they are active at dawn, which is that period of time when the sun is rising. Crepuscular animals avoid bright light and the heat of the day. Rattlesnakes, poisonous lizards such as gila monsters, and some desert animals are crepuscular. Rabbits and brown bears are crepuscular. Dogs and cats are diurnal but they were once nocturnal or crepuscular.

1. Why might nighttime be safer than daytime for animals?

_____

_____

_____

2. Fill in the boxes in the frame matrix to compare diurnal, nocturnal, and crepuscular animals.

Animals	Time of Day When Active	Reason for Being Active During a Certain Time of the Day	Examples
Diurnal			
Nocturnal			
Crepuscular			

Credit: Clipart.com.

3. Which of the following animals would you most likely see in the middle of the night?

   a. Rabbit

   b. Crow

   c. Raccoon

   d. Horse

4. Which of the following animals would you most likely see in the middle of the day?

   a. Bird

   b. Gila monster

   c. Skunk

   d. Bat

5. When would you most likely see a brown bear?

   a. Just after sunrise

   b. About noon

   c. Just before sunset

   d. In the middle of the night

6. Why are desert animals nocturnal or crepuscular? Use information from the article to help you answer the question.

_____

_____

_____

_____

7. In what way are diurnal and crepuscular animals similar?

a. They live mainly in the desert.

b. They avoid bright sunlight.

c. They are mainly meat-eating animals.

d. They do not hibernate.

8. In paragraph 1, the word *nocturnal* means having to do with

a. the sun's heat.

b. hunting for food.

c. night.

d. where animals live.

9. In paragraph 1, the word *avoid* means

a. stay in the dark.

b. keep away from.

c. look toward.

d. make plans for.

10. Are you mainly nocturnal, diurnal, or crepuscular? Explain your answer.

_____

_____

_____

11. Why do you think dogs and cats switched from being nocturnal to being diurnal?

_____

_____

_____

_____

Lesson 87: Larks and Owls

Read the article, and answer the questions that follow it.

Larks and Owls

1   If you had your choice, when would you get up in the morning? When is the best time of day for you to tackle a difficult task? If you prefer sleeping late and working late, you are an owl. If you like to get up early in the morning and seem to have the most energy early in the day, you are a lark. Larks have a higher body temperature when they awaken than owls do. Their highest body temperature comes earlier in the day. It is highest at about 3:30 in the afternoon. Owls have their highest body temperature at about 8:30 in the evening.

2   About 10 people out of 100 are larks. Their body clocks are set early. They get out of bed early in the morning. They think better and work better early in the day. Morning is the best time for them to get work done. By late afternoon, larks are beginning to grow <u>weary,</u> and they like to go to bed early. Owls prefer sleeping late. About 20 people out of 100 are owls. Their energy peaks come in the afternoon or at night. The later it gets, the better they seem to feel. Owls get higher grades on tests taken in the afternoon than they do on tests taken in the morning. The opposite is true for larks.

3   Most people are neither <u>extreme</u> larks nor extreme owls. They are somewhere in between. They don't have much trouble getting up a little earlier or staying up a little later if they have to.

1. Fill in the boxes in the frame matrix to compare larks and owls.

Type of Person	When They Like to Go to Bed	When They Like to Get Up	When They Are Most Awake
Larks			
Owls			

2. Are you a lark or owl, or somewhere in between? Explain your answer.

_____

_____

_____

_____

3. In paragraph 2, the word *weary* means

   a. sad.

   b. tired.

   c. silly.

   d. worried.

4. In paragraph 3, the word *extreme* means

   a. at the other end; beyond what is average or normal.

   b. feeling tired; not feeling rested.

   c. early in the day; soon after the sun rises.

   d. not quite sure; making guesses.

End-of-Theme Reflection

Discuss the end-of-theme reflection that appears on the Student Pages. Ask students to tell what they learned about sleep. Discuss which creature has the strangest sleep habits. Discuss, too, how animals have adjusted their sleep habits to keep themselves safe from predators.

In order for the skills learned in this unit to transfer, it is essential that students apply them to their textbooks or other full-length materials. Suggested books are listed below. Have available copies of the suggested books, and encourage students to read them. Readability levels provided by Accelerated Reading (AR) and Lexile Framework are posted for the books. Books are on a grade 3 to 6 level. However, readability formulas do not measure concept load, the background needed to read a book, or interest level. You might want to examine the books and use your professional judgment as to whether they are appropriate for your students.

Batten, Mary. (2008). *Please Don't Wake the Animals: A Book About Sleep*. **4.9**

Culbert, Timothy, and Kajander, Rebecca. (2007). *Be the Boss of Your Sleep: Self-Help for Kids*. **6.6** (estimated by Follett Library Resources)

Feeney, Kathy. (2002). *Sleep Well: Why You Need Rest*. **3.0**

Kent, Susan. (2000). *Let's Talk About When You Have Trouble Going to Sleep*. **3.7**

Scott, Elaine. (2008). *All About Sleep from A to ZZZ*. **6.9, 1050**

Encourage students to apply their skills to the books. Using one of the books as a model, show students how they might use chapter titles and headings to help them determine the main ideas that they will be reading about. You might demonstrate how most chapter titles and chapter heads can be turned into questions, which readers then answer when they come to the end of the chapter or section. Encourage students to summarize their reading by telling the three to five most important facts they learned. Encourage, too, the use of graphic organizers to highlight essential information. They might create a frame matrix to compare the sleeping habits of different animals or use a web to show the benefits of sleep. Students might also share their books with partners or in small groups. Students might wish to pursue a particular aspect of sleep.

What did you learn about sleep? Write your answer on the lines.

_____

_____

_____

_____

What is the most surprising thing that you learned about sleep? Write your answer on the lines.

_____

_____

_____

_____

Here are some books where you can find out more about sleep:

Batten, Mary. (2008). *Please Don't Wake the Animals: A Book About Sleep*. Atlanta, GA: Peachtree. Explains how gorillas, bats, birds, and other animals sleep.

Culbert, Timothy, and Kajander, Rebecca. (2007). *Be the Boss of Your Sleep: Self-Help for Kids*. Minneapolis, MN: Free Spirit. Offers tips for getting a good night's sleep.

Feeney, Kathy. (2002). *Sleep Well: Why You Need Rest.* Mankato, MN: Bridgestone Books. Explains the importance of sleep.

Kent, Susan. (2000). *Let's Talk About When You Have Trouble Going to Sleep*. New York: PowerKids Press. Explains why sleep is important and some things you can do to get a good night's sleep.

Scott, Elaine. (2008). *All About Sleep from A to ZZZ*. New York: Viking. Tells about our need for sleep, why we dream, sleepwalking, and other related topics.

UNIT 6

Unit Six reviews previously taught skills and strategies while exploring the themes of transportation and one-room schoolhouses.

Theme A > Transportation

Lesson 88 ▸ Parachutes for Planes

Objectives: Students visualize, supply supporting details, provide explanations, and use context clues.

Introduction: Invite students to turn the title of the article in the Student Pages into a question and then read the article to answer the question. Their question might be, "What are parachutes for planes?" or "How do the parachutes work?"

Guided and independent practice: Discuss students' responses. Have them tell why it is important for a pilot of a small plane not to panic when the plane develops a problem and why Albert Kolk had a feeling of relief.

Extension: Clips of real-life experiences with parachutes saving lives can be found at BRS Aviation at http://www.brsparachutes.com/brs_aviation_home.aspx.

Lesson 89 ▸ Flying Cars

Objectives: Students provide explanations, supply supporting details, and use context clues.

Introduction: Invite students to turn the title of the article in the Student Pages into a question and then read the article to answer the question. Their question might be, "What are flying cars?" or "How can a car be made to fly?"

Guided and independent practice: Discuss students' responses. Have them tell why Fulton resolved to invent a flying car to get him to his destination.

This section reviews skills that you have already been taught and tells about cars that fly and planes that have parachutes. The articles explain how trains, trucks, and ships work together and what future trains might be like. The articles also tell you about tomorrow's planes, how cats' eyes make roads safer, and which cars can run on grease.

Lesson 88: Parachutes for Planes

Read the article, and answer the questions that follow it.

Parachutes for Planes

1 You are flying high above the mountains in a small plane. Suddenly your plane goes into a spin. You pull hard on the controls. Nothing happens. The plane is spinning faster now, and it's falling. You try to stay calm. You don't want to <u>panic</u>. You reach toward a red handle and pull it. You say to yourself, "I hope this works." You hear a popping sound as a small rocket shoots out of a hatch toward the rear of the plane. It is pulling a large parachute. You watch as the parachute opens up. A feeling of <u>relief</u> flows over you. The plane floats to the ground. There is a soft bump as the plane touches down. You climb out of the plane and say to yourself, "I'm glad my plane had a parachute."

2 Although parachutes for planes might sound like a dream for the future, they aren't. Parachutes have been made that float small planes to Earth when they get into trouble. One pilot, Albert Kolk, had his grandson and two friends in his plane when it spun out of control "like a dog chasing its tail." Kolk yelled at the boys to fasten their seat belts and grabbed the parachute handle. When the parachute opened, his feeling of fear changed to a "peaceful,

wonderful feeling." His plane floated to the ground. No one was hurt. Plane parachutes have already saved the lives of more than two hundred people.

Cost of Parachutes

3   The parachutes cost from $2,000 to $16,000, depending on the size of the plane. That might sound like a high price—until you have to use one.

Parachutes for Bigger Planes

4   So far the parachutes have been used only on small planes. Small planes only weigh about 2,000 to 4,000 pounds and go about 175 miles an hour. The company that makes the parachutes is now working on parachutes that could be used on small jets. The parachutes would have control devices, so that the pilot could guide the plane as it floated to Earth.

Credit: Cirrus Aerospace.

1. In the column on the left, draw a picture that you made in your mind as you read about how the parachute for planes works. In the column on the right, tell what your picture shows.

What I Pictured in My Mind as I Read	What My Picture Shows

2. Explain why Kolk was glad he had a parachute. Write your answer on the lines.

_____

_____

_____

3. Do you think having parachutes for planes is a good idea? Why or why not? Use information from the article to support your opinion.

_____

_____

_____

_____

4. In paragraph 1, the word *panic* means

   a. act in a fearful, out-of-control manner.

   b. make up a quick plan without doing much thinking.

   c. wonder what is happening.

   d. try to get help as soon as possible.

5. In paragraph 1, the word *relief* means

   a. trying to control one's feelings.

   b. being sad or lonely.

   c. planning for a way to solve a problem.

   d. letting go of a feeling of fear or worry.

Lesson 89: Flying Cars

Read the article, and answer the questions that follow it.

Flying Cars

1   Most people don't like to wait when they are traveling. They might grow impatient and fuss a bit. Robert Fulton <u>resolved</u> to do something about it. Robert Fulton did a lot of traveling from town to town, so he bought his own airplane. But he found that lots of time was still being wasted. First, he had to get a ride to the airport. Then he flew his airplane to the airport closest to his <u>destination</u>. And then he had to get from the airport to the place he was going. Often he had to wait around for a bus or cab. As he explained, "I'd end up kicking my airplane and say, 'Why can't you take me down the road? You have an engine, you have wheels, you have controls, all the same things as an automobile, so why can't you take me down the road?'" And then Fulton came up with a very strange idea. Why not invent a car that could fly? That way he could fly to an airport or landing field and then drive to his destination. There would be no waiting around.

Building the Airphibian

2   Fulton worked on his idea for several years. A lot of people thought that his idea wouldn't work, but it did. He called his flying car the "Airphibian." It looked just like any other plane, except that its landing gear had four wheels. Most small planes have just three wheels. When the Airphibian was driven on the ground, its back part was removed. Built into the back part were the

tail and wings of the plane. The propeller was also removed. The tail, wings, and propeller were left at the airport until they were needed. When it was used as a plane, all the parts had to be firmly attached. If they weren't attached properly, the engine wouldn't start. As a car, the Airphibian could hit speeds of 55 miles an hour. As a plane, it flew 110 miles an hour.

Problems with the Airphibian

3   The Airphibian worked. It could be driven and flown. But there were some problems. Changing it from a car to a plane and back again took a lot of time. And it was a slow-flying plane. The parts needed to make it a car added to the weight of the plane. It was heavier than planes that were just planes, and that slowed it down. Fulton and some friends started a company to build and sell Airphibians. But only eleven Airphibians were built. Fulton and his friends ran out of money and had to give up on the idea of a flying car.

1. Why did Fulton build the Airphibian?

_____

_____

_____

2. What were the problems with the Airphibian?

_____

_____

_____

3. In paragraph 1, the word *resolved* means

    a. acted in an angry or rude manner.

    b. thought carefully about for a long time.

    c. fixed a part on a broken machine.

    d. firmly made up one's mind to do something.

4. In paragraph 1, the word *destination* means

    a. a box for storing tools.

    b. a place where one is going.

    c. a large map.

    d. a very long road or highway.

Lesson 90 ▸ Aerocar

Objectives: Students visualize, compare and contrast, substantiate an opinion, supply supporting or explanatory details, and use context clues.

Introduction: Invite students to turn the title of the article in the Student Pages into a question and then read the article to answer the question. Their question might be, "What was the Aerocar?"

Guided and independent practice: Discuss students' responses. Have them tell what inspired Moulton to work on a flying car and what major problems he faced.

Extension: Students can find out more about the Aerocar by going to the Air Venture Museum at http://www.airventuremuseum.org/collection/aircraft/Taylor%20Aerocar .asp. Video clips show the Aerocar in operation.

Lesson 91 ▸ Skycar

Objectives: Students visualize, compare and contrast, substantiate an opinion, supply supporting or explanatory details, and use context clues.

Introduction: Invite students to turn the title of the article in the Student Pages into a question and then read the article to answer the question. Their question might be, "What is Skycar?" or "How does Skycar work?"

Guided and independent practice: Discuss students' responses. Have them tell what Moller devised so that the Skycar could be flown vertically and could also hover.

Extension: Students can find out more about Skycar by going to the Skycar Web site at http://www.moller.com/. Demonstration videos show Skycar in flight.

Lesson 90: Aerocar

Read the article, and answer the questions that follow it.

Aerocar

1   The Airphibian gave Molton Taylor an idea. In 1946 Molton Taylor met Robert Fulton. The two discussed the Airphibian. Inspired by the conversation, Taylor became interested in the idea of a flying car. Taylor thought that he could make a better flying car. A major problem with the Airphibian was that after you took the back of the plane and the propeller off, you left them behind at the airport. To make the car into a plane again, you had to return to the airport where you left the back part of the Airphibian and the propeller. Taylor devised a flying car that was more practical than the Airphibian. He called his invention the "Aerocar." The wings, propeller, and tail of the Aerocar were built in one piece in such a way that they could be attached to the back of a regular car. The propeller is in the rear of the plane and the wings fold back, so that when the Aerocar is used on the road, they don't stick out. The part of the Aerocar that had the wings, tail, and propeller had wheels so that the plane part could be towed just like a trailer. That way, the driver didn't have to go back to the airport to change the Aerocar from a car into a plane. That meant that the Aerocar could be changed into an airplane and could take off from any location.

2   Another major problem with the Airphibian was that it took a long time to change it from a car into an airplane. The Aerocar could be changed from a car into a plane in just five minutes.

3   The Aero's top speed on the road was 60 miles an hour. Top speed in the air was double that, at 120 miles an hour. In the air, the Aerocar could travel as far as 300 miles.

4   Over the years, Molt Taylor kept on making improvements to the Aerocar. A few Aerocars were sold and flown. Molt Taylor died in 1995. But at least one of his Aerocars is still being flown.

1. In the column on the left, draw a picture that you made in your mind as you read about how the Aerocar looked as it was being driven on the road. In the column on the right, tell what your picture shows.

What I Pictured in My Mind as I Read	What My Picture Shows

Credit: Norma Kable.

2. Fill in the boxes of the frame matrix to compare the Airphibian and the Aerocar. Write your answers in the boxes.

	Wings	Propeller	Changing from Car to Plane	Where Wings and Propeller Could Be Kept While Car Was on the Road
Airphibian				
Aerocar				

3. Use information from the frame matrix to help you explain which air car was better: the Aerocar or the Airphibian. Give reasons for your choice. Write your answer in the boxes.

Opinion	Supporting Reasons

4. Explain how Taylor solved the following problems when devising a flying car.

Problem	Solution
Back part of plane and propeller had to be left behind.	
Took a long time to change from car to plane.	

5. In paragraph 1, the word *inspired* means

    a. asked about; questioned slowly and carefully.

    b. believed in fully; was very sure of.

    c. hoped for; asked for in a firm manner.

    d. gave someone the idea or desire to do something.

6. In paragraph 1, the word *major* means

    a. hard to change; difficult to fix.

    b. have lots of; plenty.

    c. main; most important.

    d. hidden; difficult to find or locate.

Lesson 91: Skycar

Read the article, and answer the questions that follow it.

Skycar

1   Like Robert Fulton and Molt Taylor, Paul Moller also had an idea for a flying machine that could be driven. His invention is known as the Skycar M 400. The Skycar M 400 will be able to hold four passengers and fly at speeds of up to 375 miles an hour. It will be able to use gasoline made from corn and will get up to 20 miles a gallon. It will have a range of 750 miles. The range is how far the Skycar will be able to fly.

2   The Skycar is a <u>vertical</u> lift aircraft. It is a bit like a helicopter. It will be able to fly straight up and straight down. The Skycar won't need a landing field. Owners of the Skycar will be able to land it in their driveways or backyards. The Skycar would be powered by engines that force air onto movable vanes. Vanes are metal plates that direct the flow of air. Directing the air downward pushes the Skycar upward and allows it to <u>hover,</u> or stay in one spot. To move the Skycar forward, the vanes are turned so that the air flows straight out and propels the Skycar ahead.

3   The Skycar is better in the sky than it is on the road. It can be driven short distances. But on the road it hits speeds of only about 35 miles an hour.

4   The Skycar will be very safe. It can still fly even if an engine fails. And if all the engines fail, it has a parachute built into it. The parachute will float it to the ground.

5   The first Skycars will probably need a trained pilot. But future Skycars will be built in such a way that computers will do most of the flying. All you will need to do is to start up the Skycar and let it know where you want to go.

6   The Skycar isn't ready to fly yet. Moller has been working on it for almost forty years. And he has spent more than $100 million on his invention. But he hopes to have a finished Skycar within a few years. Keep your eyes on the sky. One of these days you might just see a Skycar flying overhead.

1.   In the column on the left, draw a picture that you made in your mind as you read the article. In the column on the right, tell what your picture shows.

What I Pictured in My Mind as I Read	What My Picture Shows

2. Fill the boxes in the frame matrix to compare the Aerocar and Skycar.

	Engine	Takeoff and Land-ing	Speed on Land	Speed in the Air	Range	Safety
Aerocar						
Skycar						

3. Explain what has been done to make the Skycar extra safe.

_____

_____

_____

4. Explain how the Skycar's engine works.

_____

_____

_____

5. Would you buy a Skycar? Why or why not?

_____

_____

_____

6. In paragraph 2, the word *vertical* means

    a. far away.

    b. straight up and down.

    c. a far distance.

    d. having a lot of power.

7. In paragraph 2, the word *hover* means

    a. leave a place suddenly.

    b. move at about the same speed.

    c. stay or float in the same spot in the air.

    d. hit into without meaning to.

Lesson 92 ▶ Rocket Planes

Objectives: Students visualize, supply supporting or explanatory details, compare and contrast, and use context clues.

Introduction: Invite students to turn the title of the article in the Student Pages into a question and then read to answer the question. Their question might be, "What are rocket planes?" or "How do rocket planes work?"

Guided and independent practice: Discuss students' responses. Have students tell how compressed air is used by a scramjet so that it can fly incredibly fast.

Lesson 93 ▶ The Catseye

Objectives: Students visualize, supply supporting or explanatory details, substantiate an opinion, and use context clues.

Introduction: Invite students to turn the title of the article in the Student Pages into a question and then read the article to answer the question. Their question might be, "What is a Catseye?"

Guided and independent practice: Discuss students' responses. Have students tell how catseyes on a road are helpful when visibility is poor and how the eyes of a real cat saved Shaw's car from falling down a steep hill.

Lesson 92: Rocket Planes

Read the article, and answer the questions that follow it.

Rocket Planes

1 Someday we might be able to fly across the United States in less than a half hour. Scientists are now experimenting on a rocket-like plane known as a scramjet. Regular rockets require lots of fuel. They need hydrogen gas and large tanks of oxygen. Scramjets are rocket-like planes. They don't need large tanks of oxygen. Scramjets have openings on their undersides that pull in air. The air is pulled in at a very high speed. Once it enters the engine, it slows down and is <u>compressed</u> by the forward movement of the jet. Being pressed into a smaller size causes the oxygen in the air to heat up. The hot oxygen starts burning the hydrogen fuel. This pushes the scramjet forward.

2 Scramjets are <u>incredibly</u> fast. Test scramjets have flown at almost ten times the speed of sound. That's 7,000 miles an hour. Scramjets may one day fly at fifteen times the speed of sound. That is more than 10,000 miles an hour. Scramjets would be able to rocket across the country in just fifteen minutes. They could go from New York to China in about an hour and could travel around the world in about two hours. Scramjets are so fast and so powerful that they also could be used to rocket into space.

1. Show how a scramjet works by filling in the missing steps.

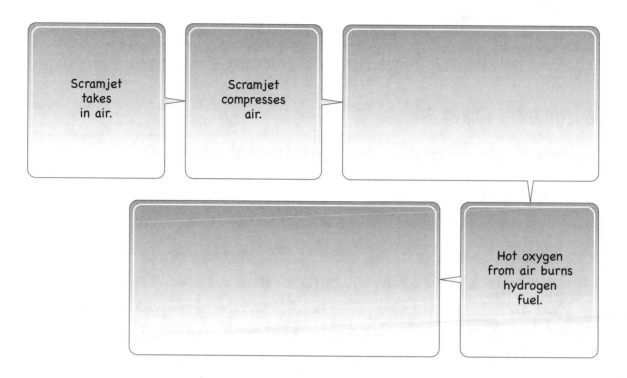

2. Tell what a scramjet can do today and might be able to do in the future by filling in the blank circles in the web.

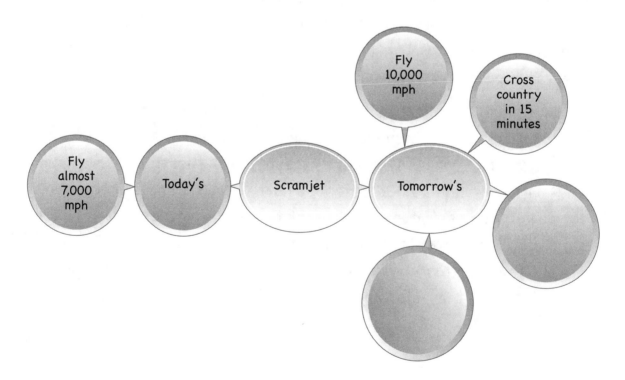

3. How is a scramjet better than a rocket? Write your answer on the lines.

_____

_____

_____

4. In paragraph 1, the word *compressed* means

  a. heavier than surrounding objects.

  b. moved ahead or forward.

  c. caused to be very cold or frozen.

  d. pushed together and made smaller.

5. In paragraph 2, the word *incredibly* means

  a. high above the Earth.

  b. very fast.

  c. difficult to do.

  d. hard to believe.

Lesson 93: The Catseye

Read the article, and answer the questions that follow it.

Catseye

1   A cat's eyes saved hundreds of lives. In 1933 Percy Shaw was driving home. He had worked all day fixing roads and was tired. <u>Visibility</u> was poor. The night was dark and foggy, and the road was narrow and winding. Suddenly Shaw saw two bright lights ahead of him. He stopped his car and saw a cat sitting on a fence. What he had seen were his headlights reflecting off the cat's eyes. Looking to his right, Shaw saw that he was on the edge of a <u>steep</u> hill. If he hadn't stopped to look at the cat's eyes, he would have gone off the road and rolled down the hill.

2   As he thought about how the cat's eyes had saved him, Shaw wondered what if there were little devices about the size of a cat's eyes in the road that would reflect light from a car's headlights. They could be placed in the road to show where the road was. It was a simple idea, but it took Shaw a while to get it to work right. The device that he created was made up of four glass beads set on an iron base and covered by a rubber molding. When a car drove over the device, the rubber molding pushed the glass beads down so they wouldn't be crushed. After the car was gone, the glass beads popped up again.

3   The design was a good one, but there was a problem. Sooner or later, the glass bead reflectors would get dirty and would no longer reflect light. Shaw made a spot in the base where rainwater would

Copyright © 2010 by John Wiley & Sons, Inc.

collect. When a car ran over the reflector, the rubber molding pushed down on the rainwater, and the rainwater was squirted onto the glass beads and cleaned them. Shaw named his device "Catseye."

4   Shaw started a company to make and sell the device. Today these reflectors are built into roads all over the world.

1. In the column on the left, draw a picture that you made in your mind as you read the article. In the column on the right, tell what your picture shows.

What I Pictured in My Mind as I Read	What My Picture Shows

2. Fill in the missing steps to show how Catseye reflectors came to be used around the world.

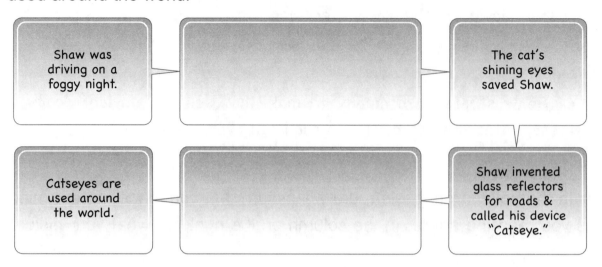

Shaw was driving on a foggy night.		The cat's shining eyes saved Shaw.
Catseyes are used around the world.		Shaw invented glass reflectors for roads & called his device "Catseye."

3. Why don't the glass beads in the Catseye get crushed? Write your answer on the lines.

_____

_____

4. What keeps the glass beads clean? Write your answer on the lines.

_____

_____

5. Why did Shaw call the device "Catseye"? Write your answer on the lines.

_____

_____

_____

6. In paragraph 1, the word *visibility* means

    a. being rough or rocky; having many bumps.

    b. being cautious; being very careful.

    c. bad or stormy weather; an upcoming storm.

    d. distance that one can see; being able to be seen.

7. In paragraph 1, the word *steep* means

    a. having a very slanted slope; almost straight up and down.

    b. having many trees; a thick forest.

    c. full of large rocks; a rough piece of land.

    d. not easy to see; hidden in the dark.

Lesson 94 ▶ Grease Mobiles

Objectives: Students supply supporting or explanatory details, substantiate an opinion, and use context clues.

Introduction: Invite students to turn the title of the article in the Student Pages into a question and then read the article to answer the question. Their question might be, "What are grease mobiles?" or "How do grease mobiles work?"

Guided and independent practice: Discuss students' responses. Have students tell why running cars on used vegetable oil is economical and why restaurant owners are delighted when they are able to get rid of used vegetable oil.

Lesson 95 ▶ A Better Idea

Objectives: Students visualize, supply supporting details, and use context clues.

Introduction: Invite students to turn the title of the article in the Student Pages into a question and then read the article to answer the question. Their question might be, "What was the better idea?"

Guided and independent practice: Discuss students' responses. Have students tell why Malcolm McLean's idea was a better one for filling the hold of a ship faster and why he purchased a number of ships.

Extension: To get an idea of what container ships look like, students might refer to the Wikipedia article on container ships. Although the text in the Wikipedia article on container ships is sophisticated, the article is accompanied by a number of photos of container ships. If possible, read the text with students. The article can be found at http://en.wikipedia.org/wiki/Container_ship.

Lesson 94: Grease Mobiles

Read the article, and answer the questions that follow it.

Grease Mobiles

1   Instead of filling up at a gas station, some car drivers stop by restaurants to fill up. They run their cars on the vegetable oil that is left over after being used to cook French fries and other foods. The car owners have diesel (DEE-zuhl) engines. Diesel engines run on diesel fuel rather than gasoline. Both diesel fuel and gasoline are made from oil. But diesel fuel is easier to make and gets more miles to the gallon. Diesel engines can also run on used vegetable oil. Vegetable oil is used for cooking. Before a car can run on vegetable oil, it must have a special kit. The kit has a tank for holding the vegetable oil. The tank also needs a filter so any dirt in the oil is removed.

2   There are some problems with using vegetable oil. It gets hard when it is cold, so cars that run on vegetable oil require a special heater to keep the oil warm. Drivers also need to use regular diesel fuel to start their cars. Once the car has warmed up, the driver can switch to vegetable oil.

3   Unused vegetable oil can be used to run diesel engines, but unused vegetable oil is expensive and costs as much as or more than diesel fuel. Used vegetable oil is free. In fact, restaurant owners are <u>delighted</u> to give it away. If they don't give it away, they have to pay to have someone remove it. Using old vegetable oil is <u>economical</u>. It saves money for car owners and restaurant owners too.

1. Fill in the blank circles to show what changes need to be made to a diesel car so that it can run on used vegetable oil.

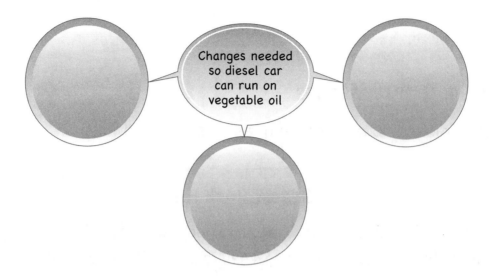

Changes needed so diesel car can run on vegetable oil

2. If you owned a car, would you run it on vegetable oil? Why or why not? Use information from the story to support your opinion.

_____

_____

_____

3. In paragraph 3, the word *delighted* means

   a. very pleased; happy.

   b. thoughtful; having something on one's mind.

   c. forgetful; not able to remember things.

   d. ready to leave; wanting to leave.

4. In paragraph 3, the word *economical* means

   a. very small; not very large.

   b. difficult to build; having many parts.

   c. hard to find; can't be located.

   d. saving money; making good use of money.

Lesson 95: A Better Idea

Read the article, and answer the questions that follow it.

A Better Idea

1 The owner of a truck company found a way to help trains and ships carry freight (frayt) faster and cheaper. Steel, coal, tires, and other things carried by trucks, trains, and ships are known as "freight." In 1937 Malcolm McLean owned a small trucking business. He had just driven a load of cotton bales to the port of Newark, New Jersey. Now he was waiting to have his truck unloaded. He waited a whole day. In those days, unloading trucks was very slow. Each bale of cotton was placed in a sling by workers. Then it was lifted onto the ship. Once on the ship, each bale of cotton had to be stacked in the ship's <u>hold</u>. As he waited and watched, McLean thought that there had to be a better way. And then he thought of a better way. Why not load the trailer part of the truck onto the ship? That way every crate or box or bale would not have to be loaded piece by piece. Both loading and unloading would be faster and easier.

2 As the years passed, McLean worked on his idea. With money he made from his trucking business, he <u>purchased</u> some ships. Now that he had ships of his own, he could try out his idea. At first he loaded truck trailers, wheels and all, onto his ships. Then he came up with the idea of using containers that would fit onto the trailers of trucks or onto railroad cars. Little by

little, trucking companies, the railroads, and shipping companies began following McLean's lead. Today there are five thousand container ships carrying goods around the world. Most of the world's freight is moved in containers.

1. In the column on the left, draw a picture that you made in your mind as you read the article. In the column on the right, tell what your picture shows.

What I Pictured in My Mind as I Read	What My Picture Shows

2. Fill in the boxes to show how McLean put his idea into action.

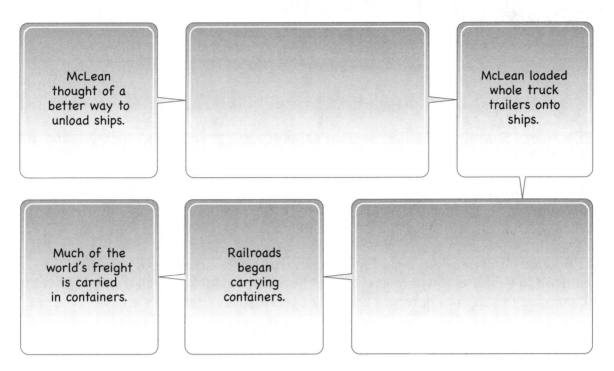

| McLean thought of a better way to unload ships. | | McLean loaded whole truck trailers onto ships. |

| Much of the world's freight is carried in containers. | Railroads began carrying containers. | |

3. In paragraph 1, the word *hold* means the

    a. part of the ship where meals for the crew and passengers are cooked.

    b. part of the ship where passengers have cabins.

    c. part of the ship where the crew sleeps and has their meals.

    d. place where steel, tires, and other goods being carried by a ship are kept.

4. In paragraph 2, the word *purchased* means

    a. bought.

    b. borrowed.

    c. loaded.

    d. painted.

Objectives: Students visualize, supply supporting or explanatory details, and use context clues.

Introduction: Invite students to turn the title of the article in the Student Pages into a question and then read the article to answer the question. Their question might be, "What will Planetran be like?" or "What will make Planetran a superfast train?"

Guided and independent practice: Discuss students' responses. Discuss how intense heat from a subterrene will melt rock and how the tunnel for Planetran will have the air pumped out so that there will be little or no resistance from air.

Assessment: Note students' overall performance on this and previous exercises in this review unit. Have they mastered key skills? If not, provide additional instruction and practice as needed.

Lesson 96: Planetran: Tomorrow's Superfast Train

Read the article, and answer the questions that follow it.

Planetran: Tomorrow's Superfast Train

1   Planetran will be more like a rocket than a train. It will swoosh across the country at a top speed of 14,000 miles an hour. At that speed, it will take just 21 minutes to rocket from New York to Los Angeles, a distance of nearly 2,800 miles.

2   Shaped like a long, thin cigar with a tip at each end, Planetran will be powered by supermagnets. Powerful magnetic waves will lift Planetran up off its rails and shoot it forward.

3   Planetran will rocket through long tubes built into plastic-coated tunnels up to a mile underground. Pumps built into the tunnel would draw out just about all the air. One of the reasons Planetran would reach such high speeds is that there would be little air <u>resistance</u> to slow it down.

4   To build such a long tunnel, special tools would be needed. Laser beams and high-powered jets of water would be used. The hardest of rock would be melted by a subterrene. A subterrene is a drill that produces such <u>intense</u> heat that it turns the hardest rock into red-hot liquid.

5   Will Planetran ever be built? Highways and skyways are becoming more and more crowded. To carry more freight and people, more trains and faster trains will be needed. In the years to come, you might find yourself rocketing underground on Planetran or other superfast train.

1. In the column on the left, draw a picture that you made in your mind as you read the article. In the column on the right, tell what your picture shows.

What I Pictured in My Mind as I Read	What My Picture Shows

2. In the column on the right, write the causes of the effect that is shown on the left.

Effect	Causes
Planetran would be very fast.	1.
	2.

3. In the column on the right, write the solution to the problem that is shown on the left.

Problem	Solution
Tunnel will be difficult to dig.	

4. In paragraph 3, the word *resistance* means

    a. an activity that is unusual.

    b. a force that slows down another force.

    c. an idea that is difficult to explain.

    d. something that is very large.

5. In paragraph 4, the word *intense* means

    a. very great or strong.

    b. very dangerous.

    c. very soon.

    d. very close or nearby.

End-of-Theme Reflection

Discuss the end-of-theme reflection that appears on the Student Pages. Discuss with students what they learned about transportation from the articles. Have them list all the inventions and devices that they read about in the unit. Have them tell which one was the most interesting, which was the most surprising, and which the most useful. Ask students what questions they still have about transportation.

Have available copies of the suggested books that follow and other books related to the theme, and encourage students to read them. In order for skills learned in this unit to transfer, it is essential that students apply the skills to their textbooks and other full-length materials. Have available copies of the suggested books, and encourage students to read them. Readability levels provided by Accelerated Reading (AR) and Lexile Framework are posted. The books are on a grade 4 to 7 level. However, readability formulas do not measure concept load, background needed to read a book, or interest level. You might want to examine the books and use your professional judgment as to whether the books are appropriate for your students.

Atkins, Jeannine. (2003). *Wings and Rockets*. **6.5**

Masters, Nancy R. (2009). *Airplanes*. **6.1**

O'Brien, Patrick. (2003). *Fantastic flights*. **6, 990**

Oxlade, Chris. (2006). *Airplanes*. **7.1**

Petrie, Kristin. (2009). *Airplanes*. **4.8**

West, David. (2007). *Why Things Don't Work: Plane*. **4.6**

West, David. (2007). *Why Things Don't Work: Train*. **4.3**

Will, Sandra. (2006). *Transportation Inventions: From Subways to Submarines*. **4.7**

Encourage students to apply their skills to the books. Using one of the books as a model, show students how they might use chapter titles and headings to help them determine the main ideas that they will be reading about. You might demonstrate how most chapter titles and chapter heads can be turned into questions, which readers then answer when they come to the end of the chapter or section. Encourage students to summarize their reading by telling the five most important facts they learned. Encourage, too, the use of graphic organizers to highlight essential information. Students might also share their books with partners or in small groups. Students might wish to pursue a particular aspect of transportation. Instead of or along with reading the books, students might consult one of the Web sites listed in the Extension sections of the lessons. Web sites tend to be more difficult than books; however, Web site text can be read by a text-to-speech feature available on most computers.

What did you learn about transportation? Be sure to tell about the most surprising thing that you learned. Write your answer on the lines.

_____

_____

_____

_____

_____

How might we be traveling in the future? Write your opinion below. Give reasons for your opinion. Write your answer on the lines.

_____

_____

_____

_____

_____

What questions do you have about transportation? What would you like to know or find out? Here is where you can go to find out more about transportation.

Atkins, Jeannine. (2003). *Wings and Rockets*. New York: Farrar, Strauss. Tells about women pilots and astronauts.

Masters, Nancy R. (2009). *Airplanes*. Ann Arbor: MI: Cherry Lake. Gives a history of airplanes and describes ways in which airplanes are used.

O'Brien, Patrick. (2003). *Fantastic Flights*. New York: Walker. Pictures and describes seventeen fantastic flights including the first flight and the landing on Mars.

Oxlade, Chris. (2006). *Airplanes*. Buffalo, NY: Firefly. Using many pictures and diagrams, gives a history of airplanes and explains how airplanes work.

Petrie, Kristin. (2009). *Airplanes*. Edina, MN: ABDO. Explains the history and workings of airplanes.

West, David. (2007). *Why Things Don't Work: Plane*. Chicago: Raintree. Explains how planes work by showing what needs to be done to fix a broken plane.

West, David. (2007). *Why Things Don't Work: Train*. Chicago: Raintree. Explains how trains work by showing what needs to be done to fix a train.

Will, Sandra. (2006). *Transportation Inventions: From Subways to Submarines*. New York: Bearport. Which came first: the bicycle or the skateboard? This book asks which-came-first questions about pairs of transportation inventions.

Theme B ▷ One-Room Schoolhouses

Lesson 97 ▶ A Day in a One-Room Schoolhouse

Objectives: Students identify the main idea, identify and supply supporting details, identify facts and opinions, use context clues, compare, and summarize.

Introduction: Invite students to turn the title of the article in the Student Pages into a question and then read the article to answer the question. Their question might be: "What was a day in a one-room schoolhouse like?"

Guided and independent practice: Discuss students' responses. Have them tell how they think the teacher managed to instruct students of so many different ages and why the students only took hikes occasionally.

Lesson 98 ▶ Teacher in the House

Objectives: Students identify the main idea, use context, identify facts and opinions, and supply supporting details.

Introduction: Invite students to turn the title of the article in the Student Pages into a question and then read the article to answer the question. Their question might be: "Why was there a teacher in the house?"

Guided and independent practice: Discuss students' responses. Have them tell why having a teacher residing in the house provided opportunities for the children who lived there.

This theme reviews skills that have already been taught and tells what school was like many years ago. The articles are about a day in a one-room schoolhouse, how students got to school before there were school buses, and what their teachers were like.

Lesson 97: A Day in a One-Room Schoolhouse

Read the article, and answer the questions that follow it.

A Day in a One-Room Schoolhouse

1   In the 1800s and early 1900s, most children went to school in one-room schoolhouses. At that time, most people lived on farms. The farms were spread out. One-room schoolhouses were built because there weren't many children in the farm areas. Most of the one-room schoolhouses only had about fifteen to twenty children. But some had as many as forty. The one-room schoolhouses had just one teacher. That teacher <u>instructed</u> all students from the age of five or six up to ages thirteen or fourteen or even older. The teacher also taught all subjects.

2   School started at nine and ended at about four o'clock. In the morning, the children studied reading, writing, spelling, and math. At lunchtime they played outside. In spring they might play baseball or another game. When the teacher rang the bell, the students went back inside and spent the afternoon studying geography and history. <u>Occasionally</u> they would take a hike up the mountains or into the forest to study the animals and plants that lived there. It is too bad there are very few one-room schoolhouses left.

Credit: Clipart.com.

1. This article tells mostly

    a. what a day in a one-room schoolhouse was like.

    b. what the inside of a one-room schoolhouse looked like.

    c. how it was possible to teach children of different ages.

    d. why students went to school for only seven months.

2. From information in the article, you can tell that in the 1800s and early 1900s, most people lived

    a. on farms.

    b. in small villages.

    c. in towns.

    d. in cities.

3. Which of the following is an opinion?

    a. In the 1800s and early 1900s, most children went to school in one-room schoolhouses.

    b. The one-room schoolhouses had just one teacher.

    c. Most of the one-room schoolhouses only had about fifteen to twenty children.

    d. It is too bad there are very few one-room schoolhouses left.

4. In paragraph 1, the word *instructed* means

    a. asked.

    b. taught.

    c. helped.

    d. begged.

5. In paragraph 2, the word *occasionally* means

    a. at least once a week.

    b. nearly every day.

    c. once in a while.

    d. sooner or later.

6. Think about what a day in your school is like and what a day in a one-room schoolhouse is like. Use the frame matrix to compare your school day with that of a day in a one-room schoolhouse. Then in the frame matrix, tell what is similar and what is different between your school and the one-room schoolhouse.

	My School	One-Room School-house	Similarities Between My School and the One-Room School-house	Differences Between My School and the One-Room School-house
What the teacher teaches				
Whom the teacher teaches				
What subjects the students learn				
Field trips				
How long the school day is				

Copyright © 2010 by John Wiley & Sons, Inc.

7. Using information from the frame matrix, fill in the boxes.

Tell briefly about a day in your school.	
Tell briefly about a day in a one-room schoolhouse.	
Compare your school and the one-room schoolhouse. How are they the same? How are they different?	

8. Write a paragraph comparing a day at your school with a day in a one-room schoolhouse. Use information from the article to support your answer.

_____

_____

_____

_____

_____

Lesson 98: Teacher in the House

Read the article, and answer the questions that follow it.

Teacher in the House

1   Some children took their teachers home with them. In the late 1800s, many teachers lived in the homes of their students, and they ate the food cooked by their students' mothers. In many places that had one-room schoolhouses, there were no hotels or apartments. The teachers lived in their students' homes. This was known as "boarding." Sometimes a teacher would stay in the same home for the whole school year. In other places, the teacher <u>resided</u> in a different home each month.

2   Boarding a teacher was a way for a family to make extra money. The teachers paid about ten dollars a month for a place to stay and food to eat, and the children had the <u>opportunity</u> to get some extra help with their homework. Having a teacher in the house was a great idea.

1. Paragraph 1 tells mostly

   a. where teachers lived and why they lived there.

   b. why there were no hotels or apartment houses.

   c. what homes were like in those days.

   d. what kind of food the mothers cooked.

2. In paragraph 1, the word *resided* means

    a. lived in.

    b. fixed up.

    c. thought about.

    d. helped out.

3. In paragraph 2, the word *opportunity* means

    a. time to rest and relax.

    b. a difficult time.

    c. late in the day.

    d. a good or helpful chance.

4. Write one fact and one opinion included in paragraph 2.

Fact:

_____

_____

_____

Opinion:

_____

_____

_____

5. Write two details that the author included to show that boarding a teacher was helpful to some families.

Detail 1:

_____

_____

_____

Detail 2:

_____

_____

_____

A Young Teacher's First Day on the Job

Objectives: Studentsidentify the main idea, identify facts and opinions, identify details, summarize, make connections, and use context.

Introduction: Invite students to turn the title of the article in the Student Pages into a question and then read the article to answer the question. Their question might be, "What was the teacher's first day on the job like?" For English learners, discuss the italicized expression in the following sentences: "Everybody *pitched in* to help. By talking to the students and looking at their books they had used with the previous teacher, the new teacher was able to *figure out where they were* in their schooling and what they needed to learn."

Guided and independent practice: Discuss students' responses. Have them tell what Mary Bradford's salary was and why it was important for her to look at the books the students had used with the previous teacher.

Lesson 99: A Young Teacher's First Day on the Job

Read the article, and answer the questions that follow it.

A Young Teacher's First Day on the Job

1   Some of the teachers in the one-room schoolhouse weren't much older than the students they taught. Mary Bradford was just sixteen years old and had finished only two years of high school when she began teaching. Her father had become ill. Because he was very sick, he couldn't work. Now the family needed money. That was back in the 1860s. At that time people could become teachers just by passing an exam. Mary Bradford took the teacher's exam and passed and taught for a few months. Her <u>salary</u> was twenty-five dollars a month. She should have been paid more.

2   On her first day as a teacher, Mary Bradford arrived at the schoolhouse early in the morning. The schoolhouse had been closed for several weeks and was filthy. Dirt and dust were everywhere. When the children arrived, she told them that there could be no schooling until the building was cleaned. Everybody pitched in to help. Once the school was clean, Mary Bradford started figuring out what she should teach her students. There were sixteen of them. The youngest student was six. The oldest was nineteen, three years older than the teacher. By talking to the students and looking at their books they had used with the <u>previous</u> teacher, Mary Bradford was able to figure out where they were in their schooling and what they needed to learn.

3   The youngest student was a beginner. He had to learn his ABCs. The nineteen-year-old wanted to learn an advanced kind of math known as algebra. Mary Bradford didn't know very much algebra herself. She had to study the algebra book.

Credit: Clipart.com.

1. Why did Mary start teaching even though she was just sixteen years old?

   a. To buy new clothes

   b. To help out her family

   c. To pay for high school

   d. She was tired of going to school

2. Paragraph 2 is mostly about

   a. what the schoolhouse looked like.

   b. what the students were like.

   c. what the students were learning.

   d. what Mary Bradford's first day on the job was like.

3. Which of the following is an opinion?

   a. Mary Bradford was just sixteen years old when she began teaching.

   b. Mary Bradford had finished only two years of high school when she began teaching.

   c. Mary Bradford was paid twenty-five dollars a month.

   d. Mary Bradford should have been paid more.

4. In paragraph 1, the word *salary* means

   a. how much people are paid.   c. a book.

   b. a bill.   d. rent.

5. In paragraph 2, the word *previous* means

   a. was there before or happened before.

   b. was older or not as young as.

   c. knew more about schools and other subjects.

   d. was coming back in a little while.

6. Imagine that you are Mary Bradford. Using information from the article, write a brief paragraph on your first day of teaching that could have appeared in your journal.

_____

_____

_____

_____

_____

_____

7. Think about a person you know or have heard about who is hard working and does her or his best to help everyone. Using information from the article, explain how that person is or is not like Mary Bradford. Use the writing organizer to help you answer the question. Write down Mary Bradford's main qualities and how she showed them. Then write down the main qualities of the person you know and how the person shows them.

	Main Qualities	How She or He Showed the Qualities
Mary Bradford		
The person you know		

Lesson 100 ▶ Study Time

Objectives: Students identify the main idea, use context clues, summarize, and make connections.

Introduction: Invite students to turn the title of the article in the Student Pages into a question and then read the article to answer the question. Their question might be, "What happened during study time?" or "What was study time like?"

Guided and independent practice: Discuss students' responses. Have them tell why students probably had to spend a lot of time studying. Discuss what spelling bees were like and some ways in which yesterday's schools differ from today's schools. Discuss, too, what your students like and don't like about one-room schoolhouses.

Assessment: Note students' overall performance on this and previous exercises in this unit. Have they mastered key skills? If not, provide additional instruction and practice. Also note in particular how well they are able to apply skills and strategies introduced in this text to reading in the content areas and any voluntary reading that they do. Provide review sessions and reminders as necessary.

Extension: Students can obtain more information about one-room schoolhouses at One-Room Schoolhouse Center at http://www2.johnstown.k12.oh.us/cornell/dayinlife.html.

Lesson 100: Study Time

Read the article, and answer the questions that follow it.

Study Time

In one-room schoolhouses, students did a lot of reciting and memorizing. Reciting means that they said something out loud that they learned. The teachers would ask a question, and the students would stand up and recite the answer. Students also did a lot of memorizing. They were often asked to memorize poems. This means they could say the whole poem word for word without looking at the poem. Some poems were short, but others were <u>lengthy</u>. The students had to memorize famous speeches and important facts, too. Students also memorized their spelling words. Once a week or so, students would <u>participate</u> in spelling bees. Students would study their spelling words, and then the teacher would give students turns spelling words out loud. Students had to sit down when they misspelled a word. The winner was the last student standing.

1. Write two details that the author included to show that students probably had to spend a lot of time studying.

Detail 1:

_____

Detail 2:

_____

2. In the paragraph, the word *lengthy* means

   a. interesting.

   b. funny.

   c. long.

   d. difficult.

3. In the paragraph, the word *participate* means

   a. go away from.

   b. take part in.

   c. remember for a while.

   d. think about.

4. Using information from this and previous articles on one-room school-houses, list the things you like about one-room schoolhouses and the things that you don't like.

Things I Like About a One-Room Schoolhouse	Things I Don't Like About a One-Room Schoolhouse

End-of-Theme Reflection

Discuss what students learned about one-room schoolhouses. Talk about what students liked best and what they liked least. Have them tell what was most surprising about one-room schoolhouses.

In order for skills learned in this unit to transfer, it is essential that students apply the skills to their textbooks or other full-length materials. Have available copies of the suggested books, and encourage students to read them. Readability levels provided by Accelerated Reading (AR) are posted for the books. However, readability formulas do not measure concept load, background needed to read a book, or interest level. You might want to examine the books and use your professional judgment as to whether the books are appropriate for your students.

Graves, Kerry (2002). *Going to School in Pioneer Times.* **5.9.** Other books in the series are: *Going to School During the Civil War: The Confederacy*; *Going to School During the Civil War: The Union*; *Going to School During the Depression*; *Going to School During the Civil Rights Movement*; and *Going to School in Colonial America.*

Kalman, Bobbie. (1994). *One-Room School.* **5.3**

Nelson, Robin. (2003). *School Then and Now.* **2.9** (Follett estimate)

Rau, Dana Meachen. (2007). *Going to School in American History.* **3.8**

Encourage students to apply their skills to the books they read. Using one of the books as a model, show students how they might use chapter titles and headings to help them determine the main ideas that they will be reading about. You might demonstrate how most chapter titles and headings can be turned into questions, which readers then answer when they come to the end of the chapter or section. Encourage students to summarize their reading by telling the main facts about the one-room school or era that they are reading about. They might focus on how the schools of yesteryear were the same or different or how they have changed over the years. They might also note statements that are factual and statements that are opinions. Encourage, too, the use of graphic organizers to highlight essential information. Students might also share their books with partners or in small groups. Students might wish to read more about yesterday's schools. Instead of or along with reading the books, students might consult the Web site listed in the Extension section of Lesson 100. Web sites tend to be more difficult than books; however, Web site text can be read by a text-to-speech feature available on most computers.

What did you learn about the schools of long ago? Write your answer on the lines.

_____

_____

_____

_____

_____

What was the most interesting thing that you learned? Write your answer on the lines.

_____

_____

_____

_____

Here is where you can go to find out more about yesterday's schools:

Graves, Kerry. (2002). *Going to School in Pioneer Times*. Minneapolis, MN: Blue Earth Books. Tells what schools were like while the West was being settled. Other books in the series are: *Going to School During the Civil War: The Confederacy*; *Going to School During the Civil War: The Union*; *Going to School During the Depression*; *Going to School During the Civil Rights Movement*; and *Going to School in Colonial America.*

Kalman, Bobbie. (1994). *One-Room School*. New York: Crabtree. Tells what it was like to attend a one-room school. Includes students' pranks, jokes, and their punishments.

Nelson, Robin. (2003). *School Then and Now*. Minneapolis, MN: Lerner. Compares yesterday's schools with today's schools.

Rau, Dana Meachen. (2007). *Going to School in American History*. Stamford, CT: Weekly Reader. Tells how schools have changed over the years.

Answer Key

Discuss students' answers so that you gain insight into their thought processes and also so that you can prompt and guide their thinking. Where appropriate, sample responses have been supplied for constructed responses. Answers to most constructed responses can vary. Accept responses that are reasonable and are supported by details from the article being assessed. In some situations, there might be more than one plausible answer to multiple-choice questions.

Lesson 1

The topic sentences are:

Birds sing for a number of reasons.

The way a bird sings depends on where it is.

Some birds can sing more songs than others.

The pygmy marmoset is the smallest monkey in the world.

African Gambian pouch rats are the largest rats in the world.

The cheetah is built to go fast.

Lesson 2

The topic sentences are:

Nile crocodiles are good parents.

Should an enemy appear, the mother crocodile has an unusual way of keeping her babies safe.

Nile crocodiles help each other.

The supporting details are:

When a school of fish is headed their way, crocodiles work together. They gather in a half circle and force the fish to swim toward the middle, where they are easily snapped up.

Nile crocodiles also work together when it gets very hot. They dig large dens where they can go to get away from the heat.

The topic sentence is:

Nile crocodiles are in danger from people.

The supporting details are:

Nile crocodiles are hunted for their hides, which can be used to makes shoes and boot and belts. Their meat can be eaten, and oil from their bodies can be used to make medicines.

Farmers sometimes hunt Nile crocodiles because they attack their sheep, cows, and other animals.

435

Lesson 3

1. b
2. d

Lesson 4

1. d
2. a

Lesson 5

1. d
2. a

Lesson 6

1. b
2. b

Lesson 7

1. b
2. upside down; walking

3. c
4. flatfish; stonefish; pipefish

Lesson 8

1. a
2. grasshoppers; rub back legs against wings. termites; beat on wooden homes.

Lesson 9

1. pointed forward, danger; pointed backward, anger.
2. The main idea of this article is that a zebra's ears show <u>how it is feeling.</u> The main idea is supported by information from the article. The article explains that if the zebra's ears are straight up, the zebra is feeling <u>calm.</u> If the zebra's ears are pointed forward, <u>a zebra is afraid.</u>

Lesson 10

1. The main idea of the article is: The whale shark was named for its size.

    Supporting details:

    A whale shark is about 30 feet (9 meters) long.

    Some whale sharks have grown to be 60 feet long (18 meters).

A whale shark can weigh as much as 72,000 pounds (32,658 kilograms).

The only sea creatures bigger than the whale shark are the large whales.

2. The main idea of this article is that the whale shark <u>is very large.</u> The main idea is supported by information from the article. The article explains that the whale shark is <u>30 to 60 feet long</u> and <u>weighs as much as 72,000 pounds</u>.

Lesson 11

1. The main idea of the article is: Some fish have unusual ways of keeping themselves safe.

   Supporting details: (1) Puffer fish puff themselves up to twice their size so they look frightening and are harder to eat. (2) Porcupine fish double their size and their needles stick out.

2. The main idea of this article is that some fish <u>have unusual ways of keeping themselves safe.</u> The main idea is supported by information from the article. The article explains that the puffer fish can <u>puff itself up to twice its size.</u> This helps the puffer fish because <u>it then looks frightening and makes them harder to eat.</u> The porcupine fish can <u>double its size and make its needles stand up.</u> This helps the porcupine fish because <u>any enemy who tries to bite a porcupine fish gets a mouthful of cuts.</u>

Lesson 12

1. See the sample answer.

2. Answers will vary but should incorporate the idea of animals helping each other and should be supported with information from the article.

Lesson 13

Answers will vary but should incorporate the idea that parrotfish have a clever way of keeping themselves safe while they sleep and should be supported with information from the article.

Lesson 14

1. b

2. d

3. The section mainly tells how meerkats protect themselves from their enemies.

Lesson 15

1. *Supporting details:* (1) The heads might want to do different things or go in different directions and end up doing nothing or going nowhere. (2) The heads fight over food. (3) One head might try to eat the other.

2. Two-headed snakes are better off in a zoo than they are in the wild because in the wild while they're fighting or figuring out which way to go, another animal might grab them and eat them.

Lesson 16

1. a

2. Grasshopper mice can eat poisonous snakes and scorpions because grasshopper mice aren't harmed by the poison of scorpions and snakes.

3. A grasshopper mouse is said to be like a tiny wolf because it is a fierce fighter and can catch its prey in a flash.

Lesson 17

1. Answers will vary but should include an essential part of the article.

2. The anglerfish has a body part that looks like a fishing rod with lighted bait on the end. When other fish stop to look at the lighted bait or try to eat it, the anglerfish snaps them up.

3. It is dark deep in the ocean where the anglerfish lives. The fake bait has to be lighted so the fish can see it.

4. Anglerfish have large jaws, so they can eat fish that are as big as or even bigger than they are.

Lesson 18

1. Answers will vary but should include an essential part of the article.

2. The Goliath birdeater can stick its prey with sharp hairs and bite it with its sharp fangs. The fangs carry venom that poisons their prey.

3. Another title for this article might be "The Killer Spider." The article tells what kinds of animals the Goliath spider can kill. The article also tells how the Goliath spider kills its prey.

Lesson 19

1. Answers will vary but should include an essential part of the article.

2. The squid shoots out a blob of black ink.

   The squid squirts water out of its funnel and jets away.

3. It is very dark deep beneath the sea. The giant squid uses its giant eyes to find food.

Lesson 20

1. Robots make good workers.

2. Robots, it seems, have a number of ways of moving around.

Lesson 21

1. d

2. b

3. Sample answers: Sawfish puts its arms around the bottom of the tree's trunk. Sawfish saws across the bottom of the tree. After tree has been cut through, Sawfish lets it go and bag carries tree to surface.

Lesson 22

1. d

2. <u>Robots on Mars</u> is a good title because it tells the readers what this article is going to be about. The article tells why the robots <u>are on Mars</u>. The article tells how the robots <u>use cameras to take long shots and close-ups of Mars</u> and how the robots <u>use instruments to analyze samples of the soil.</u> The article also tells <u>how the robots move around on Mars.</u> These details show that the title tells the main idea of the article.

3. b

4. b

5. b

6. d

7. d

Lesson 23

1. Answers may vary but should encompass the main idea of the article.

   This is a good title because the article tells that <u>the T-52 has been built to rescue people.</u> The article also tells how <u>the T-52 is able to go into a burning building and pick up people or objects.</u> These details show that the title tells the main idea of the article.

2. a

3. c

4. a

5. b

Lesson 24

1. a   3. b

2. b   4. d

Lesson 25

1. b

2. b

3. a

Lesson 26

1. b   3. b

2. a   4. d

5. Answers may vary but should incorporate the main idea of raising dogs to help people who have disabilities.

Lesson 27

1. b

2. c

3. d

Lesson 28

1. See sample answer.

2. c

3. a

Lesson 29

1. Wording may vary but should encompass the underlined ideas.

   Morris Frank and Buddy were the reason The Seeing Eye was started in the United States. After hearing about guide dogs helping the blind in Germany, Morris Frank <u>sent a letter asking for a guide dog.</u> Morris was given <u>a guide dog by the name of "Buddy."</u> After hearing what a good job Morris's dog was doing, Mrs. Eustis <u>started The Seeing Eye.</u>

2. c

3. b

4. Sample answers: A friend read an article to Morris about Mrs. Eustis.

   Mrs. Eustis started The Seeing Eye.

5. a

6. b

Lesson 30

1. The Seeing Eye has a puppy-raising program for young people. Puppy raisers take care of <u>their puppies for fourteen to eighteen months.</u> The puppy raisers feel sad when <u>they have to give their puppies back to The Seeing Eye.</u> But they feel happy and proud because <u>they were able to help raise a puppy so a blind person would have a better life.</u>

2. b

3. a

4. c

5. a

Lesson 31

1. People become acquainted with their dogs.

   People take trips with their dogs.

2. People who are getting guide dogs stay at The Seeing Eye for a month so they can <u>become acquainted with their dog</u> and learn to <u>handle their dog.</u> They learn how to cross streets, take buses, and to go to many different kinds of <u>places with their dog</u>.

3. b

4. c

5. d

Lesson 32

1. Answers may vary. Possible answers are listed below:

   have an instinct for helping the blind

   are smart

   can be trained to perform all the tasks and jobs that a guide dog is required to do

   better at spotting danger

   stronger than dogs

   can walk long distances without getting tired

   live longer

   don't chase cats or get fleas

2. c

3. d

Lesson 33

1. c

2. a

3. The dog touches its owner with its paw.

   The dog leads its owner to the door.

   The dog is given a reward.

4. d

5. c

6. b

7. d

Lesson 34

1. In Paws for Reading, dogs help students become better readers by <u>listening to them read</u>. Students like reading to dogs because <u>the dogs don't notice if the students get a word or two wrong and it gives the students a chance to be with a dog</u>.

2. c

3. c

4. b

5. b

Lesson 35

1. Answers may vary. Possible answers are listed below:

      smart

      easy to train

      small

      don't eat much

      aren't strong enough to hurt a person

      live a long time

      can pick up things with their hands

2. Capuchin monkeys can be good helpers. They are smart and easy to train. They are small and don't eat much and are not likely to hurt a person with a disability. They live a long time and can pick up things with their hands.

3. Answers may vary. Possible answers are listed below:

      can turn lights on and off

      can get their owners a drink or a snack

      can microwave food

      can clean up spills

      can put things in the trash

      can put a CD in a CD player or a DVD in a DVD player

      can bring their owner a book and turn the pages

      can pick up dropped objects and give them to the disabled person

      can carry out approximately fifty commands

4. a

5. c

6. b

7. a

8. a

Lesson 36

1. b

2. a

3. b

4. b

5. Answers may vary. Possible answers are listed below:

    people feel calmer

    hearts beat a little slower

    makes them forget about being sick

    feel a little less lonely

    feel more like talking

    might remind them of a time when they had a dog of their own

    start talking about happy times

    have a way of turning sad faces into happy faces

    help make older people more active

6. Summaries may vary but should include these essential details:

    Therapy dogs help sick people in a number of ways.

    They help sick people feel calmer and less lonely.

    They help sick people feel happier and more talkative.

    Therapy dogs also help sick people become more active.

7. Answers may vary. Possible answers are listed below:

    show that they are friendly around strangers

    can sit still while being petted or brushed

    demonstrate that they can walk by the owner's side, come when called, and sit when told to do so

    must be able to go into crowded places without getting nervous

    must pass by food without stopping to eat it

    must pass by other dogs without chasing or fighting with them or playing with them

Lesson 37

1. Bonnie decided to train dogs to help people who had disabilities.

    Bonnie started the Assistance Dog Institute.

2. Answers will vary but should highlight the main steps in the creation of the Assistance Dog Institute. The topic sentence might be: Bonnie Bergin started the Assistance Dog Institute.

3. c

4. b

5. a

6. d

7. b

Lesson 38

See sample answers.

Lesson 39

1. happy (or a similar feeling)

2. A smile broke across his face.

3. Dan West's plan was a good one for the following reasons. First, the children would have milk every day. Second, mothers and fathers would feel better because they would be feeding their own families.

4. b

5. b

Lesson 40

1. Dan West planned carefully so that he could help as many families as possible. Each family that was given a heifer was asked to give away a heifer calf when their heifer grew a little older and had calves of her own.

2. *Reason 1:* Other families would have a cow and so would be better able to take care of themselves. *Reason 2:* You would feel happy and proud that you would be able to help a family in need.

3. c

4. a

Lesson 41

1. Answers will vary. Sample answer: Dan West was out to change the world. He wanted to put an end to hunger. He wanted to help poor families all over the world feed themselves.

2. Dan West followed his dream. His dream was to help poor people feed themselves, so he started Heifer International. Heifer International has helped more than 9 million families in 125 countries.

3. c

4. a

Lesson 42

1. Heifer International gave away many different kinds of animals for people who had different needs.

2. a

3. c

4. Answers will vary but should be supported with appropriate reasons.

Lesson 43

1. Answers will vary. Sample answer: Heifer International teaches families how to take care of the animals that are given to them. They even make sure the animals that are given to families have proper shelter. These actions indicate that many families who are given animals may not know how to take care of them. Otherwise Heifer International would not have to teach the families.

2. Heifer International wants the animals it gives away to have good care. Heifer International teaches families how to feed and care for the animals. Heifer International makes sure that the animals have the proper shelter.

3. d

4. b

5. Answers will vary. Sample answer: "Helping People Help Themselves and Others" is a good slogan for Heifer International. First, people were given a heifer or other animal so they could start producing their own food. Instead of just being given food, they were given a way to produce their own food. Then when their heifer had calves, they could give one away so others would be helped to produce their own food.

Lesson 44

1. Craig felt upset (or a similar emotion).

   Supporting details:

   Craig couldn't get Iqbal Masih out of his mind.

   Craig read the article about Iqbal Masih over and over.

   After school, Craig went to the library and got as much information as he could find on child labor.

   Craig told the class about Iqbal Masih and about the millions of children who were forced to work in factories and mines.

2. Answers will vary. Predictions should be supported.

3. b

4. c

Lesson 45

1. Answers will vary.

2. Craig formed a group to find out more about child labor. Craig and the group started Free the Children and raised enough money to build a school.

3. They held bake sales and garage sales and collected money from other kids and from adults. They raised $7,000. Raising that much money would take a lot of work.

4. d

5. b

Lesson 46

1. Free the Children has raised a lot of money.

   Free the Children has raised enough money to build five hundred schools.

2. tools for farming; sewing machines; machines that polish gems, other small machines

3. Answers will vary. Sample answer: Free the Children helps people help themselves. Free the Children donates farm animals for the families and tools for farming. They also supply sewing machines, machines that polish gems, and other small machines that can be used to earn money.

4. d

5. a

Lesson 47

1. Answers may vary. Possible answers are listed below:

   sends health supplies

   helps them keep their water clean

   trains health workers

2. Answers will vary. Sample answer: Free the Children asked governments and people not to buy rugs and other products made by children. If nobody bought products made by children, then the children would not have to work and could go to school.

3. b

4. a

Lesson 48

1. Answers will vary. Sample answer: Craig and his brother started Youth in Action groups. They also established a number of programs that Youth in Action Groups could take part in. These groups and programs also help children. This shows that Craig keeps on looking for ways to help children.

2. a

3. b

Lesson 49

1. *Example 1:* Sister Teresa ate the same food that the poor people did. *Example 2:* Sister Teresa had only two rough saris.

2. c

3. d

Lesson 50

1. Answers will vary. Sample answer: Sister Teresa and the other missionaries took care of people whom no one else would care for. They bandaged their wounds and fed them and

gave them a clean bed to lie in. With their love and caring, they eased their loneliness and sorrow. Sister Teresa started a school for the children who lived in the poorest parts of Calcutta and started a home for children whose parents had died or who were unable to take care of them.

2. Any two of the following reasons: (1) Sister Teresa and the other missionaries found very sick people lying in the gutter. (2) Sister Teresa and the other missionaries took care of people whom no one else would care for. (3) Sister Teresa and the other missionaries started a home for children whose parents had died or who were unable to take care of them.

3. b

4. a

Lesson 51

1. Two reasons: (1) Mother Teresa was given a medal and $190,000. She used the money to help the poor. (2) Mother Teresa asked the Nobel committee to cancel the dinner being held in her honor and use the money to feed the poor.

2. Mother Teresa said that the money for the dinner would feed four hundred children for a year.

3. Answers will vary. Sample answer: Mother Teresa lived with and took care of the poorest of the poor in Calcutta, India. Mother Teresa also started a school for the children who lived in the poorest parts of Calcutta and started a home for children whose parents had died or who were unable to take care of them. Mother Teresa and the Missionaries of Charity started homes for the poor in a number of countries.

4. d

5. c

Lesson 52

1. Craig could see that Mother Teresa had a big heart and she told him, "We must always realize that we can do no great things, only small things with great love."

2. Answers will vary but should include the idea that what is important in helping others is having love in our hearts.

3. a

4. d

Lesson 53

1. Brandon seemed to be feeling bored. First, he hoped the meeting would be over soon. Second, the more the people talked, the more he wiggled.

2. c

3. a

Lesson 54

1. Answers will vary but should be plausible.

2. Brandon was able to tell that the home where his mom worked needed books.

3. b

4. c

Lesson 55

1. BookEnds has helped more than 100,000 young people donate more than 1 million books.

2. c

3. c

Lesson 56

Young people can help others.

Lesson 57

1. Any three of the following examples: (1) Ryan washed windows. (2) Ryan cleaned his neighbor's yard. (3) Ryan vacuumed for a dollar. (4) Ryan did chores for four months.

2. Answers will vary but should be plausible.

3. d

4. b

Lesson 58

1. When he learned that the $70 he collected would buy only a hand pump, Ryan started doing more chores.

2. Sample answer: Ryan isn't the kind of person who gives up easily. When he learned that the $70 he collected would buy only a hand pump, Ryan started doing more chores and giving talks asking for money until he accumulated $2,000.

3. a

4. b

Lesson 59

1. Examples: (1) The people of the village lined up to greet Ryan. (2) The people of the village had a big celebration as a way of showing they were grateful.

2. b

3. b

Lesson 60

1. Two examples: (1) The students didn't have much to share with others. (2) The people didn't have enough money for a well.

2. Answers will vary.

3. d

4. b

Lesson 61

1. Sample answer: Jimmy escaped from rebel soldiers, but his life was still in danger. Suppose the soldiers found him? Ryan's parents invited Jimmy to come to Canada, where Ryan and his family lived.

2. Sample answer: Ryan's parents were kind (loving). When they learned that Jimmy was in danger, Ryan's parents invited Jimmy to come to Canada. Ryan's parents made Jimmy one of the family.

3. b

4. a

Lesson 62

1. Two examples: (1) Greg helped many of Korphe's sick people. (2) Greg promised to build a school.

2. People would have to walk for two days to get to the nearest doctor.

3. d

4. d

Lesson 63

1. Two examples: (1) Greg kept on trying to collect money even when only 1 person out of 560 answered his letter asking for help. (2) Greg collected money for the bridge when he found that a bridge would have to be built before work could be started on the school.

2. Greg sold his car and just about everything else that he owned, and then bought an airline ticket.

3. c

4. d

Lesson 64

1. opinion	5. fact—observe	9. fact—measure	13. fact—observe
2. fact—observe	6. fact—observe	10. fact—observe	14. opinion
3. opinion	7. opinion	11. fact—count	15. opinion
4. fact—count	8. fact—measure	12. fact—observe	16. opinion

Lesson 65

1. b

2. b

3. c

4. a

5. d

6. *Supporting details:* Spencer Silver discovered a glue that was weak but could be used over and over again. Art Fry coated the top of small pieces of paper with the glue and made sticky notes.

7. *Possible facts:* Chances are you have used these sticky notes. Millions of pads of sticky notes are sold each year. Can you guess the name of Art Fry's invention? If you said "Post-it® Notes," you are right. *Opinion:* Post-it® Notes are a great invention.

Lesson 66

1. b

2. b

3. c

4. a

5. a

6. c

7. b

8. About 1 billion Popsicles® are sold each year.

9. Popsicles® come in thirty flavors.

10. *Facts:* Today Popsicles® are still being sold. About 1 billion Popsicles® are sold each year. Popsicles® come in thirty flavors. The most popular flavor is orange. *Opinion:* The best-tasting flavor is strawberry.

Lesson 67

1. b

2. b

3. b

4. In 1883 his factory turned out 30,000 earmuffs. By 1936 the factory was making 400,000 earmuffs a year.

5. Each December there is a Chester Greenwood Parade in Farmington.

6. It is cold in December, so it is a good time to wear earmuffs. No one needs earmuffs in June or July.

7. Supporting details: Chester Greenwood invented earmuffs, a steel-toothed rake, a spark plug for cars, a mousetrap, a new kind of rubber band, a hook for lifting doughnuts out of boiling oil, and a whistling tea kettle. Chester Greenwood was named as one of America's fifteen most outstanding inventors.

8. Answers will vary. Sample answer: I went ice skating today. It was very cold today. My ears were freezing. I wrapped a scarf around my head, but the scarf was itchy and my ears were

still cold. I made a covering for my ears, and then I used a wire to hold the covering in place. That kept my ears warm. When I got home, I asked Grandma to sew pieces of fur over the earpieces. The fur should keep my ears good and warm.

9. *Facts:* Making earmuffs gave jobs to hundreds of people in and around Farmington, Maine. Farmington, Maine, is known as the earmuff capital of the world. Each December there is a Chester Greenwood parade in Farmington. Everyone in the parade wears earmuffs. The state of Maine set aside December 21 as Chester Greenwood Day. Chester Greenwood passed away in 1937. *Opinion:* The parade is a lot of fun.

Lesson 68

1. c

2. a

3. *Supporting details:* Chester Greenwood was just fifteen when he invented earmuffs. Louis Braille was the same age as Chester Greenwood when he devised braille. Philo Farnsworth was just fourteen when he got an idea for transmitting and receiving moving pictures. Margaret Knight was just twelve years old when she got an idea for making machines that spun cotton more safely. Frank Epperson was just eleven when he created a frozen fruit juice treat.

4. a

5. c

6. *Facts:* Chester Greenwood was just fifteen years old when he invented earmuffs. Over the years, thousands of earmuffs made in his factory were sold. Louis Braille was the same age as Chester Greenwood when he devised braille. Braille is a way of writing that uses raised marks so that blind people can read with their fingertips. Philo Farnsworth was just fourteen years old when he got an idea for transmitting and receiving moving pictures. His idea was used in the invention of television. Margaret Knight was just twelve years old when she got an idea for making machines that spun cotton more safely. Frank Epperson was just eleven years old when he created a frozen fruit juice treat. He developed the frozen fruit juice treat into the Popsicle. *Opinion:* Television is one of the world's most important inventions.

Lesson 69

1. a

2. c

3. a

4. d

5. It took three years for de Mestral to get his invention to work.

6. *Supporting details:* During a walk, burrs attached themselves to de Mestral and his dog. De Mestral wondered how the burrs had become attached to him and his dog and why they didn't fall off. De Mestral took a look at one of the burrs under a microscope.

7. *Facts:* Over the years, hundreds of uses have been found for this versatile fastener. Today the hook-and-loop fastener that de Mestral invented is sold around the world and is found on hundreds of products. *Opinion:* Velcro® is a wonderful invention.

Lesson 70

1. b

2. a

3. b

4. d

5. d

6. *Supporting details:* In 1917 Rohwedder's workshop burned down. All his work was destroyed. Rohwedder rebuilt his workshop and his slicing machine. It took him another eleven years, but at last, in 1928, his bread-slicing machine was finished, and it worked.

Lesson 71

1. a

2. c

3. a

4. c

5. c

6. c

7. d

8. Davis didn't have enough money to get a patent for his invention.

9. The rivets worked well, and the miners liked them.

Lesson 72

1. a

2. b

3. d

4. a

5. a

6. Answers may vary but should reflect the main idea of the article.

   The article tells how the mouse works and how it was invented and that it made computers easier to use.

Lesson 73

1.

	African Elephants	Asian Elephants
Where they live	plains	forests
Weight	14,000 pounds	12,000 pounds
Height at shoulder	12 feet	9 feet

	African Elephants	Asian Elephants
Ears	very large	not so large
Trunk	two fingers at tip of trunk	one finger at tip of trunk
Tusks	males and females have tusks	only males have tusks
Toes	4	5
Forehead	no bumps on forehead	two bumps on forehead

2. b

3. c

Lesson 74

1.

	Savanna Elephants	Forest Elephants
Where they live	flat grasslands	forests
Size	14,000 pounds	10,000 pounds
Ears	large	smaller
Tusks	curved	shorter and straight

2. b

3. d

Lesson 75

1.

	Dugongs	Manatees
Habitat (where they live)	warm, shallow water where sea grasses grow	warm, shallow water in streams, rivers, and canals
Size	10 feet; 900 pounds	12 feet; 1,500 pounds
Senses	poor eyesight but keen hearing, whiskers are feelers	good hearing and eyesight
Food	sea grasses	plants that grow at the bottom of streams, rivers, and canals
Life expectancy (how long they live)	70 years	60 years

2. d

3. c

Lesson 76

1.

	Alligators	Crocodiles
Overall appearance	long snout, rows of sharp teeth, and long tails	long snout, rows of sharp teeth, and long tails
Habitat	warm places near the water	warm places near the water; more likely to be found in salt water
Movement	use long tails to swim; can run fast for short distances	use long tails to swim; can run fast for short distances
Food	variety of creatures	variety of creatures
Snouts	broad snout that is shaped like a U	narrow snout that is shaped like a V
Coloring	bluish	green or a greenish brown
Teeth	a lot of very large teeth, fourth tooth fits inside jaws	a lot of very large teeth, fourth tooth protrudes
Behavior	bolder	shyer, likely to hide from people

2. c
3. b

Lesson 77

1.

	Squid	Octopuses
Habitats	under water	under water
Overall appearance	bullet shaped; has 10 long armlike body parts known as tentacles, two of which are longer than the others; large eyes; and sharp beak	rounded body; 8 long tentacles; large eyes; and sharp beak
Movement	propel through the water by squirting water out of a tube	propel through the water by squirting water out of a tube
Shell	inside shell	no shell, tough covering known as a mantle
Defense	can change color to match their surroundings and can squirt ink	can change color to match their surroundings and can squirt ink

2. b

3. c

Lesson 78

1.

	Frogs	Toads
Habitat	in or near water	in fields or near water
Overall appearance	big protruding eyes, long tongues, and strong back legs	big protruding eyes, long tongues, and strong back legs
Skin	smooth, moist skin	dry, rough skin that is full of small bumps
Movement	hop on land or swim through the water	hop on land or swim through the water
Food	insects	insects
Defense	have a poison on their skins	have a poison on their skins

2. d   3. a

Lesson 79

1.

	Mikan	Aaron
Sport played	basketball	baseball
Reason turned down	too clumsy	too small
Accomplishments	helped DePaul win national championship, led the Lakers to five league titles, known as one of basketball's greatest players	set 11 records and hit 755 home runs

2. b   3. b

Lesson 80

1.

	Clementine Hunter	Grandma Moses
Occupation (kind of work done)	cook	housewife
Age when she began painting	age 50	in her 70s

	Clementine Hunter	Grandma Moses
Kinds of paintings	outdoor scenes	farm scenes
Accomplishments	5,000 paintings, special showings of her paintings	hundreds of paintings
Honors	president honored her	president honored her
How long she lived	102	101

2. d

3. c

Lesson 81

1.
	Dunbar	Wright Brothers
Work habits	hard worker	hard workers
Interests	words, poetry	machines, flying
Accomplishments	wrote books of poetry, became famous poet	invented airplane, first flight

2. The Wright brothers and Paul Dunbar were similar in at least one way. All three were hard workers. In later years all three boys became famous. The Wright brothers were the first to fly a heavier-than-air machine powered by a motor. Paul Dunbar wrote several books of poetry and became a famous poet.

3. The Wright brothers were different from Paul Dunbar. Paul Dunbar liked to work with words. He wrote books of poetry and became a famous poet. The Wright brothers liked to work with machines. They invented the airplane.

4. c

5. d

Lesson 82

1.
Kind of Sleep	Eyes	Breathing	Heart Rate	Dreaming	Amount of
REM	move rapidly	does not slow down	does not slow down	dream	2 hours
Non-REM	do not move rapidly	slows down	slows down	little or no dreaming	6 hours

2. *Supporting details:* In REM sleep, our eyes move rapidly and we dream. We are in REM sleep about two hours every night. In non-REM sleep, our eyes do not move rapidly, breathing

slows down, and our heart beats more slowly. We do little or no dreaming. We are in non-REM sleep for about six hours.

3. Answers may vary. Sample answer: Non-REM sleep seems more restful because our heart and breathing slow down, our eyes don't move rapidly, and we do little or no dreaming.

4. d

5. a

Lesson 83

1.

	Kind of Animal	Where They Sleep	How Long They Can Stay Under Water	How They Get Air While Sleeping
Dolphin	mammal	under water	30 minutes	come up for air
Hippo	mammal	on land or under water	30 minutes	come up for air

2. Dolphins and hippos are <u>mammals</u>. Both sleep under water. Both can stay <u>under water</u> for <u>thirty minutes</u>. They get air by <u>rising to the surface</u>.

3. Both are mammals. All mammals need to breathe air.

4. c

5. b

Lesson 84

1.

	Where They Sleep	How They Sleep	How Long They Sleep	How They Can Block Out Noise and Light
People on Earth	in a bed	lying down	8 hours	ear plugs and eyeshade
Astronauts	sleeping compart-ment or bag	don't have to lie down—can float	8 hours	ear plugs and eyeshade

2. Sleeping in space is different. Because there is very little gravity in space, astronauts do not have to sleep <u>in a bed</u>. They can sleep <u>in a special sleeping compartment or in a sleeping bag</u>. In some ways sleeping in space is similar to sleeping on Earth. Both astronauts and people on Earth <u>can use eyeshades and ear plugs and sleep for about 8 hours</u>.

3. c

4. a

5. c

Lesson 85

1.

Group	Amount of Sleep	How They Sleep	How Easily Awakened
Ten-year-olds	11 hours	sleep through the night	are not easily awakened
People in their sixties and older	8 hours	sleep is interrupted; don't sleep as soundly	easily awakened

2. Answers will vary. Sample answer: Ten-year-olds sleep more soundly and are not easily awakened by noises. They sleep about 11 hours a night. Older people don't sleep as soundly, are easily awakened by noises, and only sleep for about 8 hours.

3. b

4. Young people should get plenty of sleep. First, <u>sleeping gives their bodies a chance to grow</u>. Second, <u>sleep also rests children's brains</u>. Finally, <u>children are active, and their bodies need extra rest</u>.

5. c

6. d

Lesson 86

1. They are harder to see at night and there are fewer animals hunting.

2.

Animals	Time of Day When Active	Reason for Being Active During a Certain Time of the Day	Examples
Diurnal	day	can see better during the day; might be easier to find food during the day	people, most birds
Nocturnal	night	have sharp senses so they can hunt at night and avoid enemies; might be very hot during the day	raccoons, skunks, possums, owls, bats, rhinoceroses, tigers, and some other big cats
Crepuscular	dawn and dusk	stay away from bright light and the heat of the day	rabbits, brown bears, rattlesnakes, poisonous lizards, such as the gila monsters, and some desert animals

3. c

4. a

5. a

6. They escape the heat of the day, and this is a better time to hunt for food.

7. b

8. c

9. b

10. Answers will vary.

11. Because people are diurnal, dogs and cats gave up being nocturnal after being around people.

Lesson 87

1.

Type of Person	When They Like to Go to Bed	When They Like to Get Up	When They Are Most Awake
Lark	earlier in the night	early in the morning	3:30 in the afternoon
Owl	later at night	later in the morning	8:30 in the evening

2. Answers will vary.

3. b

4. a

Lesson 88

1. Answers will vary but should focus on an essential part of the article.

2. Albert Kolk had his grandson and two friends in his plane when it spun out of control. The parachute saved them.

3. Answers will vary but should include information from the article.

4. a

5. d

Lesson 89

1. Fulton built the Airphibian so that he could turn his plane into a car and drive to wherever he was going.

2. Changing it from a car to a plane and back again took a lot of time. And the Airphibian was a slow-flying plane.

3. d

4. b

Lesson 90

1. Answers will vary but should focus on an essential part of the article.

2.

	Wings	Propeller	Changing from Car to Plane	Where Wings and Propeller Could Be Kept While Car Was on the Road
Airphibian	could not be folded	front of plane	took a long time	at airport
Aerocar	could be folded	back of plane	took only five minutes to change	in trailer

3. Answers will vary.

4.

Problem	Solution
Back part of plane and propeller had to be left behind.	The part of the Aerocar that had the wings, tail, and propeller had wheels so that the plane part could be towed just like any regular trailer.
Took a long time to change from car to plane.	The Aerocar could be changed from a car into a plane in just five minutes.

5. d

6. c

Lesson 91

1. Answers will vary but should focus on an essential part of the article.

2.

	Engine	Takeoff and Landing	Speed on Land	Speed in the Air	Range	Safety
Aerocar	car engine	regular	60 miles per hour	110 miles per hour	300	no special devices
Skycar	engines that force air onto movable vanes	vertical takeoff and landing	35 miles per hour	375 miles per hour	750	can still fly even if an engine fails; has a parachute

3. The Skycar will be very safe. It can still fly even if an engine fails, and it has a parachute built into it.

4. The Skycar would be powered by engines that force air onto movable vanes. Directing the air downward pushes the Skycar upward and allows it to hover or stay in one spot. To move the Skycar forward, the vanes are turned so that the air flows straight out and propels the Skycar ahead.

5. Answers will vary but should be supported with reasons.

6. b

7. c

Lesson 92

1. Oxygen is heated up. The scramjet is pushed forward.

2. go from New York to China in an hour; fly around the world in two hours

3. Scramjets don't need as much fuel as a rocket does and don't need big fuel tanks.

4. d

5. d

Lesson 93

1. Answers will vary but should focus on an essential part of the article.

2. Shaw saw two bright lights and stopped.

   Shaw started a company to make and sell the device.

3. When a car drove over the device, the rubber molding pushed the glass beads down so they wouldn't be crushed.

4. Shaw made a spot in the base where rainwater would collect. When a car ran over the reflector, the rubber molding pushed down on the rainwater and the rainwater was squirted onto the glass beads and cleaned them.

5. Shaw named his device "Catseye" because the device worked like the cat's eyes that had saved him.

6. d

7. a

Lesson 94

1. a tank for holding the vegetable oil; a filter to remove dirt in the oil; a special heater to keep the oil warm

2. Answers will vary but should be supported using information from the article.

3. a

4. d

Lesson 95

1. Answers will vary but should focus on an essential part of the article.

2. Malcolm purchased ships.

   Malcolm loaded containers onto ships.

3. d

4. a

Lesson 96

1. Answers will vary but should focus on an essential part of the article.

2. Causes: (1) Powerful magnetic waves will lift Planetran up off its rails and shoot it forward. (2) Pumps built into the tunnel would draw out just about all the air so that there would be little air resistance to slow Planetran down.

3. Laser beams and high-powered jets of water would be used. The hardest of rock would be melted by a subterrene. A subterrene is a drill that produces such intense heat that it turns the hardest rock into red-hot liquid.

4. b

5. a

Lesson 97

1. a   5. c

2. a   6. Answers will vary.

3. d   7. Answers will vary.

4. b   8. Answers will vary.

Lesson 98

1. a

2. a

3. d

4. *Facts:* Boarding a teacher was a way for a family to make extra money. The teachers paid about ten dollars a month for a place to stay and food to eat. The children had the opportunity to get some extra help within their homework. *Opinion:* Having a teacher in the house was a great idea.

5. *Supporting details:* (1) Boarding a teacher was a way for a family to make extra money. (2) The children had the opportunity to get some extra help with their homework.

Lesson 99

1. b

2. d

3. d

4. a

5. a

6. Answers may vary. Sample answer: Today was an exciting day for me. It was my first day as a teacher. I got to the schoolhouse early. It had been closed up and was filthy. I started to clean up. When the children arrived, I told them they all needed to help. We couldn't have any lessons until the schoolhouse was clean. They pitched right in. There are sixteen children. The youngest is just six. The oldest is nineteen. Why, he's three years older than I am! I spent most of the day figuring out where everybody is and what they need to learn next. I had the students show me what books they had been using and where they had left off. Tomorrow I'll have lessons for all of them.

7. Answers will vary but should highlight substantive comparisons.

Lesson 100

1. *Supporting details:* (1) Students were often asked to memorize poems. (2) The students also had to memorize famous speeches and important facts. (3) Students also memorized their spelling words.

2. c

3. b

4. Answers may vary but should include pertinent details from the articles.

References

Afflerbach, P., Pearson, P., & Paris, S. G. (2008). Clarifying differences between reading skills and reading strategies. *Reading Teacher, 61*, 364–373.

Gunning, T. (2010). *Assessing and correcting reading and writing difficulties* (4th ed.). Needham Heights, MA: Allyn & Bacon.

Hansen, J., & Pearson, P. D. (1982). *The effects of inference training and practice on young children's comprehension* (Tech. Rep. 166). Urbana: University of Illinois, Center for the Study of Reading.

Marzano, R. J., Gaddy, B. B., & Dean, C. (2000). *What works in classroom instruction.* Aurora, CO: Mid-Continent Research for Education and Learning.

Maynard, T. (2007). *Komodo dragons.* Mankato, MN: Child's World.

Smith, L. (2006). Think-aloud mysteries: Using structured sentence-by-sentence text passages to teach comprehension strategies. *Reading Teacher, 59*, 764–773.

Terman, L. M. (1916). *The measurement of intelligence.* Boston: Houghton Mifflin.

Wade, S. (1990). Using think-alouds to assess comprehension. *Reading Teacher, 43*, 442–451.

Wilder, L. I. (1935). *Little house on the prairie.* New York: HarperCollins.

Yuill, N., & Oakhill, J. (1991). *Children's problems in text comprehension: An experimental investigation.* Cambridge: Cambridge University Press.

NOTES

NOTES

NOTES

NOTES

NOTES

NOTES

NOTES